# SAIL

TIMOTHY JEFFERY

Quarto is the authority on a wide range of topics.
Quarto educates, entertains and enriches the lives of
our readers— enthusiasts and lovers of hands-on living.

www.QuartoKnows.com

First published in Great Britain
2016 by Aurum Press Ltd
74–77 White Lion Street
Islington
London N1 9PF
www.aurumpress.co.uk

ISBN  978 1 78131 533 0

10 9 8 7 6 5 4 3 2 1
2020 2019 2018 2017 2016

Designed by
theurbanant.com

Printed in China

# SAIL

TIMOTHY JEFFERY

# Contents

# Foreword

Sailing is my course through life; it has shaped my world from when I was a kid. You can't change the direction or the strength of the wind, but you can use it to reach your goal. That's why sailing is the best sport on Earth. It can challenge you or relax you. It can frustrate and it can reward. If you allow yourself to think for a moment that you are on top of it, sailing will remind you, with the next crashing wave, that there is always more to learn.

Ever since my parents pushed me off in an Optimist dinghy in the upper reaches of a Cornish harbour, my life has revolved around what, in *Moby Dick*, Herman Melville called the 'watery parts of the world'. For every little of bit of effort I've given to win a gold medal or the America's Cup, those watery parts have repaid me with so much more.

As a kid I grew up hearing of my dad's experience when he organized a group of friends to race in the very first Whitbread Round the World Race. They had an amazing experience, from an epic party in Rushcutters Bay in Sydney – where nearly 30 years later I was based for the Olympic sailing competition – to their 22-m ketch being knocked down by a massive squall at Cape Horn.

You can master a boat, but you can never truly master the wind and the sea. Every time you leave land behind and go afloat, it's a new experience. Race a high-performance boat at the pinnacle of our sport and you take the wind on. It's a tool to use more efficiently than your rivals. Turn the tempo down, go cruising and you can just go with the flow, setting a course where the wind can make your sailing the most enjoyable.

When I started racing, I became aware of my first hero in sailing. The self-bailer in most dinghies was an 'Elvstrøm', and the racing rules guides I referred to were Elvstrøm's. The famous Dane, Paul Elvstrøm, was an inspirational figure to me.

He earned his success in the Olympics by working harder and training longer, so that he got himself in a position where success was pretty much inevitable.

This total focus was something that Russell Coutts, another sailor I admire, was famous for, and I was fortunate to see it first hand as a teammate during the 2013 America's Cup in San Francisco. Some people say I have similar intensity, but as far as I'm concerned, if you don't compete hard, fast and fair, with 100 per cent commitment, then you are not competing to your maximum potential.

The beauty of sailing, though, is that you can step on a boat with no intention other than enjoying the pure pleasure of being on the water. I feel as at home there as on land, and the simple pleasure of enjoying a boat moved along by wind is satisfaction at an elementary level. Good company on a boat is one of the best ways of chilling out that I know.

Peter Blake, another hero of mine, once said that when he was completely exhausted after racing around the world, he would wind down by hoisting a pair of oars over his shoulder and walking inland until he met the first person who asked him what he was carrying. I know many competitors who can relate to that need to get away from something you have lived for in every waking moment for several years. I also know that Blakey always went back to messing around on boats.

I can't imagine a time not wanting to step on board and turn the bows away from land. Sailing is that rare thing in sport. You can do it throughout your life, throughout the world, in any shape or form of boat, in any informal or organized way, with whomever you like and whenever you want. It is pure joy.

Ben Ainslie

# Introduction

We 'go down' to the sea. The phrase is there in hymn, verse and common usage. In geographical terms, it makes sense. Land is always higher – or it was until man learnt to construct walls, polders and levées.

Yet anyone who has tried it will tell you that going to sea is an elevating experience. That sense of leaving land for the first time, the stillness of wind power, the whistle of strong winds, the menacing roar of a foaming crest, the stars overhead, the phosphorescence streaming behind from the rudder blade, the chill before the dawn and the hint of warmth at sunrise; these experiences lift the heart, enhance the senses and fuel the memory.

Necessity rather than pleasure first lured man afloat. It was a means of communication, travel and transport. In many instances it was easier and faster than overland travel. Long before the voyages of exploration by the Portuguese, Spanish, Italians, British and Dutch from the 16th centuries onwards, the Vikings, Polynesians and Chinese were considered the earliest ocean voyagers. Even before this, man had fashioned boats from trees and animal skins for inland and coastal use. Somewhere, sometime, small personal boats grew into craft big enough to carry loads. Often, it's the Egyptians who are credited with boatbuilding on the Nile, around 3500 BC. Indeed, the Egyptian civilization probably created the first pleasure boats, the royal vessels used by the pharaohs and their court. The origins of the sailing boat might reach even further back in time to the Old World, as fragments of pottery showing a boat and a sail have been found in the modern-day Arabian peninsula.

The word 'yacht' comes from the Dutch *jacht* or *jaghte*, the origin of which means 'chasing'. *Jachtschepen* were the faster boats used to carry men, messages and pilots to and from the bigger trading vessels. A widely accepted view is that when Charles II returned from the Netherlands to England to reclaim the throne in 1660, he travelled by *jacht*, and so the word 'yacht' came into usage. From a quirk of history, we now have a recreation that knows no boundaries around the world. We also have a sport that is enjoyed by ordinary people in simple boats yet is also practised by professionals who, at the elite level, can earn million-dollar salaries and be garlanded with Olympic medals. Such big earnings are not just the currency of the last couple of decades, however – the best professionals in the 19th century could also earn substantial incomes.

Many would argue that for sheer breadth of skills, often demonstrated in arduous and sometimes dangerous conditions, today's leading pro sailor is vastly underappreciated compared with those can drive a ball down a fairway, serve an ace on match point, throw a ball with piercing accuracy down field or dunk it through a hoop. But the true beauty of sailing is that it offers an equal chance for ordinary people to do extraordinary things, just as extraordinary sailors can make the superlative seem deceptively easy.

Bringing these great sailors, great experiences and great races together for this book has been fascinating and fulfilling, as enjoyable in many ways – almost – as actually being under sail, at sea. We have tried to include the essential selection of races, sailors and boats. It is, inevitably, a subjective selection, but hopefully you will find much to enjoy, educate and entertain. Each race profile includes a route map and a fact file; the section on sailors includes a brief biography; and the chapter on boats aims to be a comprehensive reference section with all the information you could need. Enjoy – and then get out on the water.

# The Races

Pinnacles of Sailing
# The America's Cup

## Route tracker

San Francisco
2013

New York
1870–1920

Newport
1930–1983

Isle of Wight
1851

Valencia
2007–2010

Bermuda
2017

San Diego
1988–1995

ATLANTIC
OCEAN

INDIAN
OCEAN

PACIFIC
OCEAN

Fremantle
1987

Auckland
2000–2003

## Vital stats

### America's Cup

**What:** Series of match races between two yachts

**Where:** Home country or alternative chosen by current holder

**How often:** 3–4 years

**Boat type:** Class of boat chosen by holder and challenger (currently catamarans)

**Crew:** Fully crewed

▷ The yacht that gave her name to the pinnacle event of the sport: *America*, winner of an 1851 race. The America's Cup is the oldest trophy in international sport.

It is the oldest trophy in international sport; the pinnacle of yacht racing; the most prestigious prize in sport; and a competition so tough in which to triumph that only four nations have succeeded in more than 30 events over 160-odd years. It's also the competition whose name is known worldwide yet of which very few have detailed knowledge – in part because there is so much history, dating all the way back to 1851.

Back then, the world was a very different place. Europe was dominated by the Russian, Ottoman, Austro-Hungarian and British Empires. Germany was still a collection of small states. In America, the Gold Rush in San Francisco was under way, but the schism of the Civil War was still ten years away, as was the transcontinental railroad that would link the old east with the new west.

In Britain, Queen Victoria's forward-thinking husband, Prince Albert, promoted the Great Exhibition of the Works of Industry of All Nations. The USA, still flexing its wings after independence in 1776, was represented by items both practical and prosaic, such as Samuel Colt's self-loading firearms and a reaping machine. It also sent a yacht called *America*, whose victory over the best of British yachts in a race around the Isle of Wight was to create history.

In the lead-up to the Great Exhibition, five members of the newly formed New York Yacht Club (established in 1844) decided not only to commission a boat that demonstrated the speed and seaworthiness of the American hull form, but, in the manner of sport at the time, planned to race her for wagers.

Commodore John Cox Stevens replied to

*'Britannia rules the waves, and America waives the rules.'*

*New York Herald Tribune* headline
America's Cup, 1934

an invitation to come to England from the Royal Yacht Squadron: 'Some four or five friends and myself have a yacht on the stocks, which we hope to launch in the course of two or three weeks. Should she answer the sanguine expectations of her builder, we propose to avail ourselves of your friendly bidding, and take with a good grace the sound thrashing we are likely to get by venturing our longshore craft on your rough waters.'

Proof that Stevens, his brother Edwin, J. Beekman Finlay, James Hamilton and George L. Schuyler were sharp as tacks came in the contract for *America* ordered from shipbuilder William H. Brown. If the new *America* were not faster 'than any vessel in the United States brought to race with her', then the agreed $30,000 would not be paid. *America* was pitted against another Stevens yacht, *Maria*, and though 31m (100ft) long as opposed to *America*'s 30m (97ft), *Maria* was designed for inshore waters, carried more sail and a larger crew. She was faster, and the

Stevens' syndicate knocked *America*'s price down by a third.

On arrival in Cowes, England, *America* attracted considerable interest. She was different from the deep-gutted, 'cod-head, mackerel-tail' style of English yacht, with their bluff bows and tapering stern. *America* was the opposite: fine forward, shallow bodied and broad aft. *The Illustrated London News* pronounced *America* 'a rakish, piratical-looking craft', arguing that she 'seemed rather a violation of the old established ideas of naval architecture.' The Marquis of Anglesey, senior member of the Royal Yacht Squadron, noted sagely: 'If she is right, then we're all wrong.'

So it proved. In a race around the Isle of Wight, off the south coast of England, and with Cowes, 'the home of yachting', at its heart, the 170-ton *America* beat 14 of the best British yachts, ranging from the 44-ton *Aurora* to the 390-ton *Brilliant*.

The effect of her performance was likened to 'a sparrow hawk amongst pigeons'. *America* performed adequately on the light-air downwind leg from Cowes to the east of the Isle of Wight, but in turning into the wind across the back of the island, her narrow bows sliced into the seas, her raked masts and flat-cut sails propelling her forward.

By the evening, with the wind lightening and the haze growing, the anticipation at the Cowes finish line was keen. Queen Victoria, aboard the royal yacht *Victoria and Albert*, when told *America* was first, enquired: 'Who is second?' The response, true or apocryphal, was: 'There is no second'. And so the first of numerous America's Cup legends was born.

Not long after, a dinner was held in Manhattan, at which the owners of the yacht *America* considered what to do with the 'Hundred Pound Cup' they had won in Cowes. An ornate ewer made by Robert Garrard & Sons, the Crown jewellers, it was a standard Victorian cup, not a specially commissioned item, and typical of the Royal Yacht Squadron's prizes at the time.

One idea mooted by the syndicate of *America*'s six owners was to melt down the sterling-silver trophy and make medallions as a keepsake of their successful 1851 foray across the Atlantic. Fortunately that never happened. Instead, *America*'s owners decided to donate the trophy via a Deed of Gift. On 8 July 1857, it was donated as a challenger trophy to promote 'friendly competition among nations', and a new race was born.

Events spanning the three centuries since have proven the contest frequently fierce, sometimes one-sided and not always friendly – the perfect recipe for a great and enduring sporting competition.

To this day the Deed of Gift, registered in a New York court, remains the governing document of the competition, although there are many commercial and sporting supporting regulations bolted on to it.

Though venerable, the Deed, notably in the revisions made in 1887 by the last surviving member of the *America* syndicate, George

Schuyler, was a far-seeing document. Qualifications to be a bona-fide challenger are few, and the actual rules of any given match are infinitely flexible provided that the holder/defender agrees them with the challenger.

This concept of mutual consent has worked well. Chameleon-like, the competition has evolved in response to different circumstances, surviving the American Civil War, two World Wars, the Wall Street Crash and many economic downturns.

For 132 years, the United States was the holder of the America's Cup, defending first in the waters of New York and then later, Newport, Rhode Island. Throughout its history there have been several distinct phases in the competition.

## The first challengers

The first challenge after *America*'s 1851 triumph came in 1870 from James Ashbury of Britain, who faced a fleet of 17 American yachts. He challenged again in 1871 but this was a bitter match, Ashbury complaining about the legality of racing a fleet instead of one opponent, how the races were scored and the actions of the race committee. Though the Americans offered one defender for Ashbury's *Livonia* (named after the Russian province where he'd built a railway) to race, the yacht was chosen on the day of each race, a handy tactic when *Colombia* was dismasted after two races. Already public interest was running at high levels. All manner of vessels were on the water, and thousands of spectators lined the shore.

After Ashbury, it was quite possible that no other Briton would challenge. The America's Cup could have withered and died, save for Canada providing the next two challengers. The first, *Countess of Dufferin*, was under-prepared and under-financed; the second, *Atalanta*, more so. She was dragged through the Erie Canal by mules and dubbed 'rough as a fence post' by one newspaper.

Two acrimonious challenges by Ashbury and two below par ones from Canada's George Cuthbert prompted the NYYC to ask Schuyler to redraft the Deed of Gift. A key change was that challengers had to sail to New York to prove their seaworthiness.

△ The apogee of extreme America's Cup monohulls was in 1903, when Nathanael Herreshoff's American defender *Reliance* met Sir Thomas Lipton's *Shamrock III*.

## The gentlemen and the Big Boats

The next seven contests were for yachts designed to the NYYC Rule and then the Seawanaka Rule, which sought to end competition between wildly differing yachts scored by crude handicap. It ushered in the era of the single-masted yachts.

Initially the yachts were still more akin to floating country homes, such as the British challengers *Genesta* (1884) and *Galetea* (1885). The latter, when not stripped for racing, was decorated with leopard-skin rugs and featured fur throws on the sofas and china and crystal on tables and cabinets. Even when racing, her bird's-eye maple

and mahogany panelling were the epitome of a gentlemen's club. Contemporary accounts say that Mrs Henn, the wife of *Galatea*'s owner, raced with him. So did several dogs and a monkey called Peggy, pulling on ropes alongside the crew.

With the Seawanaka Rule, the yachts moved much closer to becoming racing machines, employing the latest ideas and materials. Scottish designer G.L. Watson visited the US in a scouting exercise to study the best American racing yachts. The scouting was reciprocated in what was the first example of competing syndicates trying to hide their design secrets. The Scottish yacht *Thistle*

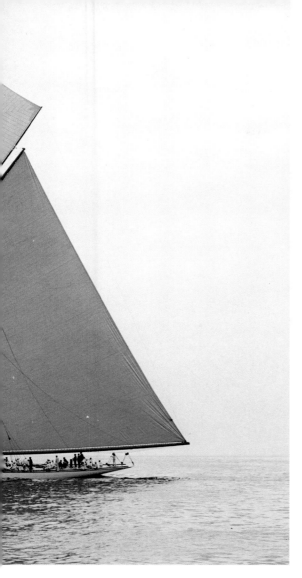

opportunity from his Cup involvement. Popular and media savvy, Lipton grew his tea business, recognizing the power of a brand name as he made tea a drink for all classes.

The apogee of this Big Boat period was 1903, when Nathanael Herreshoff produced *Reliance*. Dubbed 'the Wizard of Bristol' after his Rhode Island residence, Herreshoff was soon to become the most celebrated designer in the America's Cup. His yachts won the matches of 1893, 1895, 1899, 1901, 1903 and 1920.

*Reliance* was, and is, the biggest racing sloop ever produced. With extreme overhangs, she was 28m (90ft) on the waterline, but 43m (140ft) overall. The 5,270m² (17,000 sq ft) of sail carried on one mast was twice that of the two classes used, the J-Class and the 12-metre class.

*Reliance* featured such novelties as a hollow rudder, filled with water to balance and trim it, a telescopic topmast, under-deck winches and gear employing worm-drives and ball bearings. Herreshoff was not shy of innovation, experimenting with materials such as Tobin bronze (a metal resistant to sea water) and aluminium as well as steel. *Defender*, the 1895 defender, experienced the little-understood phenomenon of electrolysis as her cocktail of metals reacted in salt water. Although she didn't quite fizz when her aluminium deck, steel frames and bronze plating hit the water, her corrosion was so bad that she was broken up after a life of six short years. However, the construction method did save 17 tons in a vessel weighing 151 tons.

With the likes of Lipton spending £500,000 to build their yachts, and the American syndicates including scions of the Iselin and Morgan banking families and the Vanderbilt railroad dynasty, the immense cost and short life of the Big Boats was heading in only one direction. Nathanael Herreshoff soon drafted new rules to produce more wholesome yachts, known as J-Class. And the new rules were not the only change. The NYYC moved the racing from New York to Newport, Rhode Island, the summer yachting playground of America's elite.

was covered in tarpaulins when she launched, something repeated in the US. American interest was so piqued that one newspaper employed a diver, who then described the yacht – inaccurately – to an artist. This was espionage, 1887 style.

The following year, Sir Thomas Lipton (the founder of Lipton tea) launched the first of his five bids to win the Cup. None was ever successful and he was knocked back in other ways, being denied membership of the Royal Yacht Squadron for being 'the king's grocer'. But Lipton, a shrewd and charming man, thought the same way as America's owners had originally done, leveraging commercial

### The J-Class

The new J-Class featured single piece, single masts known as Marconi rigs, because of their resemblance to radio aerials. Mainsail booms no longer overhung the stern, allowing fixed backstays, and simple rigging allowed smaller crews of 30 in place of the 50 to 60 of the Big Class. Today, the J-Class embodies the popular ideal of the America's Cup yacht: long, narrow and with a fineness of line that defies their weight, sail area and power.

After a hiatus between 1903 and 1930, following the First World War and its aftermath, including financial crashes in the US and UK, one of the best chances yet seen for a challenger to defeat the Americans came with *Endeavour* in 1934. Aviation pioneer Sir T.O.M. Sopwith loaded his yacht with technology, including wind instruments. To Sopwith's torment, *Endeavour* was 2:0 up before the Americans bounced back with shrewder, subtler and tougher tactics to win 4:2.

In 1937, the US defended with the 'super J', *Ranger*. Her development was the result of extensive tank testing of a full series of hull concepts. She marked the debut of designer Olin Stephens, who, incredibly, was central to every successful defender bar one from 1937 to 1980. Collaborative efforts and the growing size of design teams mean that no one individual has subsequently held such an influence as Stephens.

### The twelves

Again, a devastating world war caused a pause for thought, an even longer 19-year gap this time. Economics then determined the need to downsize, with the 20–22m (65–70ft) yachts of

▽ Sir T. O. M. Sopwith took a 2:0 lead in the 1934 America's Cup in the J-Class *Endeavour* (shown below), but failed to win. Restored and modified, she is still racing today.

the International 12-metre class chosen.

The term '12-metre' referred to a complex formula of sail area, length and weight, the result of which was 12, rather than their actual length. The International Rule was not new, with 6-metres, 8-metres and 12-metres all used in the Olympic regatta before the First World War.

American dominance continued, but this period was notable as new countries other than Canada and Britain entered for the first time. Britain teed off the first post-War challenge in 1958, but the next three decades had an Australian accent. By 1970, would-be challengers were numerous enough for the NYYC to permit multiple entrants and a challenger elimination series.

From 1983 onwards, this was known as the Louis Vuitton Cup.

winged keel under her hull, *Australia 11* caused one of the biggest upsets in sport, finally ending the 132-year grip of the US on the America's Cup.

Defeat ushered in an even greater level of professionalism. One rival converted the hours of two-boat testing carried out by defeated skipper Dennis Conner into miles and reckoned the total was equivalent to sailing around the world. Being beaten drove Conner even harder, and he became not just the first US skipper to lose the America's Cup, but the first to win it back. He did so in Fremantle, Australia, in 1987. Fêted around the world, he made the cover of *Time* magazine and received a ticker-tape parade in Manhattan.

### The America's Cup class

A delay in announcing the venue, class of boat and conditions for Conner's defence back in the USA

◁ *Australia II*, the first ever challenger to win the America's Cup. Her victory meant that the longest winning streak in any sport ended after 132 years in 1983.

In 1970 *Gretel 11*, owned by Australian media magnate Frank Packer, beat *France*, owned by Baron Bich (of pen and razor fame), to become challenger. Sweden joined the fray in 1977, and with two Australian challengers and the French, the numbers were swelling.

Amongst them was Alan Bond, who in 1983 swept aside six other challengers with his *Australia 11*. With John Bertrand at the wheel and a radical

saw New Zealand launch a surprise challenge for the 1988 race. Sir Michael Fay's team dusted off the Deed of Gift and realized that if they challenged with a 28-m (90-ft) waterline vessel, the Americans would have to accept their bid as legitimate.

They did so only after the acrimonious 27th match went all the way through the New York court system. Conner's team responded to the giant 41-m (133-ft) monohull from New Zealand with a 20-m

(65-ft) wingsailed catamaran. Conner's cat trounced the big monohull in a mismatch of yachts sailed amid a nasty atmosphere between the teams, a result finally affirmed at the end of further court action.

This Deed of Gift match meant all other challengers were excluded, adding more ill feeling to the atmosphere. Out of it came a renaissance with a new class of boat. The America's Cup Class was bang up to date, with the latest monohull thinking – meaning higher performance, skinny high-lift appendages and built from the latest composite materials.

When normal service was resumed in 1992 there were two defence teams and eight challengers, a sign of good health. The US kept the Cup, but Conner lost the defence trials to Bill Koch's impressive *America³*.

After three attempts to win in 1987, 1988 and 1992, the fourth incarnation of a Kiwi team got everything right. Team New Zealand (TNZ) walloped all the other challengers, including John Bertrand who made a return bid in the Cup after his 1983 victory.

His hopes sank, literally, as *AUS 35* suffered catastrophic structural failure, folding in half and sinking below the Pacific waves of San Diego.

TNZ triumphed at home in 2000, displaying all that is best about the America's Cup and using the hosting of the event as a catalyst to redevelop a dilapidated part of the Auckland waterfront. Yet in triumph, TNZ imploded during the transition of power from Sir Peter Blake to skipper Russell Coutts. The powerbrokers behind TNZ failed to manage the change effectively and Coutts quit, headhunted by pharmaceutical/biotech billionaire Ernesto Bertarelli for a brand new start-up team from Switzerland.

◁ A long and bitter legal dispute between New Zealand and the US saw the 1988 match contested by two extraordinary but mismatched boats. The New Zealand boat, *KZ-1* (shown here) was a 41-m (133-ft) monohull.

## Did you know?

Not only is the America's Cup the oldest active trophy in international sport – predating the Ashes in cricket and the modern Olympics by decades – but it is also the hardest trophy in international sport to win. Since its inception in 1851, only four nations have won it: Australia (once), New Zealand and Switzerland (twice) and the USA (28 times).

In the space of 30 months, Coutts created a team and skippered *Alinghi* to victory. It was a remarkable achievement. Landlocked, the Swiss held a bidding process to find a venue, eventually picking Valencia in Spain. A strong challenger field attracted returning nations as well as debutants Germany, South Africa and China. A rift with Bertarelli saw Coutts sit out the defence but *Alinghi* won, defeating Team New Zealand.

### The multihull era

Multihulls returned to the Cup in 2010 because, as in 1988, the competition became mired in a legal dispute fought in the New York courts. This time, American software billionaire Larry Ellison, already a two-time challenger, objected to how Ernesto Bertarelli planned the next competition.

Instead of negotiating the match conditions with a challenger, Ellison argued that Bertarelli had created a compliant paper yacht club to rubber-stamp the Swiss rules for the competition. It was a bitter dispute, and despite the Cup's reputation for litigation, this was only the second time in three centuries that the matter was taken to the New York courts.

The outcome was that both teams resorted to yachts 28m (90ft) on the waterline under Deed of Gift conditions. This time both built multihulls, with Ellison's boat sporting the biggest wing ever built. At 72m (232ft) high, it was larger than anything seen on a Boeing 747 or Airbus 380.

A string of court decisions went Ellison's way, including questioning the correctness of Bertarelli's wish to sail the contest in the little-known emirate of Ras-al-Khaimah, whose territorial waters bordered Iran. A greater stretch from New York or Newport could be not imagined.

Skippered by Jimmy Spithill, Ellison's *USA 17*

trounced *Alinghi 2:0*. It was the fourth win masterminded by Russell Coutts in five attempts. What followed Ellison's win in Valencia was the biggest shake-up in the America's Cup history, with the flexibility built in to the Deed of Gift making sweeping changes possible. Coutts and Ellison aimed to modernize and popularize the Cup.

Out went monohulls as the designated class (as opposed to the two Deed of Gift match aberrations) and in came foiling catamarans with wingsails. Out went long races sent out on the open ocean, and in came short, intense races run off the city front. The single biggest innovation of the Ellison era was onscreen graphics, which demystified the racing by tagging boats and showing wind, currents and advantage lines, etc. in superb clarity for the TV and online audience.

If this wasn't enough to engage new audiences, the climactic events of September 2013 certainly were. In San Francisco Bay, Ellison's team looked under-prepared and far from their potential. Team New Zealand stretched to an 8:1 lead in the first-to-nine series. The America's Cup, it seemed, was going back to New Zealand for a second time.

Spithill pondered a crushing defeat at the hands of the Kiwis. 'Imagine if these guys lost from here, what an upset that would be...That would be one hell of a story, one hell of a comeback, and that's what I'd like to be a part of.'

So it happened. 'The biggest comeback in all sport', it was dubbed, and another chapter in the rich and fascinating history of the America's Cup was written.

△ Jimmy Spithill steers the 2010 winner, the *BMW Oracle Racing*, a 35-m (112-ft) trimaran whose towering hard wing is the biggest in history.

## Pinnacles of Sailing
# The Olympic Regatta

▽ Apart from the year 2000, the two-man, Star-class keelboat was part of each Olympic regatta from 1932 to the London 2012 sailing competition in Weymouth, shown here.

Until the Sydney Olympics of 2000, it had always been known as yachting. After that, it was sailing.

The name change was important, as for 100 years of the modern Olympics the sport had been dominated by countries from Europe, North and South America and Australasia. In the early days, the boats were yachts, some requiring as many as 12 crew members, and participation in an expensive sport was limited to those individuals or governments who could afford it.

The key to modernizing Olympic sailing and widening its participation was nothing to do with a rebranding, however. It was down to including windsurfing and the Laser dinghy. These were cheap, identical craft that could be bought off the shelf and were light and easy to transport. The number of countries participating exploded. At London 2012, the top ten places in the Laser men's lightweight singlehander included athletes from Cyprus, Croatia, Uruguay and Guam.

Today's Olympic regatta is very different from that of years past, as the following snapshots will show.

'When I look back, there are so many special memories; from that first medal in Atlanta 16 years ago to carrying the flag at the closing ceremony in London 2012. London was an incredibly special Olympics, competing on home waters and in front of a home crowd.'

**Sir Ben Ainslie** | Most successful sailor in Olympic history

## Vital stats

**Where:** Country of Olympic host nation

**How often:** Quadrennial

**Boat type:** Dinghies, catamarans and windsurfers (ten classes in 2016)

**Crew:** Singlehanded or doublehanded, men, women and mixed

## Route tracker

Worldwide

### Paris, 1900

Sailing was one of three watersports included in the first Olympics of the modern era in Athens in 1898, but it proved too difficult to stage. So yachting made its debut in the Paris games of 1900, with racing taking place on the Seine river at Meulan, near Paris, and at its mouth of Le Havre.

The records from 1900 are a little confusing, showing seven classes of yachts banded into different sizes under a tonnage rule. There was also an open class, allowing Briton Lorne Currie in his 0.5-ton *Scotia* to win two golds with one boat. Competitors came from Britain, France, the Netherlands, Germany, the USA and Switzerland and included several aristocrats.

### St Louis, 1904

No sailing was held.

### London, 1908

The Olympics were taking off. From 200 competitors in Paris, London attracted 2,000. A more scientific rule was used in place of the tonnage rule. The 6-, 7- and 8-Metre classes raced in the Solent at Ryde, Isle of Wight, while the bigger 12-Metre boats competed in Scotland on the Clyde.

Constance Edwina Cornwallis-West, Duchess of Westminster, entered her 8-Metre *Sorais* and was aboard when she took third place. She became yachting's first female medallist.

### Stockholm, 1912

The racing was staged at Nynashamm, south of Stockholm, for 6-, 8-, 10- and 12-Metre classes.

The winner of the 12-Metre class was Norwegian Johan Anker with *Magda IX*, a partner in the Anker and Jensen yard of boat builders and designers. Later, in 1927, Anker produced a 9-m (29.5-ft), three-person keelboat, the Dragon, for a competition organized by Sweden's Royal Gothenburg Yacht Club. It was intended to be a cheaper alternative to the 6-Metre-class yacht and gained Olympic selection in 1948.

### Berlin, 1916

Games cancelled due to the First World War.

### Antwerp, 1920

After the ravages of the First World War, holding the 1920 Olympic Games so close to the scene of so much destruction and loss of life was a bold step. Berlin had been scheduled to be the 1916 host, but Germany and her allies (Austria, Hungary and Turkey) were not invited to Belgium. In all, 14 countries attended, with New Zealand standing on her own feet for the first time instead of being twinned with Australia.

The yachting competition grew to 14 events, less through size of fleets and more through duplication of scoring with the Metre-boats class scored under old and new rules.

Racing was held in the North Sea at Ostend and saw the welcome introduction of dinghies for the first time to dilute the dominance of the keel boats. The 3.7-m and 5.6-m (12-ft and 18-ft) classes pointed to the future, and a shift away from heavy, costly, big keelboats towards smaller, lighter boats.

### Paris, 1924

As the entire organization of the Olympics tightened up, so the yachting regatta consolidated its operation. Racing was cut down to two keelboat classes, while a dinghy, the 3.7-m (12-ft) Voetsjol, was introduced in a forward-thinking innovation.

It attracted 16 competitors, with Portugal, South Africa, Canada, Monaco, Poland, Italy, Cuba, Spain and Argentina bringing greater representation to the regatta. As in 1900, racing was split between Meulan and Le Havre.

### Amsterdam, 1928

Racing took place on the Zuideerzee, still open to the North Sea before the extensive flooding of 1932 that led to it becoming closed off to form the IJsselmeer.

Crown Prince Olav continued Norway's steady run of medals, which started in 1908 with victory in the 6-Metre class. He was the first member of a royal household to win an Olympic

medal. His son, Harald, was later to try and repeat this success in the 1964–72 Games.

## Los Angeles, 1932

Back in the USA again, the Olympics saw sailing take place at Long Beach, a venue to be used again 60 years later when Los Angeles hosted its second Games.

1932 will always be remembered for the introduction of the two-man Star keelboat, which was to become the longest-used class of boat in Olympic competition.

Designed in the office of Garden & Cox (William Cox created the famous schooner *Atlantic*), the Star had an unbroken run (with the exception of 1976) until it bowed out gracefully after 2012.

Post-Great Depression, this was an austerity Games. That said, subsidies were offered to European countries to assist their shipping 6- and 8-Metre boats to California. None accepted other than Swede Tore Holm, who added a second gold in the 6 Metre to that won in 1920.

## Berlin, 1936

When the Games were awarded to Germany, the National Socialist Party had not yet taken power. Inevitably, though, the 1936 Games came to be called 'Hitler's Olympics', and were famous for sprinter Jesse Owens' four-medal win.

Sailing was out of the spotlight, the competition held to the north in Kiel, where it was to return in 1972. The Jolle replaced the Voetsjol as the dinghy class, and for the first time at the

△ The two-person Tornado catamaran was added to the roster of Olympic boats in the 1976 Games in Canada. For more than 30 years, it was the fastest and most spectacular Olympic boat.

Games the boats were provided by the hosts – 'supplied equipment', in current Olympic parlance.

**Tokyo, 1940**
Games cancelled due to the Second World War.

**London, 1944**
Games cancelled due to the Second World War.

**London, 1948**
With Europe ravaged by the Second World War, staging the Olympics in 1948 was no easy matter. Germany and Japan were not present, but a record 59 nations were. In the sailing world, the 1948 Games will always be remembered for the debut of the first of its great Olympians, Dane Paul Elvstrøm.

Until Ben Ainslie matched him in 2012, Elvstrøm had an unsurpassed four golds from consecutive Olympics. It might never have been, for Elvstrøm retired from the first race at Torquay after a Finnish rival lashed him verbally for a port-and-starboard incident. A shy man with a strong sense of honourable conduct, Elvstrøm did not like his first experience of the Olympics. He was just 18, and could speak no English.

Elvstrøm was competing in the 3.7-m (12-ft)

Firefly class, a two-person, hot-moulded plywood dinghy designed by Uffa Fox, but employed as a singlehander for the Olympics. Capsizes were frequent. Elvstrøm sailed without his jib, reefed the main and raced his boat while others fought theirs.

By now, the 6-Metre class were the only metre-boat class left in the regatta, as the move towards smaller, higher-performing boats accelerated. Among them was the Star. Bahamian Durwood Knowles sailed for Britain, as the Bahamas did not have separate representation. To reach the UK, Knowles shipped his boat from Nassau to Miami, trailed it to New York and would have missed his crossing on the *Queen Mary* but for a delay due to a bomb scare. Then, in Torquay, he was dismasted in one race and disqualified in another. Knowles raced for the Bahamas in 1952 and continuously until 1988.

**Helsinki, 1952**
When the Games went to Finland, yachting witnessed the introduction of the Finn single-handed dinghy, which has proven to be one of the most enduring and demanding of Olympic boats.

Seeking a satisfactory singlehander in place of the

Firefly, which was a two-person boat pressed into solo sailing, the Finnish Yachting Federation ran a trial.

Rikard Sarby designed and built the Fint (later called the Finn), although not before cutting off a couple of fingertips with an electric saw while building his prototype. The Swedish Pricken design was the front-runner in the first trials, but the Fint came through strongly in the second, windy, trials in Sarby's hands. It was selected and renamed the Finn, and Elvstrøm was its first gold medallist with a huge points lead. Sarby took the bronze.

## Melbourne, 1956

In 1956, for the first time, the Olympics moved from Europe and the USA. It was sailing's gain that it went to Australia, a great yachting country.

Racing took place in various locations on Port Philip Bay. Paul Elvstrøm won his third gold and Canada's Bruce Kirby was eighth overall in the Finns. His Olympic triumph came later when, in 1996, his creation – the Laser – was introduced to the Games.

There was another name at this Games that later earned international renown in the form of West Australian Rolly Tasker, racing in the International Sharpie class which was making

its solitary inclusion in the Games. The German world champion was the only other person in the 13-strong fleet to win a heat against Tasker and his Kiwi rival, Peter Mander. The Tasker versus Mander battle for gold continued into the last race, with Tasker thinking he'd secured the title until a tangle at the final windward mark with the French boat. Tasker didn't protest, but the Frenchman did and Tasker lost the gold despite ending up tied. Mander had three wins to the Australian's two. It was New Zealand's first sailing gold.

## Rome, 1960

Despite Rome being host city, the yachting took place in the southern city of Naples. It was a notable regatta, as no country won more than one gold and 11 nations shared the 15 medals won. It was an encouraging sign for those wanting to see the competition open up.

Elvstrøm secured his fourth gold and third in the Finn class. Timir Pinegin's gold in the Star was the USSR's first in sailing, his boat built by Skip Etchells in the USA. Etchells was to go on to create one of the most popular three-person keelboats in sailing, the E-22.

Greece issued a stamp to commemorate

▽ Star-class dinghies in action during the London 2012 Olympics at Weymouth Bay in Dorset, UK.

△ Tornado catamarans try and steal every bit of the strong easterly breeze off each other during the final qualifier for the 2012 Olympics in Weymouth, UK.

Crown Prince Constantine's victory in the Dragons, his country's first-ever yachting medal. Queen Frederica embraced her son after the final race, and then playfully pushed him into the water in front of King Paul. Constantine's grandfather had been one of those who worked tirelessly with de Coubertin to bring the modern Olympics to life.

### Tokyo, 1964

The first Asian Olympics were held in Japan, with the sailing based at Enoshima on Sagami Bay. This was the Games that saw the success of competitors who were to go and build significant companies in the marine industry. Elvstrøm had already shown the way and formed a business to leverage his success and sell some of his innovations, such as the low-drag self-bailer.

The founder and future president of North Sails, the Americans Lowell North and Peter Barrett, took bronze in the Dragon and silver in the Finn classes respectively. Briton Keith Musto and American Harry 'Buddy' Melges scored silver and bronze in the Flying Dutchman dinghy before becoming leading clothing manufacturers and

boatbuilders in the industry.

Willie Kuhweide's gold medal in the Finn and Peter Arendt's in the Dragon were scored under Unified Germany, even though the Berlin Wall had gone up three years earlier to divide the country.

### Mexico City, 1968

Paul Elvstrøm returned to sailing at this Games, after his own desire to excel and the expectation that he could not win a fifth gold after 1960 led him to stay away from Olympic sailing. Switching to the Star, he won only one race and finished fourth in the regatta held at Acapulco.

Lowell North won the Star gold convincingly. In the Finn, much was expected of Brazil's three-times world champion Gold Cup winner and bendy-rig pioneer Jörg Bruder, but he didn't make the podium. Instead, 30-year-old Valentin Mankin, who'd been in the class for 15 years, won his first gold. Mankin was to become one of the most fêted Olympic sailors behind Ainslie and Elvstrøm, with three golds and a silver in three classes.

Winning silver behind Mankin was Austrian Hubert Raudaschl, whose first Games was in

1960 and his ninth and last in 1992, by which time he'd won another silver (1980, Star). A nice touch was Switzerland's Louis Noverraz winning a silver in the 5.5s at the ripe age of 66. He had just missed victory in 1936 at Kiel, when he was eliminated under the amateur rule. The IYRU rule rescinded the verdict in 1965 and Noverraz 'won' retrospective silver.

## Munich, 1972

The Olympics returned to a Germany that was now divided between the federal west and the socialist east. At Kiel, the hosts built a marina and housing complex to rival that of Japan eight years earlier. It needed to be big: there were 152 boats from 42 nations on site.

Both East (Paul Borowksi in the Dragon) and West Germany (Uli Libor in the Flying Dutchman) scored medals. Valentin Mankin won a second gold, having moved from the Finn to the Tempest, his boat the only one in the USSR.

## Montreal, 1976

In a bid to modernize Olympic sailing, two venerable keelboats, the Star and the Dragon, were replaced. Their substitutes were the modern, glass-fibre, trapezing 470 dinghy, designed by Frenchman Andre Cornu, and a multihull with the Tornado class. The Tornado was designed by Rodney March and had won trials held by the International Yacht Racing Union to select an Olympic catamaran.

Like Rikard Sarby had done with the Finn, Reg White, already a winner of the Little America's Cup, blended his intimate knowledge of the class (having built and raced the Tornado prototype in the trials) with his ability to win the first gold medal with a race in hand, crewed by his brother-in-law John Osborn.

East Germany was among the medals, with Jochen Schümann winning the Finn-class gold on his way into the pantheon of medalists. He eventually matched Russia's Valentin Mankin's three golds and a silver, after moving to the Soling class.

Schümann had never won a major Finn event

◁ A postage stamp, devoted to the Summer Olympics in Montreal, depicts the Regatta course in Brandenburg, circa 1976.

before the Games, but a sports-science student, he used an early VMG (speed made good to windward) indicator to develop his sails, settings, tune and steering. A rudimentary recording device and basic computer had allowed post-test analysis. Although they didn't know it at the time, the paths of Australian John Bertrand, bronze in the Finn, and Dennis Conner, bronze in the Tempest, were later to become inexorably linked in the historic 1983 America's Cup

## Moscow, 1980

Politics overtook the Moscow Olympics as the USA led a boycott over, ironically, the Soviet Union's invasion of Afghanistan.

The effect was felt less in the yachting competition, as individual countries and federations made their own decisions about participation. Some 80 nations competed where there had been 92 and 121 in Montreal and Munich. In sporting terms, the notable absentees were the USA, Japan and West Germany and along with these three, Australia, Britain, Canada and France were missing from the sailing competition. Competitors were reduced, too, with only 83 boats contesting the six classes – the smallest total since 1956. The Tempest was dropped after just two Games to make way for the Star's return, with Valentin Mankin and Hubert Raudaschl winning the gold and silver.

## Los Angeles, 1984

The USA-led boycott of the Moscow Games was reciprocated by the USSR leading a Soviet Bloc refusal to attend the Los Angeles Olympics.

The USA was dominant, winning medals in every class – something not seen from a host country since 1912. This was the first of four

△ New Zealand's Russell Coutts on his way to his gold medal at Long Beach in the 1984 Los Angeles Games.

Olympic regattas that the host country was to dominate, in 1984, 1992, 2000 and 2012. Sailing gained a seventh event with the introduction of windsurfing. Despite the boycott this was the biggest sailing competition yet, with 82 countries competing.

This was Paul Elvstrøm's last Games, coming out of retirement at the age of 56 to sail a Tornado with his youngest daughter, Trine. They finished fourth. Just one place better in any race would have secured the bronze that so many wanted the Elvstrøms to win. Spain's Luis Doreste won the 470 gold, yet many remember 1984 as the year when Briton Cathy Foster, crewed by Pete Newlands, won a race against an all-male fleet in an open Olympic class, finishing seventh overall in a 28-boat competition.

### Seoul, 1988

The low numbers of women in Olympic sailing was addressed by adding an eighth event, a 470 division for females. Americans Allison Jolly and Lisa Jewel were the first winners in the 21-boat fleet. All this took place in Pusan, South Korea's second city after the capital Seoul.

Two of the all-time greats in the Soling class, Jochen Schümann (from what was still East Germany) and Dane Jesper Bank sandwiched American silver medalist John Kostecki. The Schümann versus Bank contest was to run all the way through to the final leg of the final race of the 2000 Olympics in Sydney, after which the Soling was dropped.

### Barcelona, 1992

For once, the sailing competition was right at the heart of the host city. A run-down quarter of the Catalan city was revitalized with the main Olympic Village just across the road from a vast new marina, from which the public could view from platforms and the breakwater.

Spain won four golds and a silver from nine

classes, which had grown thanks to the addition of a women's windsurfer event. The Spanish team started training at the venue early, even while the marina was being built. Big cash bonuses were on offer to the medal winners, too.

The gold medalists were Luis Doreste and Domingo Manrique in the Flying Dutchman; Theresa Zabell and Patricia Guerra in the women's 470 and Jordi Calafat and Kiko Sánchez Luna in the men's fleet and Jose Marie van der Ploeg in the Finn. The silver went to Natalia Via Dufresne in the newly introduced women's singlehander, the Europe.

### Atlanta, 1996

From being centre stage in Barcelona, sailing at the Atlanta Games became remote and well-nigh impossible for spectators to enjoy.

It took place in Savannah, 240 miles southeast of Atlanta. The administration base on Tybee Island was created five miles out of town, from where another three-mile ferry journey was needed to reach the temporary Olympic Marina on Wilmington Island. Further still was a day marina, built out of barges towed around from the Mississippi, and moored near Williamson Island. Finally contestants sailed into the shallow, murky waters of Wassaw Sound for the racing.

For American fans, there was massive disappointment. Only two bronzes left the hosts in fourth place in the medal table – off the bottom.

Lee Lai Shan won the windsurfing women's gold. Hong Kong was in transition from British colony to autonomous region of China and it was the tiny Asian state's first gold in any sport.

### Sydney, 2000

Sailing was back, front and centre. A great natural amphitheatre, Sydney harbour was a tricky place to sail, though many of its patterns could be learnt. The most difficult courses proved to be the one just inside the Heads, where the wind swirled and waves rebounded, and the outside course in the Tasman, which often featured a rolling swell under a weak breeze.

The Australian Yachting Federation hired Ukrainian 470 coach Victor 'Medal Maker'

Kuvalenko and it produced a host nation bonanza. Reigning world champions Tom King and Mark Turnbull won the men's fleet and Jenny Armstrong and Belinda Stowell the women's fleet. John Forbes, the 1992 Tornado bronze medallist, teamed up with Darren Bundock to take silver. Britain just pipped Australia as top nation, setting a run of success that carried on to Beijing 2008.

For many, Sydney will be remembered for the epic battle in the Laser with Briton Ben Ainslie match racing Brazil's Robert Scheidt for the gold and Denmark's Jesper Bank passing Germany's Jochen Schümann on the last leg in front of the Opera House to win the Soling-class gold.

This was the Soling's last Games. Making its debut was the radical-looking 49er two-man skiff, designed by Aussie Julian Bethwaite.

### Athens, 2004

Athens was another city venue where the sailing was close by. Regrettably, despite refurbishing a vast marina with a breakwater ideal for viewing, the authorities restricted spectators to boats.

Having outgrown the Laser, Ben Ainslie had moved into the Finn, jumped straight to the top of the class and was clear favourite for another gold. His first two races were weak, with conservative starts and some missed shifts. Then he tangled with Guillaume Florent, whom he crossed on port tack believing the Frenchman had waved him through. Ainslie was disqualified and was 19th after two races, his two discards effectively used. He responded with a breathtaking display of sailing.

Having won the IYRU Olympic selection trials, an old class, the 1967 Yngling, was brought in for 2004 as the women's fleet racing keelboat. It had been designed by Jan Linge, hot on the heels of his larger Soling. It drew many former Europe-class competitors, with Briton Shirley Robertson winning with a race to spare. It was her second gold.

### Beijing, 2008

2008 marked the first time that the Medal Race format, featuring the top ten competitors competing in a final double-points race, was used at the Olympic Games. China won its

first ever gold medal in sailing, Jian Yin in the men's RS:X windsurfer, backed up by Lilja Xu's bronze in the Laser Radial which had replaced the Europe as the women's singlehander. Alessandra Sensini of Italy became the first female sailor to win four Olympic medals, and a total of 18 nations won medals.

The regatta at Qingdao, 500 miles from Beijing, was marred in the build-up by the Yellow Sea turning green with huge areas of algae bloom. A massive operation saw the course area 'swept' each day by a vast fleet of boats.

### London, 2012

In 2012, Britain lost its crown to Australia as top sailing nation, not that the host country (which still won medals in five of the ten events) was disappointed. Ben Ainslie, in a nail-biting competition that was not decided until the penultimate leg of the last race, became the most successful Olympic sailor of all time.

Ainslie's silver, gold, gold, gold and gold from five successive Games moved him ahead of Paul Elvstrøm in the medal tally. Though remote from London in Weymouth and Portland, the sailing competition was specially geared up for viewing and some 60,000 spectators watched the medals decided at a hugely successful Games.

▽ The two-man 49er high-performance skiff, which made its debut at the 2000 Olympics in Sydney, bringing new levels of speed and athleticism.

# Offshore Races

▽ The competing yachts are off to a picture-perfect spinnaker start, as they steam out of Victoria during the 2010 Victoria–Maui race.

'The Vic–Maui race gives you a lot of support to go offshore for the first time. They do a lot of safety checks and make sure the boat is really well equipped for offshore and give you a lot of support out there. It's a great way to start an offshore adventure.'

Al Bartlett | Skipper of *Starlight Express*, Victoria–Maui 2008

## Route tracker

NORTH PACIFIC OCEAN

Victoria

Maui

## Vital stats

**What:** 2,308-mile offshore race

**Where:** Victoria (Canada) to Lahaina (Hawaii)

**How often:** Biennial

**Boat type:** Monohulls

**Crew:** Fully crewed

888

*Querida*
SIDNEY B.C.

Of the two major races run from the west coast of North America, the Victoria–Maui race is younger but longer than the Transpac, run from Los Angeles, USA.

The Victoria–Maui Race is a 2,308-mile event run from the island and city of Victoria, British Columbia, on the beautiful northwestern seaboard of Canada. It finishes off Lahaina on the island of Maui, the second-largest island in Hawaii. 2016 marks the 50th anniversary of the race, which is held every two years and is run by the Royal Victoria Yacht Club.

For the crews, the race has two distinct phases. First, they have to negotiate the light winds of the high-pressure area that sits over the northern Pacific in summer before tucking into the second phase, the tradewinds that will speed their yachts towards the Hawaiian islands. Getting the routing right in dealing with the Pacific high is the key to a rewarding second part of the race.

The race was the brainchild of Jim Innes, both a member of the Royal Victoria Yacht Club and a pilot for Canadian Pacific airlines. When he managed to persuade three other yachtsmen to sail to Hawaii in 1965, the race was on.

Jim Innes had a Lapworth 36 called *Long Gone*, Lol Killam the 14-m (45-ft) *Volaris*, Ron Ramsay another 14-m (45-ft) boat called *Norena of White*, while from just over the border in the US, Boo Paskal brought his 22.6-m (73-ft) ketch *Tatoosh*.

The *Vancouver Times* painted a pen portrait of the first race: 'A jet can reach Hawaii in six hours. But a group of British Columbia sailors preferred to do it the adventurous way – the hard way, if you like. They took 16 days and pioneered an honest-to-God ocean race that will stand as a test to BC yachtsmen as long as the wind blows.'

They faced what would become typical conditions for the race, nosing into westerlies in the Juan de Fuca strait, and then following the Washington, Oregon and California coast down to the parallel of San Francisco before gaining westing and picking up the northeasterly trades and carrying spinnakers to Hawaii.

The three smaller boats took 15 days to make the passage, reaching Hawaii within 15 hours of each other. Meeting them at the finish line in Kahalui harbour was the crew of *Tatoosh*, who'd used the engine and so retired from the competition. They greeted the other crews with mai tais on the dockside. Fittingly, Innes's *Long Gone* was the winner.

Before heading home from Maui, Innes talked to local yachtsmen who were in the formative stages of creating the Lahaina Yacht Club, and back in Canada he persuaded his own club and the new one in Hawaii to formalize the running of the race.

Noting that the first Transpac had attracted just three boats when it was first run, before developing into a major event, Innes set a target of 15 runners for the next Vic–Maui. The second race was run in 1968 and brought 14 yachts to the start line.

## A race of two halves

The 2002 race stood out for its distinctly contrasting conditions. So light were the winds in the Juan de Fuca strait that many in the fleet were forced to anchor to avoid being pushed backwards on the flood tide.

Then, off Washington's Cape Flattery, the most northwesterly point on the contiguous USA, a low-pressure cell brought 30 hours of 55-knot winds and big seas. When conditions abated, the wind had vanished altogether. Several days of making zero progress triggered a spate of retirements. An attendance of just 250 sailors at the awards banquet instead of the expected 400 told the story.

By the time of the 25th Vic–Maui in 2014, a total of 389 yachts had taken part in the race, ranging from modest cruiser-racers such as the Pearson 30 and Tartan 10, to maxis such as Jake Woods' Mull 82 *Sorcery* (1976) and a clutch of ultra-light Santa Cruz 70s, including Bill Lee's famous *Merlin* (1978).

One, Roy Disney's *Pyewacket*, set a record in 1996 of 9d 19h, but this has since been eclipsed by James McDowell's *Grand Illusion*, which managed 9d 2h in 2000.

△ A downhill race to the delights of Hawaii has long been the Vic–Maui race's trump card.

◁ Just off Vancouver Island, the fleet of racing yachts jostle for best position during the start of the 2012 edition of the Victoria–Maui race.

# Offshore Races
# Transpacific Yacht Race
## North Pacific/Oceania

So impressive a piece of wood-carving is the 1×1.2m (3.5×4ft) Transpacific Yacht Club's Perpetual Trophy that it is known as the Barn Door, and counts as one of the most cherished prizes in the sport.

### Linked by an earthquake and a volcano

First run in 1906, the Transpacific Race is one of the oldest and longest continuously run ocean races in the world. It's linked by an earthquake and a volcano. Originally, the start was to have been from San Francisco, but the 1906 earthquake forced the three entrants to relocate to Los Angeles. Over the years, Los Angeles, Long Beach, Balboa, San Pedro, Santa Barbara, Santa Monica and San Francisco have all sent the fleet on their way. The finish is Diamond Head, east of Honolulu and one of the numerous volcanic features that shape the Hawaiian islands.

H.H. Sinclair's 26.4-m (85-ft) schooner *Lurline* was the very first winner in a time of 12d 9h 59m, the first of three successive victories. The First World War paused the race between 1912 and 1923. The race was run during the Second World War in 1939 and 1941, but the Japanese raid on Honolulu's Pearl Harbor at the end of 1941 precipitated another stop until 1947.

The 1923 race was out of step, as Papeete, Tahiti, was the finish in place of Honolulu. From 1906 to 1936 the race was biennial in even years, with a change to odd-numbered years made in 1939. The smallest fleet seen was just a pair of yachts in 1932 (the time of the Great Depression in the USA), but the largest has topped 100 several times.

For much of its life, the Transpac has drawn its entrants from the west coast and midwest of the USA. Australians Frank and John Livingstone and Magnus Halvorsen were the first non-North American entrants in 1949 and 1951 respectively. Dick Dole was another competitor in the 1951 race. His *Typee* was the local Hawaiian champion in the 1950 season, her owner a driving force behind the islands' biggest export – Dole pineapples.

The 1949 race saw *Morning Cloud* complete her last three days at sea without a rudder, the crew cutting down the spinnaker pole and using the chart table to jury rig a rudder. Even more remarkable was the experience of Ted Sierks in the 1951 race. He fell overboard from *l'Apache* 800 miles from Oahu and was rescued by the US navy after 30 hours in the water.

### It started with an idea

Clarence MacFarlane is the father of the race, for it was his idea for San Franciscan yachtsmen to race to Honolulu. At a distance of 2,225 miles,

the race is long but famous for its sleigh-ride, downwind running conditions. So dominant is the offwind sailing in the Transpac that it spawned a whole breed of yachts on the US west coast, the so-called Ultra-Light Displacement Boats (ULDBs) in the 1970s and 1980s.

Bill Lee's *Merlin* was arguably one of the most influential ULDBs built, characterized by light displacement and commensurately short rig and low sail area – more a frigate than the battleship of the prevailing design type of the era. In 1977, up against the might of heavy-brigade maxi yachts such as Bob Johnson's *Windward Passage* and Jim Kilroy's *Kialoa III*, *Merlin* set a race record of 8d 11h 1m that proved unbeatable for 20 years.

Besides *Merlin*, there have many standouts in Transpac history. One has been the Cal-40, Bill Lapworth's famous design from the 1960s. Not only did Don Salisbury, Skip Allen and John Andron's Cal-40s win the 1965, 1967 and 1969 races, but the class has also undergone a modern-day revival.

Noted round-the-world navigator Stan Honey won the singlehanded division in his *Illusion* in the 1992 Transpac. In 2003 he raced with his wife Sally, herself a top sailor, and Skip Allen and John Andron to place third on corrected time behind two racier TP52s. Sally Honey also raced with three other women in 2005.

▽ With Hawaii in sight, *Wild Oats XI* claims another victory as she heads into Honolulu for the finish of the Transpac 2015.

Another veteran has been *Dorade*, the 2013 winner in the hands of Matt Brooks but also a winner in 1936, on top of earlier Atlantic Race and Fastnet Race honours. She was one of Olin Stephen's early designs, an icon in ocean racing.

The Transpac is not exclusively downwind. Crews have to earn the sublime sailing conditions with a three-day, upwind slog at the start before they reach the Pacific High, an area of high atmospheric pressure. There they can ride the easterly winds, which blow on the underside of the High. It's a case of spinnakers up and sunhats on. And although the looping course is longer than the direct rhum-line course, it avoids the light winds closer to the core of the high-pressure zone.

Easy, though, the race is not. During the day, the breezes are a sumptuous 15–25 knots, but at night they can double in strength and the seas climb, putting a premium on accurate helming and trimming.

As Dennis Durgan, a noted west-coast helmsman and sailmaker, once commented, 'The last three days of the Transpac is like riding a derailed freight train through the tunnel of love.'

Eventually eclipsing *Merlin*'s record was Roy Disney's (nephew of Walt) *Pyewacket* in 1977. She was a ULDB-inspired Santa Cruz 70 yacht and managed 7d 15h 22m.

Disney went on to support a crew of young Transpac first-timers. From 538 applicants, 15 of them aged between 18 and 23 were given six months' training before they tackled the race. A movie produced by Disney, *Morning Light*, documented their feat.

Multihulls were added to the Transpac in 1995, with the late aviation, ballooning and sailing record-setter Steve Fossett winning in his 18.6-m (60-ft) trimaran *Lakota*.

The advent of the latest maxis, with their complex appendages (daggerboards, canting keels, etc., often handled via stored power), has seen the race record fall. The organizers welcomed these unlimited maxis, but ultimately decided to reserve the Barn Door Trophy for conventional boats.

## Offshore Races
# Fastnet Race
## English Channel/Celtic Sea

*'Hardly a week has passed in the past 20 years when I have not thought about that frigid, soaking night when white water roared down on us from every direction as we beat out to Fastnet Rock. An event that was "only a sailboat race" had left 15 people dead, hundreds in mourning, and thousands terrified.'*

**John Rousmaniere** | Author of *Fastnet, Force 10*

▽ The race-leading yachts use the strong breeze of an advancing low-pressure system to power across the Celtic Sea and round the Fastnet Rock.

Just four miles from Cape Clear on Ireland's southwestern corner, the Fastnet Rock is one of the best-known lighthouses in the world. Nowadays it is unmanned and automated, best known as the turning point of the famous biannual Fastnet Race. But for more than two centuries it was a vital navigation mark and landfall, the point of departure or arrival from Europe. To the west, there is nothing but 2,000 miles of Atlantic Ocean before reaching Newfoundland.

A race around the Rock was first mooted over a glass or two of Plymouth gin in the Royal Weston Yacht Club back in 1924 by Lieutenant Commander George Martin and yachting writer Western Martyr. They had formed the Ocean Racing Club, whose initial aim was to organize a race of not less than 600 miles.

The Britons were aware that yachtsmen in the USA already had a race to Bermuda (initially from New London, and later from New York). Indeed, Martyr had sailed in the 1923 and 1924 races.

Martyr advocated ocean racing, and the proposed Fastnet Race would start from the Solent, go around the Rock and finish in Plymouth. He wrote in *Yachting Monthly*, 'It is without question the very finest sport a man can engage in.'

Martyr won the inaugural race in 1925 in *Jolie Brise*, a former French pilot cutter built in 1913. In all, *Jolie Brise* competed in the Fastnet Race four times, winning three.

The Fastnet Challenge Cup evolved into the Fastnet Race with the trophy remaining the principal prize, though the test it poses has not changed. There are inshore and coastal phases out of the Solent and

along England's south coast, with all the tidal gates and shifting winds to be met. Beyond Land's End the colour of the sea changes and the Atlantic swell becomes apparent, as the open passage is made across the Celtic Sea to Ireland and back.

## The 1979 storm

These western approaches can deal out the severest of conditions, never more so than in 1979 when a rapidly deepening Atlantic depression swung the breeze around and created vicious breaking waves. The storm of 14–15 August that year claimed 15 lives. Of the 303 yachts that started, only 85 finished. Some 24 yachts were abandoned, five claimed by the raging seas.

The tragic events made headline news around the world, not least because former British prime minister Edward Heath was competing, as was CNN mogul Ted Turner. It was an era of paper navigation charts and not always reliable radio communications. In the tumult, crews struggled to keep their yachts on their feet and their equipment working. For the majority, racing ended two days after the start, replaced by an elemental fight for survival.

The normal functions of navigating, cooking and resting fell by the wayside. Cookers and radios failed. Those yachts that couldn't make daily radio check-ins to the accompanying escort vessel were feared missing rather than out of contact.

On land, this was also an era before even fax machines. Just getting the Telex printouts between the Land's End coastguard and Plymouth was taking three to six hours. With such communication difficulties at sea and on land, it was inevitable that inaccurate reporting would run rife. The New York Times carried a report of two US Admiral's Cup team yachts being lost. Causing more consternation was the fact that two American crewmen arrived back in Plymouth to find that their obituaries had been published.

The rescue operation mounted by British, French and Irish services was massive. Thirteen

lifeboats spent 169 hours at sea; helicopters some 411 hours in the air; fixed-wing aircraft a further 135 hours. In all, 136 sailors were rescued from yachts, life rafts and the sea.

It was tragically bad luck that such a concentration of yachts found itself in the path of an unusually severe summer storm in a location where it generated an especially confused and raging sea. In a battle against the odds, the unforgiving sea overwhelmed the fleet.

Some of the world's elite custom racing yachts, as well as ordinary series-produced cruiser racers, were laid flat or, worse, rolled through 360 degrees. Size or style was no arbiter of whether a yacht suffered in the conditions. Yachts over 15.5m (50ft) were knocked down or rolled; one of the smallest, the Contessa 32 Assent, came through it and finished.

The sport fell under a scrutiny that had not been seen before. A diligent review of the 1979 Fastnet Race brought in a host of recommendations

△ A defining image of the 1979 Fastnet Race tragedy. Fifteen sailors lost their lives, but another 136 were recovered by the rescue services.

## Fastnet speeds

The winner of the first Fastnet race in 1925 was a gaff-rigged pilot cutter named Jolie Brise. It took the boat 147 hours to finish the race. Today, yachts are competing to beat the monohull record of 42 hours 39 minutes, set by the Volvo 70 yacht Abu Dhabi in 2011.

◁ Maxi-trimaran Banque Populaire V steaming past the Needles Lighthouse off the Isle of Wight during the August 2011 Rolex Fastnet Race.

for training, procedures and equipment, which became widely adopted by other race organizers. It was a turning point in the sport of offshore racing.

Before and after events of 1979, the race prospered. It is one of the great classics in ocean racing, along with the Sydney–Hobart and Bermuda races, and its honour roll is populated by some of the most prestigious names in the sport. American Paul Hammond became the first overseas winner in 1928. In 1931, his countrymen Olin and Rod Stephens triumphed in *Dorade*, the yacht that was to launch the Sparkman & Stephens design office into a global powerhouse for the next 50 years. On the brink of war, the German navy set the fastest time for the 1939 race in *Nordwind*.

With winners coming from Britain, France, the Netherlands, Sweden, the USA, Australia and Brazil, it took until 2007 for an Irishman to win his 'home' event, with Ger O'Rouke's 15.5-m (50-ft) *Chieftain*.

Many different handicap systems have been used over the years, but the winner has normally been from the mid-to-large size range. A notable exception was in 1973, when Richard and Harvey Bagnall sailed the 10-m (33-ft) *Golden Delicious* to victory, a feat repeated by Matt Humphries in the 9-m (30-ft) *Min-o-Din* in 1991.

Times for line honours have tumbled from the 6d 3h that *Jolie Brise* first took in 1925. The fastest monohull time was set in 2007 by Mike Slade's 28-m (90-ft) *Leopard* in 1d 20h. In recent times, the monohull record was set in 2011 by the Volvo 70 *Abu Dhabi* in 42h 39m.

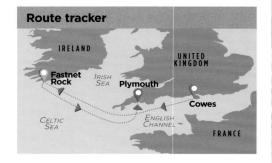

### Route tracker

IRELAND

**Fastnet Rock**

*IRISH SEA*

**Plymouth**

UNITED KINGDOM

*CELTIC SEA*

**Cowes**

*ENGLISH CHANNEL*

FRANCE

## Vital stats

**What:** 605-mile offshore race around Fastnet Rock

**Where:** Cowes (UK) to Plymouth (UK)

**How often:** Biennial

**Boat type:** IRC/non-IRC and open monohulls, multihulls

**Crew:** Fully crewed

▽ The Whitbread 60 *illbruck* reaches the Fastnet Rock in the 1999 race.

## Coastal Races
# Tour de France à la Voile
French Atlantic/Mediterranean Sea

*'The Tour is a model in French crew-handed sailing. Many young sailors have grown to top-level racing and become pro after sailing on the Tour. Multihull sailing is clearly part of the French sailing and technological culture, and now it is finally going international!'*

**Michel Desjoyeaux** | Double winner of the *Vendée Globe*

## Route tracker

UNITED
KINGDOM

NETHERLANDS

Breskens

Dunkirk
Departure

ENGLISH CHANNEL

Dieppe

Deauville

BELGIUM

Brest

Lorient

FRANCE

Saint Gilles

ATLANTIC
OCEAN

BAY OF
BISCAY

Delivery

Marseille
Arrival

La-Seyne
sur-Mer

Gruissan

Roses

MEDITERRANEAN
SEA

## Vital stats

**What:** Multi-stage
race around France

**Where:** From Dunkirk
via Breskens to Saint
Gilles, then overland
delivery to Roses via
La-Seyne sur-Mer to
Marseille

**How often:** Annual

**Boat type:** M32
catamarans

**Crew:** Fully crewed

◁ Modelled on the cycle race,
the Tour de France à la Voile
sees crews compete on the
north, west and south coasts
of France.

Take an excellent proven concept and apply it elsewhere – that's how one French legend spawned another. The famous Tour de France cycle road race was applied to the sea and first run in 1978. It was so successful that the Voile version is now a firmly established fixture in the European calendar.

Although the Tour de France à la Voile has passed through the hands of several organizing bodies and the type of boats used has varied enormously, the annual event has held true to the original concept. For this, we must thank Bernard Decré. Back in 1978 he declared, somewhat grandiosely, 'I praise God every day. He created the world. He let me create the Tour de France à la Voile.'

Fundamental to the concept was a multi-stage event, with a travelling road show supporting the race fleet as it raced between ports. Secondly, Decré expressly targeted young sailors. He wanted to give them an opportunity to enter high-level offshore racing outside the conventional and limited points of entry. Typically this meant finding an owner or yacht club to secure a crewing spot.

Just how green some of the crews were is exemplified by 18-year-old Jean-Yves le Hir, who skippered the winning Marseille boat. 'We were just over 18 and didn't have a clue about currents and navigation,' he said. 'It was an adventure. Well, we won very few legs because we often didn't know where the finish line was and had to wait for another boat to show us the direction.'

Ashore, a festival atmosphere was created with bands, performances, farmers' markets, food and drink fairs and street parties.

**One-design fleet**

A vital enabling factor to get the race up and running was to find a fleet of yachts to race, as the vision was based on identical, one-design boats. This meant significant start-up costs. Decre went knocking on the doors of Europe's boatbuilders and finance companies, eventually striking deals with Cegemar for the funding and Mallard for the Ecume de Mer boats. Towns and cities were encouraged to sponsor one of the fleet, with crews selected to make a connection with the local audiences around France.

Finally, on 1 July 1978, the first race began, with the fleet starting in Dunkirk and the finish set in Menton.

To facilitate the boats' passage between the north and west coasts of France with the Mediterranean, the Canal du Midi was used in the first race. But this proved to be slow and cumbersome, so for successive races the boats were trucked across by land. This also allowed the fleet to head further south on the Biscay coast.

Buoyed by the success of the first race, Decre went to France's biggest boatbuilder, Bénéteau, and secured a new fleet of 25 bigger, faster boats (First 30s) for the second running.

After two races, the boats were changed again. From 1982 to 1998, Jeanneau provided Rush Royales, Selections and JOD35s. Decré knew all about the value of advertising, and the branding of the boats and their spinnakers by the likes of Royale and Orangina was immaculate. However, the biggest development in the race's history has been the 2015 shift to multihulls, with the Diam 24 catamaran being used for the first time.

Throughout the 1980s, the reputation of the race climbed quickly. Eric Tabarly wished the fleet good fortune when it visited his homeport of Benodet, and established stars including Marc Pajot, Eugène Riguidel and Florence Arthaud took part. After 2000, non-French teams such as the Team New Zealand America's Cup outfit began to be attracted, with Russell Coutts sailing some of the tour.

Breaking the French domination of the podium was Adrian Stead's British crew on *Barlo Plastics* in 2000. Otherwise the roll call of winners has included many of France's top sailors. Amongst the winners have been Benoît Caignaert, Thierry Peponnet, Jean-Piere Dick and Franck Cammas. The stand-out skipper has been Bertrand Pacé, who between 1987 and 2011 recorded an unparalleled eight victories.

▷ Seven different classes of one-design monohulls were used in the Tour since 1978, until 2015's switch to multihulls with the Diam 24.

△ Boxing Day. Sydney Harbour. Massed spectators. It can only be the start of one the great ocean-racing classics – the Sydney–Hobart.

One of the 'crown jewel' ocean races, the Sydney–Hobart is defined by the open-water section in the Bass Strait. Like another of the classics, the Fastnet, it is also remembered for tragic events. In the 1979 Fastnet, 15 people lost their lives. The 1998 Hobart saw six sailors perish. Each was a major news story that transcended sailing. In both cases, events unfolded relatively close to land which, mercifully, meant huge search-and-rescue operations could be staged.

The Sydney–Hobart has worldwide renown for another, better, reason. The images of the massed fleet sailing out of Sydney harbour, against the backdrop of the Opera House and Harbour Bridge, is iconic. That it happens on Boxing Day means that not only do Sydney-siders throng the shores to savour the spectacle, but also that Australia's early slot in the world clock means that news broadcasters and outlets appreciate the images that the start generates.

The body of water between the mainland and Tasmania has a fierce reputation. The relatively shallow water combined with strong, 'Southerly Buster' winds blowing against the East Australian Current can kick up steep, breaking seas. The Sydney–Hobart's reputation as a tough race is well deserved.

It was a Briton who was instrumental in getting the first new race after the Second World War off the ground. The original outline idea was for a cruise from Sydney to Hobart. John Illingworth, a serving captain in the Royal Navy, gave a talk on ocean racing at the Royal Prince Alfred Yacht Club in Pittwater. Before his wartime service, Illingworth worked with a naval architect and gained a lot of experience in the field. He was stationed in Sydney at the end of the war.

## A boxing day race

The year was 1945. After his talk, Illingworth's Australian hosts asked if he'd like to join their cruise to Hobart in *Rani*, the 9.3-m (30-ft) boat that Illingworth had bought in Australia. Illingworth agreed, but only if it was a race. Boxing Day was selected as the ideal date in order to make maximum use of the summer holiday period. 'Keeping oneself completely sober over Christmas was,' Illingworth admitted, 'a bit of a bind.'

This first fleet of nine encountered a Southerly Buster and knew that they were in for 24–48 hours of strong southwesterlies. Some hove-to or anchored behind Gabo Island. Captain Illingworth however, contrary to popular belief, sailed close to the coast, at no time more than twenty miles out. It was heavy going. They sailed from Gabo to Cape Forestier on the north-east coast of Tasmania, making landfall exactly where planned.

### Vital stats

**What:** 650-mile offshore race

**Where:** Sydney to Hobart (Australia)

**How often:** Annual

**Boat type:** Monohulls

**Crew:** Fully crewed

### Route tracker

AUSTRALIA

Sydney

Melbourne

Tasmania
Hobart

◁ Investec Loyal's proud zebra has *Wild Oats XI* for breakfast as she manages to break the Audi-sponsored yacht's supreme reign to snatch victory during the 2011 Sydney–Hobart race.

00011806

△ The yacht *Morna*, built in 1913, was skippered to three successive line honor wins at the Sydney–Hobart race by Sir Claude Plowman, from 1946 to 1948. Under a new owner and the new name *Kurrewa IV*, she took another four line honors between 1948 and 1960, making her one of the most successful Sydney to Hobart yachts, only bettered by *Wild Oats XI* between 2005 and 2014.

Onboard *Rani*, the bilge pumps worked overtime, the crew bailing for almost 30 hours straight. Six-and-a-half days later, *Rani* reached Hobart, 17 hours ahead of the next yacht. She was the first winner, and the first legend of the Hobart.

*Rani* not only won line honours but was also the handicap winner of the race. Following her in this rarely achieved double were American media mogul Ted Turner in 1972 in his converted 12-Metre-class *American Eagle*, Californian real-estate developer John Kilroy in *Kialoa III* in 1977, Peter Blake's *Ceramco New Zealand* in 1980, Bernard Lewis's *Sovereign* in 1988 and Bob Oatley's *Wild Oats XI* in 2005 and 2012. All of them, other than *Rani*, are big boats that have made hay in fast sailing conditions and then benefitted from the wind change to a less favourable direction and angle behind them.

Eight of the nine starters finished the first race. In the second race, 19 started but only 11 reached Hobart. Over the years, however, the Hobart race has recorded a consistently high proportion of finishers, a signifier of well-prepared yachts, well sailed.

### *Morna's* hat-trick and *Wild Oats'* revolution

First to reach Hobart in the second race was *Morna*, a 1913 classic Fife design that went through a number of owners until radio manufacturer Claude Plowman took her ocean racing. The yacht took line honours in three successive Sydney–Hobarts between 1946 and 1948, before being sold to the Livingstone brothers and renamed *Kurrewa IV*. She entered a further six races between 1954 and 1960 and was first to finish four more times.

It took until 2005 for this record of three successive line honours to be matched by Bob Oatley's Reichel-Pugh-designed maxi *Wild Oats XI*. This began a spectacular run of line honours, masterminded by *Wild Oats XI*'s sailing master Mark Richards. From 2005 to 2014, the silver yacht was first to Hobart eight times out of ten starts.

It couldn't be argued that *Wild Oats XI*'s hegemony was unchallenged – Neville Crichton's near sistership *Shockwave/Alfa Romeo* and *Loyal* (the former Greg Elliott-designed *Maximus/Ragamuffin 100*) each managed to get their bows ahead on the finish line once. What the Oatley family has done is to repeatedly carry out major modifications to hull, sail and appendages. The most drastic was to cut the hull in front of the mast and lengthen the yacht for the 2015 race.

Times have tumbled over the years. The first sub-three-day time was set way back in 1975, when conditions allowed a full 45 minutes to be sliced off the race record. One of the drivers behind the modifications to *Wild Oats XI* for the 2015 race was to try and crash through the 40-hour barrier. Oatley's maxi came closest in 2008, with a time of 1d 18h.

### An (almost) entirely Australian affair

Simple geography makes participating in the Sydney–Hobart a major undertaking for any owner outside of southern Australia, but the race's star quality has drawn many overseas competitors. The first foreign winner after Illingworth came from across the Tasman. Chris Bouzaid's *Rainbow II* was the overall handicap winner of the 1967 race, perfect preparation for her European campaign which saw victory in the 1969 One Ton Cup.

That year also saw a more famous overseas winner than CNN-founder Ted Turner, when future British prime minister Edward Heath won the race in his first ocean-racing yacht, the S&S34

◁ Twelve crew were airlifted off the 12-m (40-ft) *Stand Aside* during the stormy 1998 race. Some 67 of 155 yachts retired from the race, which claimed six lives.

gusting 90. These were exceptional speeds. The position of the station accelerated the wind, but Badham was deeply concerned that the fleet was going to be hit by far more than the 40–50-knot winds that the Australian Bureau of Weather was forecasting for the Bass Strait. The Bureau revised its forecast but, as the coroner's later inquiry found out, attempts to advise the Cruising Yacht Club of Australia's race office failed because it was unmanned. How the CYCA managed the unfolding events was later to be criticized by the coroner and became the subject of lawsuits brought by the families of those who lost their lives and surviving competitors.

The race start itself was normal enough, with easy winds and sunshine. On the second day, lightning signalled the approach of the storm front as the wind swung forward. The fleet was spread over a 30-mile area. The seas built to 3.7–4.7m (12–15ft) high, interspersed with sets of waves whose heights were reported anywhere between 12.4 and 24.8m (40 and 80ft). *Stand Alone* was the first to make a Mayday call. She'd been rolled, dismasted and was taking on water. The winchman on the Helimed helicopter estimated the waves to be 18.6m (60ft) high, and the wind, easy to hear above the turbine's roar, 'sounded like a train'. Standing on the skid, he was being hit by sea spray.

The first life lost was that of British Olympic sailor Glyn Charles. *Sword of Orion* had retired and turned back towards the mainland under just a storm jib, when a 24.8-m (80-ft) wave rolled the boat. The lashed-down mainsail boom broke free and knocked Charles over the side, the force breaking his safety tether. When the boat recovered from a 360-degree roll, Charles was 30m (98.4ft) from the boat, which was knee-deep in water.

Three lives were lost from *Winston Churchill*, a competitor in the first race in 1945. Built in 1942, she'd sailed around the world twice, competed in 15 Hobarts, been extensively rebuilt and was the oldest yacht competing. Rising over a big crest, the wave broke and threw the yacht into the trough, breaking the hull. She sank in five minutes. The crew took to two liferafts. After a heinous night, in which the rafts were rolled, ripped and swamped, three were swept away in a particularly violent breaking wave. The surviving *Winston Churchill* crew were not found until the onset of the second night, still in the remains of their liferafts.

The other two lives were lost on *Business Post Naiad*. The skipper had a heart attack and another drowned while tangled in his harness, as the dismasted yacht lurched helplessly in the violent seas. 'Disaster' didn't begin to cover it.

The New South Wales coroner who investigated the lives lost in the 1998 Sydney–Hobart called it a 'disaster'. 80-knot winds cut a swathe through the 115-boat fleet and generated huge seas with foaming crests as the yachts ventured out into the Bass Strait. Six men died, five boats sank, 66 retired and 55 crew were rescued from the tumult.

It was Australia's biggest-ever maritime rescue operation, involving 25 fixed-wing aircraft and helicopters, a navy frigate, six boats and 1,000 personnel. Until 1998, only two lives had been lost in the race. The cause was a weather 'bomb', when a low-pressure system suddenly deepened with dramatic effect. Abnormal summer weather had already been affecting southwest Australia that year, including snowfalls. But the storm that hit the race far exceeded what was expected before the start.

Noted Australian weather forecaster and yachting meteo guru Roger 'Clouds' Badham started to check his 20 years of race data when, after the start, he heard that the weather station on Wilson's Promontory was recording 70-knot winds,

△ The organ pipes are an icon of the Tasmanian landfall for crews crossing the Bass Strait.

*Morning Cloud.* Turner's win in 1972 saw him pace restlessly ashore in Hobart, watching the arrivals after *American Eagle* to see which, if any, would deny him the double. American boatbuilder Bob Derecktor summed up Turner: 'Some people put in a lot of time, some people put in a lot of money and some put in a lot of effort. But nobody puts in as much of all three as Turner. He has the drive. Nobody wants to win as badly as he does.'

### Sponsors and disqualifications

A landmark year was 1999, when the Rule 26 advertising restrictions were relaxed for the first time. When Peter Blake won in 1980, his Whitbread Round-the-World racer was entered as plain *New Zealand*, rather than *Ceramco New Zealand*. Ten years later, Briton Lawrie Smith fell foul of the rules in another Whitbread racer. He didn't enter his maxi as *Rothmans* to conform,

but popped a branded spinnaker during the race. Smith's yacht was first to finish but not scored. The controversy and media coverage of such a high-profile disqualification left his sponsors measuring the column inches with satisfaction.

The most famous disqualification in the race came earlier, in 1983. Neck and neck to the finish were the two most famous maxi yachts of the day, the beautiful blue *Nirvana*, owned by American Marvin Green, and the varnished *Condor*, famous for her yellow spinnakers carrying the silhouette of the big South American bird of prey. In a match race to the line, *Condor* ran aground and protest flags were waved. *Nirvana* finished first but the jury later disqualified her for failing to give way.

This was a bitter blow for Green, as it denied *Nirvana* a never-achieved triple crown. She had set first-to-finish race records in the

Bermuda and Fastnet races that were to be unbeaten for 14 years. How Green would have cherished the Hobart line honours, too.

In 1967 Australia followed the British example of the Admiral's Cup and created its own three-boat team competition. The Hobart was the long-distance finale. Only New Zealand fielded a team other than Australian state teams. But having won the Fastnet in August, Eric Tabarly had *Pen Duick III* shipped to Sydney for the Hobart. The Frenchman was leading on handicap at the halfway stage, but an ebbing tide forced him to anchor in Hobart's Darent river. *Pen Duick III* had to be content with line honours.

Being an annual race, the Hobart has had to be adaptable to changes in rating systems and rules. A memorable race was held in 1977, when there was a standoff between the Aussies and the Kiwis. Light-displacement boats had long been a design trait favoured by the New Zealanders, but when applied to the International Offshore Rule (IOR) rules it resulted in tippy boats because of their lifting keels and internal ballast.

New Zealand's Southern Cross team of *Swuzzlebubble*, *Jenny-H* and *Smir-Noff-Agen* were Hobart race-bound and held valid international rating certificates when the Cruising Yacht Club of Australia threatened to turn down their entry. To address concerns about low righting moment of light-displacement types, the IOR's world governing body, the Offshore Racing Council, aimed to bring in a self-righting test on 1 January 1978.

The Australian race organizers wanted to go a few weeks early, hence the standoff with the Kiwis. Peace was restored when it was agreed that calculations could be used instead of a physical haul-down test, and all the boats passed. That said, of the seven light-displacement types that competed in the windy 1977 race, only *Jenny-H* finished. Her designer, New Zealander Bruce Farr, however, went on to have the best win record in the race with 15 victories.

▷ The American-owned 31-m (100-ft) maxi *Comanche*, winner of the 2016 Sydney–Hobart, is so wide at 7.8m (25ft) that she's sailed heeled, like a multihull, to reduce drag.

## The QLD

Tasmania is isolated even from Australia, which is perhaps why the racing fleet receives such a warm welcome. Sir Claude Plowman wrote in the logbook of *Morna*, the first competitor to finish the 1946 race, 'The reception we received in Hobart was amazing. The whole town appeared to be waiting for us and as we crossed the finishing line, the firing of the finish gun was the signal for an outburst of cheering and the blowing of whistles.

'We were allotted a berth in the Marine Department Dock and on tying up were boarded by hundreds of people, amongst whom were movie cameramen, press photographers and reporters.

'The facilities of the town were more or less at our disposal – in short, we were granted the freedom of the city.' The definitive Sydney–Hobart race celebration is the QLD – the Quiet Little Drink. It was the brainchild of Tony Cable and John Dawson in 1969, who believed that the ever-growing size of the race fleet would mean losing the convivial congregation of all the crews on Constitution Dock at the end of the race.

Their response was to organize a crew party at the Shipwrights Arms on Battery Point. The first order was for 200 beers. A tally was chalked up on a backboard by David Hutchen (who later co-founded Hamilton Island Race Week), totalling 1,467. Hutchen was christened 'Chalky', a nickname that stuck for years.

1972 saw a new grand total of 6,200 beers. To head off some of the stiffer yacht-club types who took a dim view of the QLD, a portion of the takings were donated as bursary for young Hobart sailors.

# Newport–Bermuda Race

North Atlantic

**'Deep-sea racing was inevitable. It simply had to come.'**

**Thomas Fleming Day** | Former editor of *The Rudder*, 1906

## Vital stats

**What:** A 635-mile offshore race

**Where:** Newport (USA) to Hamilton (Bermuda)

**How often:** Biennial

**Boat type:** Monohulls

**Crew:** Fully crewed

## Route tracker

If there were to be a crown jewels or holy trinity of ocean races, then the Newport–Bermuda race would sit alongside the Fastnet and Sydney–Hobart. It is one of the all-time classics of the sport and the oldest regularly staged ocean race in the world.

Distancing the Newport–Bermuda race is the fact that the fleet leaves land behind on the first day at sea and doesn't raise it again on the horizon until the finish, some 635 miles later. It is a true ocean-sailing test in the north Atlantic, defined by negotiating the Gulf Stream and finding an isolated, low-lying island.

By contrast, the Fastnet race course covers coastal southern England and Ireland for 50 per cent of its length, whilst the Sydney–Hobart sees the fleet tracking south down the New South Wales coast for several days before heading into the Bass Strait.

2016 is a landmark; the 50th running of the biennial race first run by the influential Thomas Fleming Day, the then-editor of the American yachting journal, *The Rudder*. Day's guiding hand was behind not only the Newport–Bermuda race but also the Fastnet and Chicago–Mackinac. That's a considerable legacy.

'Deep-sea racing was inevitable,' proclaimed Day in 1906. 'It simply had to come.'

There's no mistaking the certainty of belief espoused by Day on the eve of the first race. Yet, at the time, open-ocean voyaging by amateurs in relatively small boats was considered only one step from the deeds of the great explorers. It was not something that ordinary people attempted.

Detractors called it foolhardy, to which Day had a riposte: 'The danger of the sea for generations has been preached by the ignorant.'

### A yacht club with a royal warrant

The very first race in 1906 was Day proving the point. He created the Brooklyn Yacht Club and ran the race from New York Bay, where the Hudson river meets the Atlantic. Embracing the fleet at the other end was the Royal Bermuda Yacht Club (RBYC), the oldest yacht club outside the UK and Ireland with a royal warrant.

And a warm welcome it was, too. It was said that more than a quarter of the island's 14,000-strong population turned out to greet the yachts. Day was sailing master on the 11.8-m (38-ft) yawl *Tamerlane* and was first boat home. Thora Lund Robinson, another pioneer, was among them. She competed on the 8.7-m (28-ft) sloop *Gauntlet*. The wreaths delivered to the yachts in New York by fearful sceptics, so that decent burials at sea could be conducted, were not needed.

The race was held four times more, but moved to a biennial schedule rather than annual. After a hiatus during the First World War, the RBYC's Eldon Trimmingham, from one of Bermuda's most famous families, canvassed American support. The race resumed in 1923 with 22 yachts. This time the start had moved up from New York to New Bedford on Long Island Sound. Eventually the race start would settle in Newport, Rhode Island.

In 1926, the recently formed Cruising Club of America (CCA) took on the co-hosting of the race with the RBYC, so beginning an era of profound influence over the sport.

For the next 50 years, the CCA in the US and the Royal Ocean Racing Club in the UK each had a rating rule that shaped the ways yachts raced. This was before the birth of the International Offshore Race (IOR). The CCA favoured slightly shallower-bodied hulls and lighter forms and rated centreboards well – so much so that the designer of note of the second half of the 20th century, Olin Stephens, produced outright winners in 13 Bermuda races. Most famous of all was the 1956, 1958 and 1960 winner, Carleton Mitchell's 11.8-m (38-ft) yawl *Finistere*.

The only other three-time winner is *Carina*, another S&S design, which won under her original owner Dick Nye in 1970 and again in 2010 and 2012 in the hands of Rives Potts.

A recurring theme of the race has been the participation of yachts from the academies of the various branches of the US's uniformed services, such as the navy, the coastguard and the merchant marine. Tax-friendly schemes have meant that the services have had a good number of hot race boats donated to them over the years. The US Navy Academy in Annapolis has long had its own fleets of custom-designed boats by Luders, McCurdy & Rhodes and Pedrick.

**The Bermuda Triangle**

The race has had its share of severe weather, 1972 being among the noteworthy years. Out of the melée came Ron Amey's 14.9-m (48-ft) *Noryema*, from Britain, which became the first non-US yacht to win.

Safe landfall on a reef-shrouded island puts a high premium on safe navigation. A sextant, good sights and correct reduction-table calculations marked out good navigators as a breed apart in the early days, and are still used today by those who can. Electronic aids were available after the Second World War, first Loran, and latterly GPS. Only one yacht has been lost in the race, wrecked on the reef that obstructs the approach to Bermuda.

There has been only one further casualty. In 1932, the American schooner *Adriana* caught fire on the first night. Bobby Somerset, skippering *Jolie Brise*, brought the British schooner across *Adriana*'s stern so that her crew were able to jump across. Helmsman Clarence Kosley, the last man aboard, fell between the yachts and could not be found in the dark.

What makes navigation vital is the high proportion of the race being sailed across the easterly sweep of the Gulf Stream. Taking the water temperature remains a key indicator of the Stream, but from the 1980s, a swath of information has allowed crews to pick their way across for maximum tactical gain. Getting the first point of entry into the Stream is invariably a race-shaping move.

△ *Carina*, which first won the Newport–Bermuda in 1960 in Dick Nye's hands, then again in 2010 and 2012 under Rives Potts' ownership.

# Offshore Races
# Marblehead–Halifax Race
## North Atlantic

*'It's the granddaddy of them all [offshore races]... If you want to get challenged, this race has it all.'*

**Dave Stanfield** | Co-chair of the 2015 Marblehead–Halifax race

When it comes to one of the oldest races in the calendar, the Marblehead–Halifax earned its place in 1905. That means it had its 100th anniversary as long ago as 2005. As Dave Stanfield, co-chair of the 2015 race, likes to say, it is the 'granddaddy' of offshore races.

If the Bermuda Race has the Gulf Stream, the Fastnet Race the variable weather of the English Channel and Celtic Sea, and the Sydney–Hobart the open expanse of the Bass Strait as hurdles for race crews to negotiate, then it is the tides of the Bay of Fundy that give the Marblehead–Halifax race its distinctive mien.

The rise and fall of the Bay of Fundy features one of the biggest tidal ranges in the world, so crossing from the Gulf of Maine to Brazil Rock off Nova Scotia poses the risk of being drawn into the Bay. There is a swirl of currents in the Bay, but the big push comes from the Nova Scotia current, which heads south down the Canadian coast before surging into the Gulf of Maine.

After that, coastal navigation up the unforgiving Nova Scotia shore means that the challenge continues, particularly as fog can descend quickly. Crews can expect to wear everything from shorts and t-shirts to full battledress oilskins, thermals, boots, harnesses and lifejackets. The cold water of the Nova Scotia current can keep air temperatures low.

Another characteristic of the race is the start in one country and finish in another, although Boston and Nova Scotia have long-established links between then.

▷ The Nova Scotia coast can bring cold, rain, wind and fog.

**Vital stats**

**What:** 363-mile offshore race

**Where:** Marblehead (USA) to Halifax (Canada)

**How often:** Biennial

**Boat type:** Monohulls, handicap

**Crew:** Fully crewed and two-handed

**Route tracker**

The race was co-founded by the Boston Yacht Club in the picturesque, weather-boarded town of Marblehead. Among the first 90 members was soon-to-be renowned designer and engineer, Nathanael Herreshoff. The early events were friendly challenges between yachtsmen of the BYC as well as the Eastern Yacht Club, another prestigious Marblehead institution, and the Royal Nova Scotia Yacht Club. Dating back as far as 1837, it is one of the world's most senior clubs.

Marblehead can be considered the cradle of modern ocean racing, i.e. in yachts less than 21.7m (70ft) and sailed by amateurs, as opposed to the ocean greyhounds owned by gentlemen and manned by professionals.

In 1903 a race was run from Brooklyn to Marblehead, and it was considered by many to be the first ocean race as we now recognize the sport. The pivotal figure was Thomas Fleming Day, editor of *The Rudder*, who was also involved in the genesis of the Bermuda and Fastnet races.

The Marblehead–Halifax Race wasn't run regularly in its first three decades, but after 1939 the Boston and Royal Nova Scotia yacht clubs put it on a much more formal footing as a biennial event, running it in alternate years to the Newport–Bermuda Race. By 2015, despite being 110 years old, the race enjoyed its 36th staging.

At 363 miles it is only half of the Fastnet, Bermuda and Sydney–Hobart distances, but in the early days it was a long passage to make. Five days was typical. Nowadays, a modern, grand-prix-style boat can sail the course in 30 hours or less.

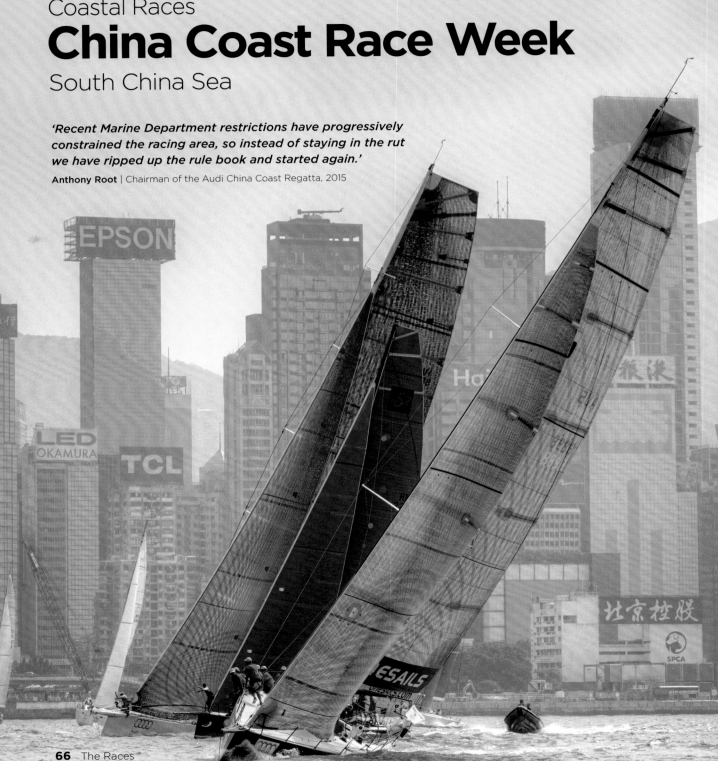

# China Coast Race Week

## South China Sea

*'Recent Marine Department restrictions have progressively constrained the racing area, so instead of staying in the rut we have ripped up the rule book and started again.'*

**Anthony Root** | Chairman of the Audi China Coast Regatta, 2015

From standalone races from Hong Kong to the Philippines and Hong Kong to Vietnam, the China coast events run by the Royal Hong Kong Yacht Club have grown into the China Coast Race Week. Measured by the calibre of its competitors and the frequency of fresh, monsoon-season winds, the regatta has a reputation for being the stiffest test of inshore racing in Asia.

The China Coast Race Week now comprises the China Coast Regatta, a three-day series of inshore races sailed in the southern and eastern waters of Hong Kong, and then the Hong Kong to Vietnam race. Competitors can enter one event or both, with each scored individually and with their own prizes. In the eyes of the Royal Hong Kong Yacht Club, they have developed a format that is now 'the best regatta in Asia'.

1993 saw the seeds of the event sown from a base in Clearwater Bay and courses set in the Ninepins area. After this, the racing was staged on Hong Kong's south side, with a mix of short windward/leeward courses, and a longer race out to the TCS2 buoy.

However, as one of the buoys was marking the traffic-separation scheme in the busy Tathong Channel, the mix of racing yachts and commercial shipping become increasingly uncomfortable bedfellows.

For 2015, the RHKYC had a rethink. In the words of Anthony Root, who chaired the China Coast Race Week committee that year, 'Recent Marine Department restrictions have progressively constrained the racing area, so instead of staying in the rut we have ripped up the rule book and started again.'

Instead of solely using fixed navigation marks, the race committee started to employ specially laid inflatable marks to bring greater choice to its course setters. So for 2015, the race area was relocated and defined by Tung Lung, Basalt Island, Ninepins, Po Toi and Waglan.

Some 40 boats turned out for the revised event, and enjoyed the full gamut of conditions from light and fading breezes to a brisk 25 knots, which kicked up a lumpy sea. The northeast monsoon coincides with the regatta and can give crews and their boats a real work-out.

## The Hong Kong–Vietnam race

Starting from Victoria Harbour and ending in Nha Trang, capital of the Khanh Hoa province, the Hong Kong–Vietnam race is a run of a challenging 673 miles found on the south central coast and one of the country's key tourist hubs.

The fleets are not large but the standards are high, and some of the most ardent competitors in the Australia/Asia offshore scene are familiar faces: Geoff Hill, Ray Roberts, Syd Fischer and David Witt.

The sou'-sou'west course from Hong Kong means that the race is downwind orientated, often leading to fast passage times. Over the years, the fleet has experienced some high-speed sailing. Plastic debris off the coast is a problem for the crews; so too is threading a path between densely packed Chinese and Vietnamese fishing boats, which are often encountered.

In 2015, the young and still relatively inexperienced Chinese crew on *ARK323* used the race as their qualifier for the Sydney–Hobart classic.

The race record is slightly complicated by the race originally starting from southeast of Lamma Island before moving to Victoria Harbour in 2013, a 656-mile race as opposed to the original 673 miles.

Grant Wharrington's 31-m (100-ft) *Wild Thing* set a record of 42h 45m 21s in 2003. Syd Fischer's *Ragamuffin 90* shaved four minutes off that in 2013 and then in 2015, in the longer *Ragamuffin 100*, cut another 27 minutes. The next barrier for the greyhounds contesting the Hong Kong–Vietnam race is to sail the course in less than 40 hours, a feat that will no doubt soon be achieved.

◁ The distinctive Hong Kong cityscape is the backdrop for the China Coast Race Week.

## Vital stats

### China Coast Race

**What:** 350-mile offshore race

**Where:** Hong Kong to Sanya, China

**How often:** Annual

**Boat type:** Monohulls

**Crew:** Fully crewed

## Route tracker

## Offshore Races
# San Fernando Race
## South China Sea

*'Given the forecasts available, the San Fernando Race Organizing Committee believe there is no alternative but to alter the destination of this year's race in the interests of competitor safety.'*

**Gerry Daughton** | San Fernando race chairman announcement regarding the development of typhoon Maysak in 2015

### Vital stats

**What:** 480-mile offshore race

**Where:** Hong Kong (China) to San Fernando (Philippines)

**How often:** Biennial

**Boat type:** Monohulls

**Crew:** Fully crewed

The San Fernando Race started as a cruise and ended as a race. This was the plan in 1977 when a group of keen sailors cruised down from Hong Kong and assembled 450 miles later in San Fernando. Then, they raced back.

In the case of the race, the San Fernando in question is not the provincial capital of Pampanga, named after Spain's King Ferdinand VI and located in Manila Bay, some 45 miles from the Philippines capital. Rather it is the port and beach resort of the same name located on the northwest coast, linked to the capital by the McArthur Freeway. The beaches were the attraction back in 1977 and remain so today.

The race requires an open-sea passage southeast through the South China Sea, with land left behind as soon as Hong Kong dips below the horizon and not raised again until the northern tip of the Philippines. As such, it is a Category One race under the banding of the Offshore Special Regulations of the World Sailing governing authority. However, in a reversal of the first race, competitors now often use the race as the spur to go on and explore the Philippine cruising grounds.

The fleet sails out of Hong Kong's Victoria Harbour, with the high-rise modern cityscape as its backdrop. In recent years the race has been run with the support of the Philippine government's Department of Tourism, and also the support of Britain's Royal Ocean Racing Club. As such there is a beneficial marriage between sport and tourism. The Philippines gratefully acknowledge the 'constant flow of tourist arrivals' the biennial race brings; meanwhile, the Royal Hong Kong Yacht Club speaks of the 'natural fit' of the race bringing visitors who wind down from the long race on the beaches of the Philippines.

There is an additional charitable element, too, with the race supporting a children's home in San Fernando. A dinner and auction are the prime fundraising activities associated with the race. In 2013, an impressive HK$500,000 was raised. The main lure of the race, however, is the night sailing – often under starry, clear, moonlit skies – and the promises of sand, sunshine and a few cool beers at the end.

The first phase of the race can be hard, with rough seas on the first night of Hong Kong. Then, as the Philippine coast is closed, the wind can become a patchwork of breeze and holes that can test the patience of even seasoned sailors. Seeing another boat close by pick up a zephyr and climb away is frustrating. Crews have to tell themselves that the lottery of breezes tends to even out over time, and there's often another one before the finish line.

The fleet typically numbers above 20, and includes yachts racing under the IRC and

Performance Handicap rating systems. The 2001 race record of 49h 55m, set by Sam Chan's 22-m (71-ft), ultra-light displacement sled *FreeFire*, has proven hard to beat. Hong Kong's Chan is one of the many regulars in the San Fernando race, most recently racing his new *FreeFire*, a TP52.

In 2003 the race was badly affected by the SARS outbreak, which imposed limitations on travel. And in 2015, the race didn't go to San Fernando at all. On the advice of the Hong Kong Observatory about the track of the unseasonally easterly cyclone 'Maysak', the race committee set the fleet for the 20th race on a 240-mile track to the east through the Lei Yue Mun Gap, rounding three 'virtual marks' established by GPS before returning to Hong Kong.

**Route tracker**

CHINA · Hong Kong · TAIWAN · Hainan · SOUTH CHINA SEA · PHILIPPINES · San Fernando · Manila · VIETNAM

▽ A clammy dawn on the South China Sea on the last morning before reaching Hong Kong during the 2013 San Fernando race.

# The Governor's Cup

## South Atlantic

### Vital Stats

**What:** 1,700-mile offshore race

**Where:** Simon's Town (South Africa) to St Helena

**How often:** Biennial

**Boat type:** Monohulls and multihulls

**Crew:** Fully crewed

### Route tracker

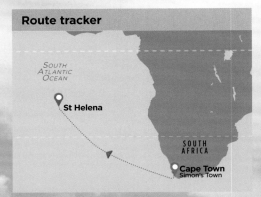

SOUTH
ATLANTIC
OCEAN

St Helena

SOUTH
AFRICA

Cape Town
Simon's Town

St Helena must rank as the remotest destination of any yacht race. Open a map of the South Atlantic and pick a point mid-distance between Africa and South America, and chances are that you'll have homed in on St Helena.

Assuming you can find it, that is. St Helena is tiny, just ten by five miles and with a population of 4,000 people. The volcanic tropical island is located 1,200 miles west of the Namibian and Angolan border, and was discovered in the early 1500s.

A British territory, the island has been dependent on sea connections for centuries. This chain of dependency, mostly on a mail-boat service running between Cardiff, Wales and Cape Town, South Africa, was broken in 2016 when a newly constructed airport brought fast connections and a boost to St Helena's economy in the shape of expanded tourism.

The round trip on the mail ship takes three weeks, testament to St Helena's remoteness. Already cruise ships stop in St Helena, and the airport has increased visitor numbers five-fold.

The Governor's Cup yacht race from False Bay, Simon's Town, was started in 1996 and remains another chapter in the island's long seafaring tradition. For a tiny and remote location, St Helena has born witness to significant events. English explorer Sir Francis Drake is said to have stopped there during his 1577–80 circumnavigation. In 1676, astronomer Edward Halley landed there and mapped the southern hemisphere sky for the first time. France's Emperor Napoleon was exiled there after his defeat by the English and Prussians at the 1815 Battle of

Waterloo. And in 1898, American Joshua Slocum, the first person to sail around the world alone, spent nine days there enjoying the hospitality of the governor, Sir R.A. Standale, towards the end of his three-year circumnavigation in *Spray*.

## The race from Cape Town to St Helena

Despite the sea being the island's overriding influence on life, sailing did not form a major part of contemporary life until 1996. The master of RMS *St Helena*, Captain David Roberts, had seen the Cape Town to Rio de Janeiro race start in early January of that year. By the time he'd reached St Helena, the idea had fermented. He pitched it to the then governor, David Smallman, knowing he was a sailor. By June, David Smallman had met South Africa's minister for sport, plans had been made and a trophy created.

The race from South Africa to St Helena was on. Given the undertaking, it was remarkable that the first race attracted 15 starters, with *Nina* winning in nine days. It was the start of something more than a race. No 'Saints' (St Helena residents) had taken part in that first race, so Governor Smallman proposed sail-training for St Helena's youngsters. Nina MacLennan, a widow of a Canadian member of the Royal Cape Yacht Club, contributed towards the cost of two dinghies. So did the Leatherseller's Company, one of London's ancient livery companies, located in St Helena Place.

Over the years, the initiative has blossomed. The old Bond Store on the wharf at James Bay became the new St Helena Yacht Club. Tie-ups

*'What could be more exciting than watching this colourful fleet sail out to the start, impatient for the gun to sound?'*

**Captain David Roberts**
Founder of the the Governor's Cup

were established with keen and supportive sailors in Cape Town, which allowed youngsters to go there to gain more experience on bigger boats. All of this resulted in ten Saints sailing in the second race in 1998.

Although the new airport was welcomed by the islanders, many were fearful that it could spell the end of the race. With aircraft replacing RMS *St Helena* as the island's lifeline, there would no longer be a ship on which to carry yachts back to South Africa. The alternative would be a hard-going, long, upwind delivery back to Cape Town. Not all competitors shipped their boats back after the last race, however, so the organizers remain hopeful that it will continue to flourish.

▽ An unlikely setting for the finish of an ocean race, St Helena is still one of the most remote inhabited islands in the world – although the newly opened airport now makes it possible to fly in a substitute crew for the return journey.

# South Atlantic Race
South Atlantic

*'I really think the course should be re-examined, and we should try to get Rio back as the finishing point.'*

**Bertie Reed** | Legendary skipper of *Voortrekker*

## Vital stats

**What:** 3,800-mile offshore race

**Where:** Cape Town (South Africa) to Rio de Janeiro (Brazil)

**How often:** Triennial

**Boat type:** Monohulls and multihulls

**Crew:** Fully crewed and two-handed

It began life as the Cape–Rio, shorthand for the Cape Town to Rio de Janeiro race. It has also been known as the South Atlantic Race, which muddies the 3,000 miles of waters somewhat. Clear enough, however, is the fact that the race is one of the longest and toughest regular races in the calendar, typically taking two weeks to complete.

Look at a wind map and it's evident that the South Atlantic High has a distinct voice in yachts sailing to and from Cape Town. Better winds are found underneath the high pressure area, but dip too far south and in place of good downwind sailing, even stronger westerly headwinds can occur – and all in a part of the world where high ocean seas can be encountered.

The start and finish are no easy pickings, either. The wind can whistle in Table Bay, and the seas on the edge of the continental shelf are rarely nice and regular. Some 3,800 miles later, lumpy seas can pile up on the South American shore, as can sloppy swells under windless conditions.

In 2006 the race ran to Salvador, Brazil, under the name of the South Atlantic Race and Rally, electing to head to a port that had also played host various times to the Mini Transat, the Clipper Race and the Route du Rhum. The Cape–Rio and the South Atlantic Race both claim parentage from the original race run in 1971, but it is the Cape–Rio that is the keeper of the flame and that is still running today under the auspices of the Royal Cape Town Yacht Club and Britain's Royal Ocean Racing Club.

### Cape to Rio

That first race in 1971 took place during apartheid-era South Africa and prior to the boycott that many sports instituted. Sailing was not one of them because, politics aside, there were no realistic alternative ports of call to South Africa for long-distance races. Not only this, but Cape Town had long been known as the Tavern of the Seas for its warm welcome in what is a hard part of

## Route tracker

BRAZIL

Rio de Janeiro

SOUTH ATLANTIC OCEAN

ANGOLA

NAMIBIA    BOTSWANA

SOUTH AFRICA

Cape Town

the world when at sea. It is windy, and the seas are properly big ocean waves.

Bruce Dalling was a rare example of an individual sportsman coming from South Africa to compete in the wider world, and his exploits in the 1968 Transat were headline-making at home and abroad. Sailing the 15.5-m (50-ft) Van de Stadt plywood ketch *Voortrekker*, Dalling's second place in the Transat was a huge boost to South African sailing. The yacht passed to the South African navy, and these two facts prompted Admiral Hugo Biermann to campaign for South Africa to host its own international yacht race. Australia was considered as a finish point, as was South America. When the Rio de Janeiro Yacht Club agreed to be a partner, the race was born.

Expectations were far outstripped when 69 boats lined up in Table Bay in 1971. It was a remarkable tally for a pioneering race. Not only this, but consider some of the sailors who participated: France's Eric Tabarly, Britain's Robin Knox-Johnston (who won line honours in 23d 42m with Leslie Williams in the 22-m (71-ft) ketch *Ocean Spirit*), and the Netherlands' Kees Bruynzeel (resident in South Africa), whose plywood had been used to construct *Voortrekker*.

Bruynzeel, then 72, competed again in 1973. Despite recovering from a series of heart attacks, he defied doctors' advice, added a nurse to the crew of his 16-m (52.5-ft) ketch *Stormy* (a smaller version of the famous 22-m/72-ft *Stormvogel*) and signed off from the sport in fine style, winning both line (21d 12m) and handicap honours.

The 1976 race was part of the Gauloises Triangle, an attempt to link St Malo, Cape Town, Rio and Portsmouth in a three-legged series of races. Line honours went to Huey Long's US maxi *Ondine*.

South Africa's political isolation saw a hiatus between 1976 and 1993, when two 'South Atlantic' events headed to Punta del Este, the Uruguayan port on the Plate river that also hosted the Whitbread/Volvo Race in the 1980s.

After South Africa's integration back into the international fold, the race was staged once more to Rio in 1993. It has run every three years since, apart a four-year interregnum between 1996 and 2000 to coincide with celebrations for the 500th anniversary of the discovery of Brazil by Pedro Álvares Cabral.

From 1993, the calibre of the fleet and crews has spiralled upwards. Hasso Plattner's *Morning Glory*, Robert McNeill's *Zephyrus*, Jim Dolan's *Sagamore* and George David's *Rambler* have all set the pace at the front. By 2014, Italy's Giovanni Soldini in his former Volvo 70 *Maserati* had brought the fastest finish down to 10d 11h 29m, less than half the time *Ocean Spirit* recorded in 1971.

▽ Nowhere is Cape Town's Table Mountain, with its distinctive tablecloth cloud, better seen than from the sea.

## Offshore Races
# Middle Sea Race
## Mediterranean

*'This must be the most beautiful race course in the world. What other event has an active volcano as a mark of the course?'*

**Ted Turner** | Skipper of *Lightnin'* in 1973 and founder of CNN

## Vital stats

**What:** 608-mile offshore race

**Where:** Start and finish in Valetta, Malta

**How often:** Annual

**Boat type:** Monohulls and multihulls

**Crew:** Fully crewed

Unusually for a long-distance race, the Middle Sea Race starts and finishes in the same place – the Grand Harbour of Malta. Malta is in the middle of the middle sea, the Latin derivation of 'Mediterranean' being 'middle of the land'. The island group is triangulated by Italy, Tunisia and Libya and its location means that it has held strategic importance for everyone from the Phoenicians, the Romans, the Moors, the Normans, the Sicilians and the Knights of St John to the Spanish, the French and the British.

For today's racers, it means departing Malta's impressive harbour for a 608-mile clockwise course that takes the fleet north around Sicily before returning to Valetta. The scenery is stunning, with the volcanic Lipari Island and Mount Etna offering their own nighttime accent to the spectacle. Indeed, Ted Turner, a formidably good ocean racer and America's Cup winner before he turned his attention to his CNN and media empire, called it 'the most beautiful race course in the world'.

Though the race is relatively young, it has always attracted famous yachtsmen and a high-calibre fleet. Famous competitors include round-the-world sailors Eric Tabarly, Sir Chay Blyth and Sir Francis Chichester; Austrian maestro Herbert von Karajan and software magnate Hasso Plattner;

Swedish internet entrepreneur Niklas Zennström; US aerospace technology boss George David; and Kiwi Volvo Ocean Race winner Mike Sanderson.

The Middle Sea Race is often ranked with the likes of the Fastnet, Sydney–Hobart and Newport–Bermuda as one of the great races to be undertaken. The link is strong, as the Middle Sea Race was co-founded in 1968 by the Fastnet Race organizer, Britain's Royal Ocean Racing Club, along with the Royal Malta Yacht Club, which was founded in 1835. It's no coincidence that the nominal distance of 608 miles is one mile greater than the Fastnet course.

Robert McNeill's *Zephyrus IV* set a course record in 2000 of 64h 49m 57s, which stood for seven years before it was smashed by George David's *Rambler* in 2007 with a new time of 47h 55m 3s. Though the race has long attracted maxis and big boats, the changing conditions have made reducing the race record an elusive goal. Light airs predominate, but the race can also lash out with big winds, waterspouts, rain, hail and crashing seas.

The Middle Sea Race might have originated as a friendly challenge between Paul and John Ripard and Malta-based Englishman Jimmy White, but it's all got a lot more serious since then.

△ The Russian Raketa 1200 racing yacht *Belka 2* at the start of the 2015 Rolex Middle Sea Race.

◁ The *Kuka-Light*, a fully carbon prototype with a canting keel, makes best use of the strong winds off the Maltese coast.

# Transat/OSTAR

## Atlantic Ocean

> **'It would be more seemly for the entrant to die like a gentLéman.'**
>
> H.G. 'Blondie' Hasler

△ H.G. 'Blondie' Hasler

Never for a moment think that cruising and voyaging is the soft side of the sport of sailing. This is the fearless sort of endeavour that led the likes of Joshua Slocum to sail singlehanded around the world alone in 1895–98. This same spirit of taking on the forces of nature was the driving force behind what became one the greatest solo races of all – the OSTAR, or Transat.

It was the British sailor Colonel H.G. 'Blondie' Hasler who came up with a pragmatic answer to the ever-rising costs of ocean racing. New boats were becoming ever more sophisticated and needed large crews. If you were an owner who could afford it, fine. Hasler could not. As a wartime commando, he led a daring and exceptionally dangerous raid in 'cockleshell' canvas canoes. Taking on the sea, dealing with risk and living on his wits was in his blood.

### Make it cheap, go it solo

In 1957 he proposed a race across the Atlantic from east to west against the prevailing winds. The expensive crew problem was solved: it would be a solo race. Fittingly, Hasler worked with the Slocum Society to set about its organization. He then took the idea to David Astor, editor of *The Observer* newspaper in London.

In his pitch, Hasler did not sugar the pill. He told Astor such a race 'would inevitably attract adverse criticism', although, in his estimation, the risk to life 'would be less than the Grand National' horse race. Astor agreed to support the race, and so it became the Observer Singlehanded Transat Atlantic Race, or OSTAR. Things went less well with the Slocum Society, unsurprising given that its members were interested in cruising and, as individuals, marching to their own beat.

So Hasler set up his own organizing committee and Sir Francis Chichester, who'd heard about the race, became its secretary. The Royal Western Yacht Club in Plymouth agreed to take on its management, which it did from 1960 all the way through to 1986. From over 100 expressions of interest, the starting line-up eventually numbered five come 11 June 1960.

They included Hasler himself in *Jester*, a specially modified 8-m (26-ft) Folkboat with a junk-rig and closed-in cockleshell deck, through which Hasler manned the yacht via a Perspex dome. Also on the starting line were Welshman Val Howells in the similar-sized *Eira*; David Lewis in *Cardinal Vertue*; Frenchman Jean Lacombe, who started three days late; and Chichester in *Gipsy Moth III*.

Look at the track of those five pioneers today, and it's a clear reminder that the race was a leap

◁ Ellen MacArthur on her Open 60 *Kingfisher*, the youngest-ever Transat winner.

boat home, seven days behind *Fleury Michon* but top monohull. In this race, *Jester*, the only yacht to have sailed in every edition after Mike Richey took her over from Blondie Hasler, sank after being overwhelmed in big seas.

Loïck Peyron repeated his 1992 win with *Fujicolor* in 1996 with *Fujicolor 2*. He was the first successive winner in the race, although he was the beneficiary of Francis Joyon's capsize while holding a lead of 300 miles. In fact, only three multihulls completed the race because of the severe conditions.

## The *Kingfisher* girl

In 2000, the proliferation of specialist solo monohulls saw a remarkable fleet of 24 Open 60 monohulls part of the entry, using the race as preparation for the Vendée Globe. Emerging victorious from this fierce contest was Ellen MacArthur in *Kingfisher*, at 23 the youngest-ever winner.

Throughout the 1980s and 1990s the race was called variously the 1 STAR, C STAR, Europe 1 STAR and New Man STAR, as sponsors came and went. Then, as now, it was hard to throw off the original OSTAR name or its French nickname, *Le Transat Anglaise*. In time, Transat has become the modern name for the race.

The 2004, the race passed into commercial hands for its management with the OC Group, which had been started by Ellen MacArthur and Mark Turner. Boston became the new finish. The Royal Western Yacht Club felt that such a heavily sponsored professional race had outgrown its objectives and resources, and so ran a second race in 2005 for what it felt was the race's original constituency, the ordinary amateur tackling the Atlantic as a personal Everest.

Mike Golding was the Transat monohull winner in *Ecover* in 2004 – giving back-to-back British wins after MacArthur's victory – while Michel Desjoyeaux took the multihull honours in *Geant* in just 8d 8h.

Where 37 yachts entered the 2004 race, only nine started the 2008 Transat. And where the race had once been the original and only solo transatlantic race, the calendar had latterly become crowded with alternatives. The Transat was put on hold until 2016, with the OC Group reformulating it to cater for the four busiest classes of boats: Class 40 and IMOCA 60 monohulls, and 15.5-m (50-ft) and unlimited 'Geant' class multihulls.

Offshore Races
# Route du Rhum
Atlantic Ocean

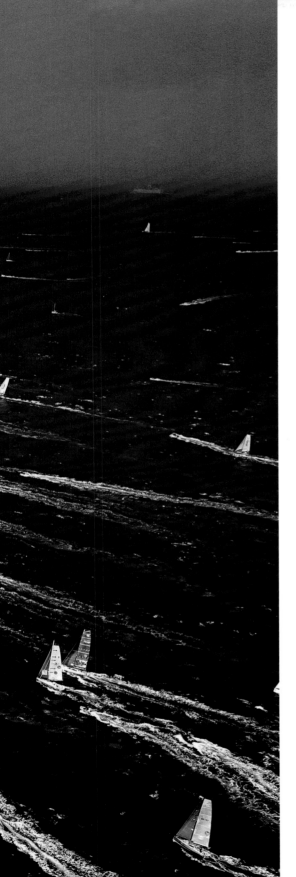

'Solo sailing is where I feel most at home, it is all in my hands. The Route du Rhum is one of the classics – it is a very well-run race. It is exciting because it's tactical. The tactics are the weather. You have got to read it right and you have got to sail your boat really hard. It's really such a buzz.'

**Sir Robin Knox-Johnston** | Skipper of *Grey Power*, Route du Rhum, 2014

The 'Rum Race' was the brainchild of Michel Etevenon, a new kind of impresario who created yacht races, something that previously had more normally been the preserve of yacht clubs.

To the yachting establishment in the 1970s, however, he was a foe, not a pointer to the future. Notably, Etevenon fought long battles with the then president of the International Yacht Racing Union (now called World Sailing), Beppe Croce, as well as the French Federation of Sailing (FFV) to allow sponsorship. At the time, a rear-guard stand was being mounted to keep advertising on yachts banned by the yacht-racing rules.

Running a small advertising agency in Paris, sponsorship was something Etevenon knew all about. His sailing experience was narrower, though he did crew in the inaugural Whitbread Round the World Race on *Kriter*. This yacht carried the name of a French sparkling wine, so Etevenon was breaking down the barriers even then.

Etevenon's efforts helped bridge the gap between sailors who had talent but no money, and companies who were attracted to the sport. He sensed that the number of wealthy owners who were the driving force behind the latest ocean racers was limited and unlikely to grow, making sponsorship vital.

◁ The Route du Rhum start – a headlong charge of competitors and media boats, with car ferries acting as floating grandstands.

△ Florence Arthaud's 1990 victory in *Pierre 1er* was a breakthrough for a woman in one of the toughest and most competitive solo races.

In 1978 he created the Route du Rhum, a non-stop solo race from St Malo in France to Guadeloupe in the Caribbean. Its success was assured from the moment when, after 23 days and with no intervening progress reports from sea, race favourite Michel Malinovsky, in the elegant, navy-blue, 22-m (70-ft) monohull *Kriter*, was passed by Canadian Mike Birch in *Olympus Photo*, a canary-yellow trimaran half the length. The winning margin at the Pointe-à-Pitre was just 98 seconds. A piece of jerky cine film, shot from a motorboat running helter-skelter alongside the two yachts, is an evocative reminder of this little bit of yacht-racing history.

The race had earned its place in the calendar, running every four years, and allowing an entire generation of French singlehanded racers to blossom.

### Size matters

The Route du Rhum's creation actually owed much to French reaction to the 1976 OSTAR, the British Plymouth–Newport classic first run in 1960, which then matured into the Observer Singlehanded Transatlantic Race. In 1976, some truly enormous

yachts had competed, none bigger than the 73-m (236-ft), three-masted schooner *Club Méditerranée* that Alain Colas raced, though only after a legion of support crew left the boat shortly before the start.

In Britain, debate raged about the safety and wisdom of allowing such yachts to take part, especially as under the strict letter of international maritime law, the skippers were unable to 'maintain a lookout at all times'.

In smaller yachts, the risk was to the sailors if they hit a ship; in *Club Méditerranée*'s case, the risk was quite possibly to other shipping. In response, the organizing Royal Western YC imposed a length limit for races after 1976, effectively legislating out the giants.

This was the opportunity that Etevenon seized: a Frenchman running a French race for predominantly French sailors and sponsors. Some 38 competitors lined up for the first race, confirmation that Etevenon had read his market right and an endorsement of his vision.

His second innovation was to offer substantial prize money. In 1978, there was a $130,000 prize pot, a sizeable sum.

Eric Tabarly's success in the 1964 OSTAR triggered an entire generation of singlehanded sailors who followed in his wake, so the timing of the first Route du Rhum was perfect. From 38 entrants, the start list grew to 52 in the 1982 race. In defiance of the overall length reduction brought into British races, the French still loved their big boats. Three of the 1980 runners were over 20m (66ft).

If there is a weakness in the Route du Rhum concept, it is one of timing. November is late to leave northern Europe with its autumn/winter weather systems, but the timing is set to match the end of the Caribbean hurricane season. In what was to become a repeating trend, there was a high retirement rate in 1980, including notable entrants Eric Tabarly (*Paul Ricard*), Jean-Yves Terlain (*Gautier III*) and Daniel Gillard (*Brittany Ferries*).

Come 1986, sponsorship dollars propelled even more big boats, and there were 13 boats longer than 23m (75ft). The race will be remembered, however, for the loss of Loïc Caradec overboard from *Royale* and Philippe Poupon's victory by 48 hours in *Fleury Michon VIII*.

By 1990, Etevenon and the French (mostly) accepted the argument that 19m (60ft) was a sensible length limit for a solo boat. The race, though, was Florence's; Florence Arthaud triumphed in *Pierre 1er* against the previous winner, Philippe Poupon, whilst in third was another young hotshot, Laurent Bourgnon.

The rate of attrition remained high. Like other solo races, a 25 per cent or higher retirement rate is normal. Seven from 27 dropped out in 1990; eleven from 25 in 1994; eight from 35 in 1998; seven from 25 in 2002, and so on.

2002 was the worst race for heavy weather, triggering a spate of capsizes, dismasting and gear damage. Only three of the 18 starters in the ORMA 60 multihull class came through unscathed and completed the course. It hastened the end of the ORMA 60 class, already under pressure from spiralling development costs.

By 2006, the Route du Rhum had attracted a huge fleet of 72 starters, helped by the addition of the new Open 40 monohull class, which

accounted for 25 yachts, to join the various multihull and monohull divisions.

For the 2010 edition onwards, the new wave of giant multihulls was accommodated once again, with veterans of round-the-world record attempts such as Franck Cammas' 31-m (102-ft) *Groupama 3* and Francis Joyon's 29.5-m (97-ft) *IDEC* the first and second boats home, shrinking the Atlantic to a nine-day crossing. In 2014, 32 years after he first competed in it, Loïck Peyron was fastest home in just over seven days.

The choice of St Malo as the start port was inspired. The walled city, rebuilt following the First World War, houses inner basins, allowing the public excellent viewing of the assembled fleet. And Cap Fréhel, a short distance to the west, gives a superb high vantage point as the fleet heads west. Typically some 200,000 people are attracted to Brittany for the race, making it one of the biggest events in the sailing calendar.

△ The trimaran *Oman Sail*, skippered by Sidney Gavignet, makes good progress on the 2014 edition of the Route du Rhum. Although one of the smaller boats, *Oman Sail* managed to finish in the very respectable time of 8d 19h 15m.

### Route tracker

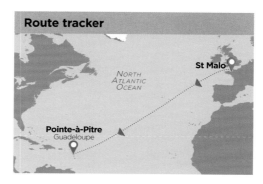

NORTH ATLANTIC OCEAN

St Malo

Pointe-à-Pitre
Guadeloupe

### Vital stats

**What:** 4,300-mile) transatlantic race

**Where:** St Malo (France) to Guadeloupe (Caribbean)

**How often:** Quadrennial

**Boat type:** Open class multihulls and monohulls

**Crew:** Solo

# Offshore Races
# Mini Transat
## Atlantic Ocean

*'I am not looking at sleeping for longer than 20 minutes as it is too risky. And I am becoming of the opinion that it is impossible to keep dry on a Mini.'*

**Pip Hare** | Competitor in Mini Transat, 2015

▽ Swiss skipper Simon Koster sets out on leg two of the 2015 Mini Transat from Lanzarote to Guadeloupe in his semi-foiling prototype scow *Eight Cube*, designed by Michel Desjoyeaux's company Mer Forte.

Briton Bob Salmon created the Mini Transat in the 1970s as an antidote to the growing size and rising costs of singlehanded racing events such as the OSTAR (Observer Singlehanded Transatlantic Race).

It was a nod over the shoulder back to 1960, when the OSTAR was first mooted as a sporting challenge between Corinthian sailors.

Meeting this ethos meant that the first Mini Transat in 1977 was run not from any of the major British yacht clubs, but from Penzance Sailing Club in Mounts Bay, Cornwall. The club was formed in 1939 and, true to its origins, it remains an excellent local club, blessed with superb sailing waters.

It hosted the first four Mini Transats in 1977, 1979, 1981 and 1983 before the race outgrew the club and the start was moved to Brest, France. The race, a very British innovation, had been more enthusiastically adopted by French 'soloists', so it was logical that it should be organized from where its critical mass was located. In due course, the event that had a 22ft maximum length limit became metricated and formalized around the Classe 6.5m.

Salmon's idea was not just to make racing alone across the Atlantic more affordable to more people, but less daunting as well. He set Antigua in the Caribbean as the finish line, with an intermediate stop in Tenerife, one of the Canary

Islands, not only breaking the long ocean crossing into two stages, but also routing boats onto a more southerly trade-wind track.

For a period the start moved further south to La Rochelle, and the finish to South America at Salvador de Bahia, Brazil. The 2013 and 2015 editions have used Douarnenez, south Brittany, as the start, and Guadeloupe as the finish.

The 2013 race was severely affected by bad weather. The scheduled 13 October start was delayed, and once underway, strong winds prompted the organizers to suspend racing midway across the Bay of Biscay, sending competitors scurrying to find shelter in Spanish havens. The race was restarted on 12 November. As a consequence and in a bid to avoid the worst of the weather, the 2015 event was brought forward to September.

Jean-Luc Garnier, Salmon's successor, developed the race programme, adding a Mini Fastnet and Trans-Gasgone race to the programme of events for the Classe 6.5m. This trend has continued so that there are now events in Valencia (Spain), Sicily, Sardinia and France to keep the sailors active in between the Mini Transat, which takes place every two years.

The evolution of a class does not always run smoothly, and so it was with the technical management of the class and the event organization merging and diverging between French and Italian bodies in the 1990s.

Through it all, the Mini Transat continued, proving to be a forcing ground for some of the most innovative boats in sailing and a stepping stone for sailors wanting to become professionals.

Past competitors read like a who's who of solo sailing. Among them have been Jean-Luc Van Den Heede, the Peyron brothers (Loïck and Bruno), Laurent Bourgnon, Roland Jourdain, Michel Desjoyeaux, Isabelle Autissier, Thomas Coville, Ellen MacArthur, Bernard Stamm and Yves Parlier.

Just as the Quarter Ton and Half Ton classes were a relatively low-cost way for emerging designers to try out their ideas in the 1970s in the inshore grand-prix racing world, so the Classe Mini has hot-housed all sorts of innovations.

## Route tracker

As long ago as 1991, Michel Desjoyeaux tried out a sideways hinging keel. Cranked up to windward, it massively increased the boat's sail-carrying power. Yves Parlier brought the first carbon-fibre mast to the start line in 1985, and the latest prototypes are experimenting with additional foils that generate lift and keels that extend as they hinge to boost righting movement.

Even by the 1980s, the Classe Mini was spawning boats that were more like offshore dinghies than baby yachts. Today, a typical Mini Transat boat looks like a 6.5-m (21-ft) boat with the rig of a 9-m (30-ft) boat. Control is vital for these overpowered boats, not just for the solo sailor, but also for extended running under autopilot. Twin rudders are the norm, as are long bowsprits to carry big offwind sails. These innovations trickled up, rather than trickled down, into bigger boats, notably the IMOCA 60s used in events such as the Vendée Globe.

By the 1990s, the entry list was split into two classes: 'Proto' for custom-designed and built boats, and 'Serie' for those series-produced.

Though the race continues to attract a predominantly French entry, the demographics have changed over the years. Interest peaked between 1995 and 2005, with the 75-slot entry list often having a waiting list as long again. Recently Spain has eclipsed Italy as the second-biggest contingent.

Casting a paternal eye over the Mini Transat scene in 2013 with its super-charged, complex, pocket-rocket boats, Salmon commented: 'I think only the technology has changed. The people haven't. It's always been a development class. Because of the cost, it's easier to develop technology more quickly.'

## Vital stats

**What:** Two-stage 4,020-mile transatlantic race

**Where:** Douarnenez (France) to Guadeloupe (Caribbean)

**How often:** Quadrennial

**Boat type:** Classe 6.5 Mini

**Crew:** Solo

mini transat
ÎLES DE GUADELOUPE
DOUARNENEZ ▸ LANZAROTE ▸ POINTE-À-PITRE

6.50 classemini

# Offshore Races
# **Transat Jacques Vabre**
## Atlantic Ocean

*'From the first night race, we had a navigation-system failure. We even thought of putting ribbons in the rigging, as we did when we sailed our 420 dinghies as nippers. We did everything without electronic help. But if you had told me before the start we would do this, I would have said not a chance. It's not possible. But we had to sharpen up our senses and make it work.'*

**Vincent Riou** | Previous race winner

**Vital stats**

**What:** 5,400-mile transatlantic race

**Where:** Le Havre (France) to Itajaí (Brazil)

**How often:** Quadrennial

**Boat type:** Open class monohulls and multihulls

**Crew:** Two crew

## Route tracker

▽ Armel Le Cléac'h down below on board the monohull *Banque Populaire*, mending sails during the Transat Jacques Vabre 2011.

It started out as the Route du Café and a singlehanded race in 1993. By the time the race was run a second time in 1995, it had become the Transat Jacques Vabre and a two-handed event.

This is because the Pen Duick organization run by Michel Etevenon had taken it over. He reshaped the race with its own clear niche to dovetail with the existing Route du Rhum rather than compete against it, as the same ORMA 60 multihulls and IMOCA 60 monohulls were the eligible boats.

What did not change was the cornerstone of the race's concept – namely linking Le Havre in Normandy (France's primary importation centre for coffee) and South America, from where the crop originated.

The Jacques Vabre coffee company and the port of Le Havre were partners in the venture, and with the company taking title sponsorship for the second edition, a long-running association was assured.

The line-up of the first race may have been only 13 competitors, but they were the elite of French singlehanded sailing, proving that there were sailors with sponsored boats and a strong following among the public with a commercial imperative to compete.

Every one of them was an established or soon-to-be star: Paul Vatine, Loïck Peyron, Yves Parlier, Alain Gautier, Jean-Luc Van Den Heede, Paul Vatine, Laurent Bourgnon, Francis Joyon, Hervé Laurent, Eric Dumont, Mike Birch, Gerry Roufs and Vincent Riou.

Vatine was the first to finish in Cartagena amongst the multihulls, while Parlier took line honours among the monohulls.

Turning the race into a double-handed event in 1995 brought ten boats to the start, and the concept was tweaked again in 1997. This time 16-m (50-ft) monos and multis could enter as well, with the multihulls given a longer course at nearly 5,000 miles via Barbados. Even so, the Bourgnon brothers, Laurent and Yves, in their *Primagaz* trimaran, finished nearly five days ahead of the best monohull pair, Yves Parlier sailing with the legendary Eric Tabarly.

For the 1999 race, an attempt to close the finish times between the monos and multis saw staggered times tried in addition to the longer course set for the faster boats.

By 2001, the finish had been relocated to Salvador de Bahia, a move from Colombia's fifth-largest city of Cartagena, with its World Heritage Site colonial-walled centre, to Brazil's eighth-largest urban area. It is also one of South America's oldest European-settled cities, colonized by the Portuguese who had arrived in 1549.

This also marked the first time a race across the Atlantic headed south of the equator. Bit by bit, the Transat Jacques Vabre was carving out its own distinct identity.

Two more classes were added for the 2003 race, for smaller monohulls and multihulls. The next

race in 2005 proved to be especially tough. Six of the ten ORMA 19-m (60-ft) trimarans abandoned the race, three due to capsizes, and others were forced to make pit-stop repairs.

By 2007, the race had taken on a very different flavour. The ORMA 60s had reached their zenith, due to spiralling costs and limited returns in development, a spate of capsizes in the 2002 Route du Rhum and 2005 Jacques Vabre events, plus sponsors looking for other projects. Only five lined up at the start.

By contrast, the IMOCA 60 monohulls were enjoying a growth spurt as teams targeted the Vendée Globe solo round-the-world race. Skippers considered a preceding transatlantic race a vital part of their preparations, so no fewer than 17 started in 2007. The monohull class was further boosted by the new Classe 40, with 30 on the start line.

Salvador de Bahia wasn't to prove the race's permanent home, moving briefly in 2009 and 2011 to Puerto Limon in Costa Rica before 2013's return to Brazil. This time, though, the finish line was Itajaí, its most southerly destination. The distance from Le Havre is 5,400 miles, but both monohulls and multihulls sailed the same direct course.

Located some 500 miles south of São Paulo, Itajai had launched an initiative to boost watersports and tourism, previously attracting the fully crewed Volvo Ocean Race in 2011/12. The benefits of bringing a big event to a small place saw 250,000 people visiting the race village, and the Transat Jacques Vabre reinforced that success.

2011 was another tough race. The start from Le Havre was delayed by three days and even then, the first week across the Bay of Biscay and around Cape Finistere was punishing. Some 15 out of 35 starters were forced out.

To date there have been nine two-time winners of the race, something tough to achieve in a race where attrition is so high. Remarkably, there have been three triple winners: Franck Cammas, Jean-Pierre Dick and Francis Escoffier.

◁ Three-times Jacques Vabre winner Jean-Pierre Dick, onboard his monohull *Virbac Paprec 3*. Together with co-skipper Jérémie Beyou, he pulled off his last win in 2011 on a northerly route, setting a new IMOCA time of 15d 18h 15m.

# Offshore Races
# Quebec–St Malo Race
## Atlantic Ocean

*'It's really the best fully crewed event one can participate in. It's a fascinating course, complex, varied and the fact of starting on a river adds something special to it. It's unique, surprising and fantastic.'*

Loïck Peyron

## Vital stats

**What:** 3,000-mile transatlantic race

**Where:** Quebec (Canada) to St Malo (France)

**How often:** Quadrennial

**Boat type:** Open class multihulls and monohulls

**Crew:** Minimum three crew

▽ The pack of yachts set off for the Quebec–St Malo on the St Lawrence river in Quebec City in July 2012.

More by happenstance than convention, races across the Atlantic seem to have evolved with shorthanded races heading west from Europe, and crewed races heading east from the North American seaboard.

This trend was pretty much cemented by the 1905 Kaiser's Race from Sandy Hook (New York) to The Lizard (Cornwall, southwest England), promoted by Kaiser Wilhelm of Germany when German, English and American owners regularly contested regattas in Newport, Cowes and Kiel in their large, handsome yachts; and later by the very first singlehanded transatlantic race from Plymouth to Newport in 1964.

### The original west-to-east transocean
The Quebec–St Malo race attempted to break this template. First run in 1984, it was hung on the hook of the 450th anniversary of Jacques Cartier's first of three voyages of discovery from St Malo, commissioned by France's King Francis I. The Breton claimed what is now Canada for his country, and went on to survey and map the Gulf of St Lawrence and upstream of the St Lawrence river to Quebec and Montreal.

The organizers of Quebec–St Malo like to say that it remains the only regular west-to-east trans-ocean race in the world. Also setting this race apart is its opening phase. A third of its overall length is sailed on the St Lawrence river, some 370 miles to Percé and open waters. The backdrop is stunning, though it presents numerous hurdles for the crews to negotiate, not the least of which are shallows, the current and shifty, variable winds affected by the topography.

Today, the Classe 40 monohull is the predominant class, though when the race was

first run, the multihulls reigned supreme. France's Loïck Peyron set a race record in 1996 that still remains today, setting a time of 7d 20h for the 3,000-mile course in his ORMA 60 trimaran *Fujicolor II*.

Peyron competed in the first race in 1984 when he joined the crew of the big catamaran *Formule TAG*. This was a notable boat for several reasons: it was one of the first large, offshore multihulls built from advanced-level, pre-impregnated carbon-fibre composites; and secondly, her skipper was Mike Birch. The Canadian had been in the vanguard of the professional skippers, his career as a yacht-delivery skipper morphing into a racing professional by dint of winning the first Route du Rhum in 1978. In that race he was aboard the much more modest 9-m (30-ft) trimaran *Olympus Photo*, having come second in the OSTAR behind Eric Tabarly two years previously.

### From the river to the sea

*Formule TAG* went on the reel off a 24-hour run of 516 miles in the first Quebec–St Malo, a figure that was quite staggering at the time. Peyron himself considers the event the top crewed race he's contested. 'It's really the best fully crewed event one can participate in. It's a fascinating course, complex, varied and the fact of starting on a river adds something special to it. It's unique, surprising and fantastic.'

The nature of the course sends the boats out into the Atlantic in proximity to Newfoundland. The Grand Banks, with fog routinely generated by the clash of the warm, northwesterly flow of the Gulf Stream/North Atlantic Drift with much

◁ Loïck Peyron aboard his ORMA 60 trimaran *Fujicolor II*. In 1996 he set a new speed record of 7d 20h for the 3,000-mile race that still remains today.

colder Arctic water, always poses a test. Even with modern ice-reporting communications, it is the small, barely awash 'growlers' that the racers of fast, light boats fear.

Loïc Caradec won the first Quebec–St Malo in 1984, his *Royale* recording a time of 8d 19h. Three races on, Loïck Peyron set *Fujicolor II*'s record, which remains an hour better than any other time achieved.

The emphasis of the race has since shifted to the Classe 40 monohulls. 2012 was a banner year for Halvard Mabire, who became the first ever skipper to win back-to-back races. His *Campagne de France*, co-skippered by Miranda Merron, won in 11d 17h in a fleet of 20 Classe 40s. This was a significant achievement, considering that *Pogo Structures* won in 2008 with a time of 13d 13h.

### The 1992 monohull record

The maxi yacht *Merit* still holds the monohull record after 20 years. In 1992 Swiss skipper Pierre Fehlmann and his crew covered the distance in 10d 15h 44m.

# Transatlantic Races

## Atlantic Ocean

*'This is yachting in earnest.'*

**Samuel 'Billy' Samuels** | Skipper, 1866
Transatlantic Race

---

### Vital stats

**What:** Variable organized race or individual record attempt of up to 2,880 miles

**Where:** Eastern seaboard (USA) to England

**How often:** Variable

**Boat type:** Monohulls and multihulls

**Crew:** Fully crewed or singlehanded

### Route tracker

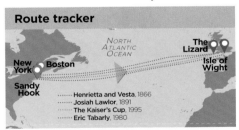

- Henrietta and Vesta, 1866
- Josiah Lawlor, 1891
- The Kaiser's Cup, 1995
- Eric Tabarly, 1980

New York · Boston · Sandy Hook · North Atlantic Ocean · The Lizard · Isle of Wight

---

'Gordon Bennett!' At some stage this exclamation entered the English language as an alternative to swearing. Gordon Bennett, father and son, were real people, however, and the younger man instigated the first race across the Atlantic in 1866.

The Gordon Bennetts ran the *New York Herald* newspaper and had a sharp news sense. They paid for salacious stories and weren't above entrapment. James Gordon Bennett Jr was equally in the public eye himself, living an extravagant and colourful lifestyle – which is probably why the family name became used as an expression of amazement.

J. Gordon Bennett was also a yachtsmen and a gambler, taking part in races from Newport's Brenton Reef lightship off Rhode Island to another at Sandy Hook. At the age of just 26, he became commodore of the prestigious New York Yacht Club in 1871.

### Raising the stakes

Before then, and wanting to raise the stakes to something higher than 200-mile races off New England, Gordon Bennett challenged his fellow owners to a race *to* England. The wager was US$30,000, the equivalent of $500,000 today. So high were the stakes that Bennett hired America's best skipper, Samuel 'Billy' Samuels, for $10,000 to take charge of his 33-m (107-ft) schooner *Henrietta*.

### Yachting in earnest

All that skill and experience was certainly necessary. Instead of a summer race, *Henrietta* was joined at the Sandy Hook start by *Vesta* and *Fleetwing* on 11 December 1866. Their crews knew that they were taking on the Atlantic in its foulest mood. The yachts' sail area was reduced. *Henrietta* and *Vesta* closed in their cockpits.

The yachts' owners agreed that only smaller working sails would be carried. It was prudent. The yachts encountered short daylight hours and full winter gales, burying their bowsprits and getting laid on their beam-ends regularly. Samuel wrote of the 'Gordon Bennett!' conditions, using the much more understated language of his time: 'This is yachting in earnest.'

On *Vesta*, a wave swept all eight of the on-deck watch overboard. Two clung on to a sail, but the other six were lost.

*Henrietta* made one day's run of 277 miles, impressive for a mid-19th-century vessel. She won the race in a fast time of 13d 21h.

So began what has become a string of occasional races and record attempts to cross the Atlantic from west to east. There was not a similar east-to-west event until the solo Transat, which began nearly 100 years later in 1960. To 2015, there have been 27 Transatlantic Races, with 12 run by the NYYC and seven by the Cruising Club of America.

Although historically sporadic, the second race followed in short order. As a means to an end, Englishman James Ashbury intended to head to the USA to try and regain the trophy *America* had won in 1851 (to become the America's Cup). He asked the New York YC if any American wanted to race his *Cambria* across.

J. Gordon Bennett accepted the challenge with his new yacht, *Dauntless*. *Cambria* won by just over

two hours in a 23-day crossing. *Dauntless* lost two crew, swept off the bowsprit. This terrible cost of eight dead in two races meant that it was 1887 before a third race was attempted.

## Son of a gun!

*Dauntless* had a new owner in the shape of Caldwell H. 'Colly' Colt, son of the inventor of the eponymous revolver.

In the 20th century, American yachtsman Alf 'The Loom' Loomis credited Colt with a profound influence on what was to become the sport of ocean racing. Colt actually raced onboard, unlike other owners who treated their yachts like racehorses, sporting possessions to be observed from the grandstand, a means to demonstrate social and financial standing. Loomis said that Colt

▽ The Currier & Ives lithograph *The Great Ocean Yacht Race Between Henrietta, Fleetwing & Vesta*, by Charles Parsons, from 1867.

THE GREAT OCEAN YACHT RACE.
BETWEEN THE HENRIETTA, FLEETWING & VESTA.
THE "GOOD BYE" TO THE YACHT CLUB STEAMER "RIVER QUEEN," 4 MILES EAST OF SANDY HOOK, LIGHT SHIP, DEC.R 11TH 1866.

THE HENRIETTA arrived off the Needles, Isle of Wight, England, at 5.45. P.M. Dec.r 25th 1866, winning the Race, and making the run in 13 days 22 hours, mean time.
The FLEETWING arrived 8 hours afterwards, and the VESTA 1¾ hours after the Fleetwing.

NEW YORK PUBLISHED BY CURRIER & IVES, 152 NASSAU STREET

raced for the simple reason that 'he knew he would have a hell of a good time.'

## Sabotage

In the third race, *Dauntless* leaked badly and lost to the newer *Coronet*. Several years after the race, when the copper cladding was stripped off *Dauntless*'s hull, skipper Samuel Samuels claimed that two neatly drilled holes had been found forward. He had no doubt that it was a deliberate act of sabotage and explained why *Dauntless* had leaked so badly that it prevented her being driven hard in the race.

## The birth of singlehanded transats

Nowadays, 1960 and the first OSTAR/Transat is considered the birth of singlehanded racing across the Atlantic. But in truth it had already been done, in 1891 and 1892. More remarkable still was that Americans Josiah W. Lawlor and William Andrews undertook a race from Boston to Europe in tiny 4.7-m (15-ft) boats, the *Sea Serpent* and the *Mermaid*, respectively. The records are sketchy, but the feat was achieved as early as 1876. Lawlor and Andrews engaged in the first race, the former winning by reaching southwest England in 45 days. Both men endured capsizes, shark attacks and

worse, but Williams suffered worst when he lost all his water and food while 700 miles from land. To his immense fortune, he was spotted by a passing ship four days later and rescued.

The year after Lawlor's win, the pair tried again, but on this voyage, Lawlor disappeared forever. Andrews undertook three more attempts, including a third with his new bride in 1901. In an ironic twist of the fate, William Andrews and his new bride were also lost at sea.

## The Kaiser's Cup

If there is one race that is still talked about today, it is the legendary 1905 Transatlantic Race. At the start of the 20th century, a number of races had been run between England and New York, Newport, Marblehead and Halifax. Some of the great America's Cup men of the era, Jacob Astor and Thomas Lipton, donated handsome trophies to encourage participation.

Some believe the 1905 race to be a monument to the aggrandizement of Germany's Kaiser Wilhelm II. Whatever the motivation, the intention was to make this race more prestigious than any other.

The kaiser had long struggled to beat his cousin, Edward, Prince of Wales, later king of England, at

▽ Captain Josiah W. Lawlor in his boat, the *Sea Serpent*. By the time he arrived in England, the rudder had been badly gnawed by a large shark that Lawlor fought off with an explosive signal candle.

▷ Captain William Andrews skippering his boat *Mermaid*. After he capsized several times he finally asked the *Elbruz* from Antwerp to take him onboard. He arrived safely in Antwerp and sold the *Mermaid* for a tidy profit and rejoined Lawlor in England two weeks after Lawlor had won the race.

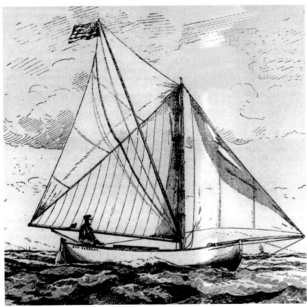

Cowes Week. So for the Transatlantic Race, he presented an impressive gold trophy, the Kaiser's Cup, and intended to present it to the winner at Kiel Week, although the race from New York was to finish at the Lizard, England's southernmost point. *Pfeil*, a cruiser from the German Imperial Navy, was stationed there to time the arrivals.

The 11 yachts were very impressive. In America, this was the Gilded Age. They ranged in size from 33m (107ft) to the largest, a gargantuan 600-ton, 91.5-m (295-ft), ship-rigged schooner called *Valhalla*, owned by Lord Crawford. Crawford came from one of the oldest of Britain's hereditary families, with a fortune from the Lancashire coalfields. *Valhalla* could seat 30 for dinner in her lavish saloon.

It was not the Kaiser's *Hamburg* (formerly the British yacht *Rainbow*) that triumphed. Rather it was Wilson Marshall's aptly named *Atlantic*, a 300-ton, 57.4-m (185-ft) schooner designed by Gardner & Cox. Exceptionally comfortable, *Atlantic* was innovative, too. She had retractable funnels so that the steam-powered electrical generators could be kept running while sailing to service the light and refrigeration. For the race, skipper Lem Miller invited the American-naturalized Scot, Charlie Barr, famous as a three-time America's Cup-winning skipper,

aboard to take command.

Both *Valhalla* and *Hamburg* made the early running before a gale broke spars, sails and gear. Through the maelstrom, Barr drove *Atlantic* hard and with great skill. Marshall, uncomfortable and concerned, ventured on deck and asked Barr to reduce sail. Instead, Barr said, 'You hired me to win this race and by God, that's what I am going to do!'

*Atlantic* finished first in a time of 12d 4h 1m. This time was not bettered for 75 years. Her best day's run was 341 miles. While riding out the two-day gale, Barr ordered bags of oil to be hung over *Atlantic*'s windward gunwales to stop the seas breaking onboard. On the helm, two men were lashed down to man the kicking wheel.

As for the Kaiser's Cup, Marshall's son auctioned the celebrated trophy to raise funds for the Red Cross during the First World War. Far from being solid gold, it turned out to be gold-plated pewter.

Since the 1905 epic, the Atlantic has been tackled as either a race (from 1928 onwards) or as a straight-out record attempt. The 1931 race was famous for *Dorade*'s victory in the hands of Olin and Rod Stephens. They were honoured with a ticker-tape parade in Manhattan.

▽ The start of the Kaiser's Cup, with the schooners *Hamburg* on the left, *Valhalla* in the centre, and *Atlantic* on the right.

„Hamburg".  „Valhalla".  „Atlantic".

Der Start zur Ozean-Wettfahrt um den Pokal Kaiser Wilhelm's II.

△ Eric Tabarly in his revolutionary trimaran *Paul Ricard* during the record-slashing race.

▷ The maxi trimaran *Banque Populaire*, skippered by Pascal Bidégorry, arrives in Manhattan for the North Atlantic record in 2009.

## New records

The fully crewed races decreased in frequency and support, as solo racing across the Atlantic in the other direction grew from the 1960s, but have undergone a revival in recent times. Interest in cracking the Atlantic record was rekindled in 1980 when *The Sunday Times* in London and *Le Point* in Paris offered a US$50,000 prize for beating the 12d 4h benchmark between Sandy Hook and the Lizard, in Cornwall.

It should be no surprise that the first to do so was as big an icon as Charlie Barr — French legend Eric Tabarly, who did it on his own and in a radical boat, the foil-assisted trimaran *Paul Ricard*. Tabarly slashed the record by nearly two days, to 10d 5h 14m.

Since then, the record has fallen ten more times to just 3d 15h 25m, set by Pascal Bidégorry's crew on the giant trimaran *Banque Populaire* in 2009. Tellingly, sailors are not just interested in the fastest time any more. The World Sailing Speed Record Council recognizes no fewer than 12 different categories of record to cover the different permutations of monohulls, multihulls, crewed, solo, women, length and powered sail-handling systems. That the record hasn't been cut since 2009 suggests that multihull and weather-routeing technology has plateaued — for the time being, that is.

# Offshore Races
# Osaka Cup
## Tasman Sea/North Pacific Ocean

*'Coming into Osaka in the dark, the traffic was extraordinary. Little ships, big ships, ferries, fishing boats – it was like lit-up ants everywhere. We got squeezed between three ships. It's the most dangerous finish to a yacht race I've ever seen!'*

**Jock MacAdie** | Skipper of winning yacht *Alex-Team MacAdie*, 2007

### Vital stats

**What:** 5,500-mile offshore race

**Where:** Melbourne (Australia) to Osaka (Japan)

**How often:** Quadrennial

**Boat type:** Monohulls

**Crew:** Two-handed

### Route tracker

The Melbourne–Osaka race began as a single race in 1987 to commemorate a significant landmark in the history of Osaka – the 120th anniversary of the opening of the Japanese city's port.

The route was unusual, as well as the fact that the event was conceived as a two-handed race. At 5,500 miles, it was a stern test of sailors, boats and the durability of each, during which the competing yachts encounter multiple weather systems and seasons as they cross the Pacific Ocean from south to north. The race record is held by *Wild Thing*, completing the race in 26d 21h in 1995.

### A tale of two cities

The race's reputation spread quickly after the first edition, and its place in the calendar seemed secure. The M20, as insiders call the race, was run every four years from 1991. The 2013 race mustered 11 entries and was won by Australians Bruce McKay and John Davies in the 12.7-m (41-ft) *Wasabi*. But declining entries saw the organizers, the ports of Melbourne and Osaka, postpone the 2017 race by a year.

With the 40th anniversary of the twinning of the two host cities marked in 2018, organizers' hopes to re-establish the race for an eighth edition appeared to be rewarded with expressions of interest from both Australian and Japanese entrants, making the 25-boat fleet the viable number they were seeking.

### Timed to avoid the worst weather

The race is a tale of two hemispheres, which means that the seasons are encountered in reverse order, from autumn in Australia to spring in Japan without either a full summer or winter in between. This timing was chosen to avoid both the end of the cyclone season in the southern hemisphere and the beginning of the typhoon season in the northern hemisphere.

Break the distance down and it turns into the equivalent of eight Fastnet, Bermuda or Sydney–Hobart races. During the three to six weeks the race can take, competitors face an extraordinary variety of conditions. Melbourne's Port Philip Bay, the Great Australian Bight and the Bass Strait are subject to stiff winds and unrelenting, heavy seas. The strong breeze is from the south, where it is super-chilled by Antarctica.

Once around New South Wales, it's north towards the equator, passing between the Solomon Islands and Papua New Guinea.

There is champagne sailing in the tradewinds before a path has to be picked through the light and variable doldrums. The final approaches to

Osaka are narrow, tidal and with winds that can be light or strong. Typically competitors cruise back at a leisurely pace, or have their yachts shipped back by cargo freighter.

The winner of the first two events was one of Japan's most experienced offshore sailors, Kaoru Ogimi in *Nakiri Dao*. Because there is so much offwind sailing in the course, designer Bruce Farr gave the boat a ketch rig with a big mizzen. Ogimi raced with American Warwick Tomkins, the pair good friends from college days in Oregon, USA. Their winning time in the first race was 31d 19h.

Kiwi Ross Field raced *Nakiri Dao* with an updated sail plan in the second race with Hideo Sugai. Field remembers the 1995 race as he and Jeff Scott, skipper and watch leader from the Whitbread-Round-the-World-Race-winning *Yamaha*, were rolled 360 degrees in 50–60-knot winds and the breaking seas of Wilson's Promontory. This was the year that Aussie Grant Wharington, ever keen to upset the established order, raced his then radical 15.5-m (50-ft) *Wild Thing* with Scott Gilbert to set the race record at 26d 21h.

The Australian boat *Gusto* managed to complete the 2007 race with just one of the crew aboard. Brian Pattinson finished alone because his friend, the co-owner of their former Open 60,

Patrick Guidice, got off the boat in Honiara, on Guadalcanal in the Solomon Islands where they'd stopped for rig repairs.

'I really don't know why, he just wanted to, so he did – there was no discussion on why', said Pattinson on arrival. The Australian explained how he managed the remaining 3,000 miles on his own: 'I tended to pull the sails down at night and sleep.'

This same situation had occurred in the 2003 race, when Giudice stepped off the boat in Eden, on Australia's southeast corner, suffering back problems and Pattinson eventually retired to Newcastle on the New South Wales Central Coast with damage.

In the same race, *Mad Max* ran aground on a reef and was lost. James Murchison and Jeff Thompson from Sydney were helicoptered safely off their stricken yacht and taken to Rabaul, Papua New Guinea.

2003 saw a win for Kiwis Brian Petersen and John Bankert on the Greg Elliott-designed *Maverick II*. This was Petersen's third race, having been placed third in 1991 on *Ikando* and second in 1995 with designer Greg Elliott on the potent wing-masted ketch *Elliott Marine*. In a nice twist, he then met his future wife, Kei Ko – who hails from Osaka.

# Offshore Races
# Clipper Cup/Kenwood Cup
## Hawaii

### Route tracker

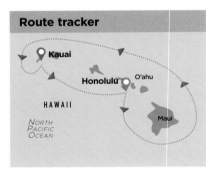

R ather like the airline from which it took its name, the Clipper Cup is no more. Neither is its successor, the Kenwood Cup.

Yet while they existed, these series gave sailors the opportunity to 'race the winds of paradise'. The mixture of tradewinds, balmy temperatures and Pacific waves made Hawaii a wonderful venue.

The event's origins lay in the Round the State race run by members of the Waikiki Yacht Club in Honolulu, a 775-mile track that looped around the island chain from Honolulu in the southeast to Kauai in the northwest.

Isolated in the middle of the Pacific, the Waikiki YC decided it would try to encourage more yachtsmen to visit Hawaii to revive its flagging local long race. At the time offshore racing was prospering, with a strong Admiral's Cup in the UK, the Southern Cross Series in Australia and the Onion Patch and Southern Ocean Racing Conference in the USA, plus a full array of level-rating events in the Ton Cup classes that were staged in different locations around the world every year.

Scheduled in August, the objective was to fit in with ocean racers considering the biennial Transpac (from Long Beach to Honolulu) or the Victoria–Maui Race (British Colombia to Lahaina).

**With a little help from Pan Am**

By 1977, the Waikiki YC knew they had to fan the embers if the Round the State race was to survive. Much of what followed was to the credit of Dick Gooch, who took the idea to Pan Am and did not let it go until the airline agreed to come on as title sponsor for a new series built around the existing long race. The format was also built around the three-boat team format pioneered in the Admiral's Cup.

Now defunct, in the 1970s Pan Am was arguably the most famous airline in the world. Gooch not only secured its marketing support – the 'Clipper' brand was synonymous with Pan Am from its flying boat days through to its premium cabins and lounges – but also ensured great coverage from the media. Such aspirational demand for the event was created that the event grew strongly from 1978 to 1984.

The format originally added three 30-mile inshore triangular courses plus an overnight race to create a longer, 775-mile race that lapped the USA's 50th state. If overnight races sound like the endurance events experienced in other parts of the world, in Hawaii it was different. Day or night, the crews raced in t-shirts and shorts; oilksins were not required.

The Pacific yachting nations supported the Pan Am Clipper Cup, with Australia, New Zealand, Japan and the USA all sending two three-boat teams. The American teams featured two maxis, Jim Kilroy's *Kialoa* and Juey Long's *Ondine*.

Two years later, in 1980, 11 teams attended. The series was notable for the Japanese 12.4-m (40-ft) *Unchu*. In the fourth race, she split from the fleet, broke free and went on to win. The Ichiro Yokoyama-designed boat had become the first ever Japanese-designed and built ocean racer to win outside of Japan in international competition.

The third series in 1982 showed that the Pan Am Clipper Cup had become a real magnet for the maxis. There was the new *Kialoa V*, plus Bob Bell's new *Condor*, both Ron Holland-designed 25-m (80-ft) boats, plus the revamped *Windward Passage*, which lost her rig in the Round the State race.

1984 was a significant regatta because of a couple of individual entries, the one-tonners *Pacific Sundance* and *General Hospital*. They placed first and second in their class and were built to Design 136 of New Zealand's Bruce Farr.

Farr had been a prolific designer of winning boats in the 1970s, but his work had been treated harshly by administrators of the International Rating Rule (IOR). After a period away, back came Farr with a new generation of fast, fractionally rigged boats that helped him become the most successful designer of the next 20 years.

## The Kenwood Cup

For 1986, the Clipper Cup turned into the Kenwood Cup, sponsored by the Japanese electronics giant. Essentially the event stayed the same, offering the highest level of offshore team racing. By 1988 there was sufficient pulling power to see owners ship their boats from Europe, including Raoul Gardini's Germán Frers-designed maxi *Il Moro di Venezia*. In all, a total of nine maxis entered, making it the glitziest series ever.

Britain entered for the first time and finished third overall, despite Mike Peacock's one-tonner *Juno* being rammed in race four by the local, and appropriately named, *General Hospital*. Peacock was awarded average points for the rest of the series. Robin Aisher's *Yeoman XXVII* from the Australia Red team, one of three Aussie teams entered, was the winner.

In the face of dwindling entries, the Kenwood Cup expired in 2014.

▷ The One Ton racing yachts compete in the Kenwood Cup on 1 November 1988 off the Hawaiian coast.

# Atlantic Rally for Cruisers

North Atlantic

*'The boats are bigger, the boats are faster and communications have changed and so has navigation. But the wind and the waves are still the same.'*

**Chris Tibbs** | Weatherman, ARC

△ Jimmy Cornell, who in creating the ARC fulfilled the dreams of thousands to make trans-ocean voyages possible.

The story of the Atlantic Rally for Cruisers (ARC) rests squarely on the shoulders of its founder Jimmy Cornell. He is the man who not only lived the dream himself (cruising around the world) but then set about making the dream possible for others.

His reasoning was that there was pent-up demand for yachts to cross the Atlantic to the Caribbean in company, as opposed to making solitary passages.

He launched the Atlantic Rally for Cruisers in 1986, linking the Canary Islands, where yachts from all over Europe could assemble, with the Caribbean. The 204-boat fleet, from 24 nations, was recognized at the time in the *Guinness Book of Records* as the largest trans-ocean event ever staged.

Every year since, some 200 boats, carrying 1,200 crew, have made the crossing, enjoying the benefits of shared information, briefings and practical demonstrations before the start, the safety net of being in touch during the two-week crossing, and parties at the start and finish. The ARC has quickly become the number-one ambition for numerous sailors.

Cornell carefully chose the word 'rally' instead of 'race', as it better fits the event's ethos. It is not a hell-for-leather dash, but rather a means of

crews going at a pace they're comfortable with. As such, it has attracted crews of all abilities, all ages (including babies) and all nationalities.

A novel feature is engine use. Crews can switch on and use auxiliary power if they are not moving along adequately by wind power alone. The engine hours are recorded and a correction applied in working out the handicap results.

Striking the right chord was no accident, as Cornell knew all about the siren call of the far horizon. He grew up in Romania, but left while his country was still in the iron grip of the communist dictator Nicolae Ceaușescu and moved to London with his British wife, working there for the BBC World Service.

He fitted out his own 11-m (36-ft) cruising boat and in 1975–77 circumnavigated the world in a 70,000-mile, 70-country voyage, accompanied by his wife and their two children. It was to prove the first of four circumnavigations Cornell was to carry out, with a fifth planned.

The knowledge and organization required to complete it was put to good use. Cornell is a bestselling author on all aspects of long-distance sailing, and he used this experience to make the template for others to follow. Not only was the ARC a runaway success, but it spawned both longer events (around the world) and shorter ones (within the Canary Islands).

Cornell sold his World Cruising company to his operations boss Andrew Bishop in 1998, though any plans to retire seem to have not survived very long thanks to his restless energy. This was partly sated by building another yacht and going on two round-the-world trips. But by 2010, Cornell was back in the event organization business, running a series of events under the Odyssey banner.

In the meantime, World Cruising has gone from strength to strength, itself organizing a panoply of events based on the same philosophy as the ARC. These range from rallies in the Baltic and Caribbean to the Classic Malts Cruise, which travels between Scotland's west-coast island distilleries.

In 1989 a racing division was added to the ARC for the more sporty crews, some of whose yachts were Caribbean bound for the northern winter season, in order to take in the springtime regattas in the islands. By 1990, the destination had shifted from Barbados to St Lucia, where the finish has remained ever since.

The nominal distance from the Canaries to the St Lucia finish is 2,700 miles, though most crews typically log a 3,000-mile passage. This is because most don't take the rhumb line course (the steady course that appears as a straight line on a cylindrical map) but seek the tradewinds before turning their bows westward. 'Head south until the butter melts,' is the old saws' advice.

In the early days there was just a radio ham net (an amateur radio net) but this has evolved into satellite tracking and position reporting. Before they start, there is now a full fortnight of activities ranging from life-raft drills and parties to engine strip downs and first aid at sea.

The ARC has had an impressive safety record given that in its first 30 years, more than 6,000 individual transatlantic crossings have been made. There have been some incidents, however. In 2007 an ARC yacht rescued a non-ARC crew from their life raft, and one ARC sailor lost his life due to a head injury.

**Route tracker**

NORTH ATLANTIC OCEAN

Gran Canaria

St Lucia

MOROCCO

WESTERN SAHARA

AFRICA

**Vital stats**

**What:** 2,700-mile transatlantic event

**Where:** Gran Canaria (Spain, Canary Islands) to St Lucia (Caribbean)

**How often:** Annual

**Boat type:** Cruisers and cruiser racers

**Crew:** Minimum two crew

▽ Small or large, humble or luxurious – the ARC caters for all types of cruising yachts wanting to cross the Atlantic.

# Round-the-World Races

# Round-the-World Races
# Volvo Ocean Race

The first race was won by a Mexican. The Netherlands has fielded more winners than any other country – three. And, yes, this is one of the pre-eminent races of them all.

It's the Volvo Ocean Race, which began life in 1973/4 as the Whitbread Round the World Race, a name it kept for the next eight editions until 2001, when its new owners rebranded it.

It was Anthony Churchill – who had navigated Edward Heath's *Morning Cloud* to win the 1969 Sydney–Hobart and published *Yachting & Boating Weekly* – who floated the idea of a fully crewed, round-the-world race to follow on from the Golden Globe. Churchill had joined forces with Guy Pearse, who had previously organized the OSTAR.

## Route tracker

Gothenburg Finish
Cardiff
Newport
Lisbon
Alicante Start
Abu Dhabi
Sanya
Recife
Atlantic Ocean
Itajaí
Cape Town
Indian Ocean
Auckland
Pacific Ocean
Pacific Ocean
Southern Ocean

## Vital stats

**What:** 27,000–38,000-mile round-the-world race

**Where:** UK or Spain to a variable finish

**How often:** Quadrennial

**Boat type:** Monohulls

**Crew:** Fully crewed

Previous page: Skippered by Grant Dalton, the Volvo Open 60 yacht *Amer Sport One* battles through heavy seas off the Cape of Good Hope during leg two of the 2001/2 Volvo Ocean Race. She eventually claimed third place overall.

At the 1969 Cowes Week, they had distributed a brochure outlining a race around the world on the traditional clipper-ship route and with stops in Cape Town, Sydney and Rio de Janeiro. Yachting magazines around the world picked up this audacious adventure. By 1971, amongst the serious enquires were those from the army and Royal Navy in Britain, plus others from Germany, Poland and Italy.

The navy interest was to prove vital, as the Royal Naval Sailing Association (RNSA) was willing to organize the race and had British brewer Whitbread interested in backing it. Today, the navy connection seems odd in an era where races are used to generate income, media interest and image. But 50 years ago, the Royal Navy used sailing as key adventure training and had an organization through sister navies to organize it.

Enlightened for the time, the RNSA decided to take a generous view of Rule 26 of the International Yacht Racing Rules, which banned advertising. They realized that the costs of entering a nine-month race around the world were a considerable disincentive to entries. Instead, they imposed their own 'good taste' rule.

### Whitbread Round the World Race

Having assembled at the naval base at Portsmouth, 17 yachts started the first race on 8 September 1973. The gun was fired by Sir Alec Rose, who five years before had sailed around the world.

The fleet was a fascinating mix. There were the already famous Chay Blyth and Eric Tabarly and the experienced but relatively unknown Les Williams (UK) and André Viant (France). Others,

such as Roddie Ainslie (UK – and later to become father of star Olympic sailor, Ben Ainslie), were good sailors clubbing their funds together for the adventure of a lifetime on the yacht they had chartered, *Second Life*. The German and Polish entries, *Peter von Danzig, Otago* and *Copernicus*, were entered by actual clubs sailed by, variously, students and shipyard workers.

There was also Mexican washing-machine millionaire Ramon Carlin. He had only taken up sailing five years before, and had gone to fabled Finnish yacht builders Nautor for *Sayula II*, one of their S&S-designed Swan 65 yachts. While the Swan 65 was the distillation of best yacht practice and the accumulated knowledge of the world's most successful yacht designers – Sparkman & Stephens – variety rang rife through the fleet.

Take Tabarly's *Pen Duick VI*. André Mauric designed her, but Tabarly insisted on a tiller in the face of conventional wisdom, which said that a wheel was essential for the helm loads of a big boat. *Pen Duick*'s keel was made from spent uranium, because it was denser than lead. The yacht's construction was a collaborative French effort. The naval dockyard in Brest built the boat for no charge; Renault supplied the engine; aluminium plate, sails, winches and so forth – Tabarly had no end of donors.

Chay Blyth, by contrast, was backed by Jack Hayward, an ardent supporter of all things English. He recovered Britain's first iron ship, SS *Great Britain*, from the Falklands and brought her back to Bristol for restoration. As a consequence, Blyth's maxi ketch was called *Great Britain II*. A former parachute sergeant, Blyth selected his crew from this regiment. Travelling to and finding a remote Scottish croft was the first of many initiative tests that Blyth used to whittle down 200 applicants to a crew of 12. When construction of the foam-sandwich maxi fell behind, the Paras split into two groups and worked 12 hours on, 12 hours off continual shifts as boatbuilders.

Out in front on leg one, *Pen Duick VI* was dismasted. Tabarly diverted to Rio de Janeiro, but not before a huge operation had been launched back in Europe. A new mast, new sails and new rigging were made and flown to Brazil in a French military plane. Also onboard was a wheel steering system to replace the Tabarly-ordained tiller.

The Royal Navy's Nicholson 55, *Adventure*, became an unlikely frontrunner. It turned out that the crew tuned into weather forecasts transmitted to ships on the high seas in Morse code. They were able to read Morse and make use of this legal and sensible aid to navigation in an era of the sextant and dead reckoning.

Leslie Williams' *Burton Cutter* was first to Cape Town. Remarkably, the much smaller *Adventure* was second, and handicap winner of the leg. That *Burton Cutter* was barely completed before she left Portsmouth proved a lifesaver a few days after the start of leg two. Faulty welding meant that her internal frames were detaching, and the front of the hull was panting in and out. Williams' crew used some of the still-to-be-fitted internal furniture to shore-up the hull as they headed straight back to Cape Town.

Leg two claimed the first of two lives lost in the race. Paul Waterhouse completed leg one on *British Soldier* and switched to the Italian *Tauranga*, where he was ejected off the foredeck when a headsail filled as he struggled with a broken spinnaker pole. Dominique Guillet was swept off by a wave breaking over *33 Export*.

It was a damaging leg. *Adventure*'s rudder failed and her crew had to use the trim tab on the keel to steer. *Great Britain II* and *Otago* lost their mizzen masts. *Kriter* broke her rudder skeg. And *Sayula II* dropped like 'there was no gravity' as she was rolled so violently a coachroof window was smashed.

On leg three towards Cape Horn, *Pen Duick VI* was pressing on at the front when Tabarly's yacht was dismasted a second time as a Southerly Buster front hit in the Tasman Sea. The reaching strut failed and the compression load of the spinnaker pole crumpled the mast.

Having come through the Buster, *Great Britain II* was changing up to bigger sails when Bernie Hosking fell overboard. He'd been overboard once already on leg one and been recovered. The crew searched for more than two hours this time, but without success. Blyth was later criticized for being

△ Eric Tabarly's *Pen Duick VI* at the start of the race, battling an early storm in the Solent.

◁ The Swan 65 yacht and handicap winner *Sayula II*, skippered by owner Ramón Carlin, nears the finish line in Portsmouth, outrunning its closest pursuer, the Royal Navy's *Adventure*.

so matter-of-fact about Hosking's loss. Allowances weren't made for this being, outwardly at least, the Paras' way. *Great Britain II* reached Rio ahead of the fleet, her first line honours of the race.

On the final leg home, *Adventure*'s canny navigation caused anxiety that she might gain time on the overall handicap leader, *Sayula II*. Ramón Carlin's crew were anxious enough anyway, as the headstay was starting to fail. A spare main halyard

▷ The final 100 miles of leg one of the Volvo Ocean Race 2014/15 prove to be the hardest as the yachts enter the ocean sprint towards Cape Town. French sailor Seb Marsset holds on during a sunset sail change onboard the US yacht *Team Alvimedica*.

was double rigged to take the load off it. By the time *Sayula II* reached Portsmouth and victory, five of the 17 strands in the wire headstay had parted.

An amazing adventure had proven to be a great race. There was no doubt in anyone's mind that it was to be repeated.

### The 1970s

So began a four-year cycle of races that produced endless drama and fascination, with reputations won and lost. Ironically, Churchill and Pearse had been organizing their own race while the first Whitbread was going on. Their FT Clipper Race in 1975/6 attracted only four entries, whereas the second WRWR in 1977/8 drew 15 boats. The standout yacht of the race was *Flyer*. She was beautifully built by Walter Huisman for experienced sailor and ship-owner Cornelis van Rietschoten. Designed by S&S, she was like a Swan 65 except improved in every single way and immaculately prepared.

*Flyer* won the overall handicap victory, through always being in the hunt. Her rivals were neither good enough nor reliable enough. Take Heath's *Condor*. Leslie Williams was back with another handsome John Sharp-designed yacht, but she was late and ill-prepared. Her crew included alternate skipper Robin Knox-Johnston and a 6ft 4in, tousle-haired Kiwi by the name of Peter Blake. *Condor* was

a contradiction – beautifully constructed in wood long after this was the material of choice for race boats, and sporting the first carbon-fibre mast. In fresh headwinds after the doldrums, the mast broke. *Condor*'s crew jury-rigged the 400 miles to Monrovia, Liberia. A new aluminium mast was stepped.

In the race, Clare Francis became the first female skipper (of the Swan 65 *ADC Accutrac*). Eric Tabarly's *Pen Duick VI*, back for a second race, was disqualified as the depleted uranium of the keel had become a prohibited material during the course of the race, even though the yacht had a rating certificate valid until 1977. It was an acrimonious decision. And John Ridgway, with whom Chay Blyth had rowed the Atlantic in 1966, took *Debenhams*, a 17.7-m (57-ft) cruising boat, so much further south than any of the fleet on leg two that the yacht was ensnared in pack ice in full gale conditions with visibility blotted out by snow. This dangerous course at 66 degrees south was criticized as foolhardy in the respected *Yachting World* magazine.

Auckland had replaced Sydney as the mid-point stop for the second race, and the thousands of spectator boats showed that

New Zealanders took the race to their hearts like no other.

Rio de Janeiro hosted the fleet again, though the stopover was marred by the prizegiving at the Rio Yacht Club. After the band stopped playing at midnight at the exclusive club, some of the crews carried on with high-jinks partying. Local officials called the riot police and broke things up with tear gas.

## The 1980s

Conny van Rietschoten was back with a new *Flyer II* for the 1981/2 race, this time a 24-m (78-ft) Germán Frers maxi. He went one better, winning not only on corrected-time handicap but also elapsed time; the double.

*Flyer II* was not the only new yacht specially created for the demands of the race. Peter Blake entered *Ceramco New Zealand*. At 21m (68ft), she was designed by Bruce Farr and was shorter, lighter and more easily driven than *Flyer I*, sporting a fractional rig with smaller headsails and spinnakers. The thinking was that the boat would be easier to push harder in the Southern Ocean.

*Ceramco*'s chances were dashed on leg one. Some 500 miles south of the Canaries, the blue Kiwi yacht was surfing easily in the Atlantic swell when a stay broke.

'Dismasted. Proceeding under jury rig to Cape Town,' messaged Peter Blake. Cape Town was 2,700 miles away, upwind. *Ceramco* could only really reach, hampered by an inefficient jury rig, so Blake sailed an additional 1,500 miles to use the winds circulating around the South Atlantic High.

Only pride was left for *Ceramco*'s crew, whose campaign was partly supported by public subscription. This was the start of widespread engagement by the Kiwi public in sailing: first the Whitbread Race and, later, the America's Cup.

*Ceramco* won two of the three next legs and excelled in the Southern Ocean. She had an epic fight with *Flyer II*, and as second boat and handicap winner into Auckland received a delirious reception. No one knew until *Flyer II*

△ Two-time winner Cornelis van Rietschoten, steering *Flyer II* in the Southern Ocean during the 1981/2 race.

finished that her Dutch owner had had a heart attack. Rietschoten was so determined to keep this secret from his rival that he refused to let the onboard medic, Julian Fuller, discuss treatment with *Ceramco*'s doctor, who was a cardiologist.

'The nearest port was ten days away, and the critical period is always the first 24–36 hours,' reasoned van Rietschoten. '*Ceramco* was already breathing down our necks. If they had known that

I had a health problem, they would have pushed their boat even harder. When you die at sea, you are buried over the side. Perhaps those *Ceramco* boys might then have spotted me drifting by. And that, I was determined, would be the only thing they would see or hear from *Flyer II* on the matter!'

Because of what had happened in Rio the race before, Mar del Plata in Argentina replaced it as the stopover port. The fleet, in a British-run race managed by the Royal Naval Sailing Association, enjoyed excellent hospitality during their stay in January 1982.

By April of that year, Argentina occupied the Falklands Islands and the two countries went to war. This prompted another stopover change for the fourth race, to Punta del Este, Uruguay.

**Pop stars and apartheid**

Pre-race attention was focused on Duran Duran pop star Simon Le Bon and his producers Mike and Paul Berrow, who had taken over a maxi project during the build stage that had been designed for former *Second Life* sailor and Chay Blyth co-skipper Rob James. Called *Drum*, the 23.6-m (76-ft) maxi had rolled like one during the Fastnet Race the month before the Whitbread started. All the crew were safe, Le Bon included, but it was very worrying for two-time Whitbread racer Skip Novak, who was skipper. It turned out that *Drum* indeed seemed nixed. In Cape Town, the hull and rudder needed extensive rebuilding.

Blake was back, in a Ron Holland-designed near sistership to *Drum* called *Lion New Zealand*. Despite the *Ceramco* experience, he'd reverted to a *Flyer* type of maxi, heavy displacement with a masthead rig. Blake raced with a crew of 22, believing he could set the tempo of inshore racing around the world. In place of tinned food, he planned to fuel his crew on freeze-dried food.

Where Blake had not gone, Switzerland's Pierre Fehlmann chose to go: Bruce Farr's design office. He got a 24.8-m (80-ft) version of *Ceramco*. Lighter than the other maxis, it had smaller sails that were easier on her gear and crew. And she was fast. *UBS Switzerland* took line honours for the race. Handicap winner was the 17.4-m (56-ft)

△ Bruce Farr-designed
*Ceramco*, skippered by
Peter Blake.

*L'Espirt d'Equipe*. Although Tabarly was back with a new maxi, *Cote d'Or*, it was Lionel Péan who had brought France its first Whitbread victory.

The fifth race of 1989/90 had to face the political reality of South Africa. The apartheid regime there had prompted a widening sporting boycott, and the WRWR followed. Replacing Cape Town was tricky, as it was a natural turning point in a circumnavigation. Instead, it was decided to go to Punta del Este on the outward track of the race, as well as the return track. To compensate, Fremantle was added to reduce the long third stage in the Southern Ocean, while a stop in Fort Lauderdale, Florida, aimed to boost the race's exposure in the American market. The nominal race distance had grown from 27,000 miles of the 1973/4 race to 32,000 miles.

### Incidents, accidents and suicides

In effect, the now longer race gave Peter Blake more stages to win. This time the New Zealander got everything right, from choice of boat (a big 26-m/84-ft fractional ketch rigged from Bruce Farr), handsomely financed by Steinlager beer, a superb crew of inshore and offshore veterans and van Rietschoten levels of immaculate preparation.

*Steinlager 2* faced only two setbacks. One was in construction, when the first hull failed to cure correctly. Blake's campaign was sufficiently forward-looking in its planning that there was time available to build a second hull. Then, on the final leg to the Southampton finish with the race seemingly in the bag, a loud crack was heard at night. Instinctively, the helmsman gybed the boat. He'd avoided a double dismasting of main and mizzen masts – the noise was the chainplate shearing.

The race was now split into four divisions to cover three varying lengths of racers and one cruising division. *Steinlager 2*'s triumph in Blake's fourth race was the greatest highlight, all the more newsworthy as Grant Dalton, who had crewed on *Flyer II* and *Lion New Zealand*, had gone toe-to-toe with his own Farr ketch *Fisher & Paykel* against *Steinlager 2*. They differed, with *Fisher & Paykel* being masthead rigged, though remarkably, on four of the six legs, the pair finished within 90 minutes of each other.

Footage shot in the Southern Ocean of the yachts under full press of spinnaker, stretching apart and surging together as they barrelled down wave after wave, is some of the most iconic in the race's rich archive.

The incident quota was particularly high in this race. Somehow, in the dying days of the Soviet

Union and with the Iron Curtain still standing, the crude, under-funded, and odd-looking maxi *Fazisi* emerged. It fell to American Skip Novak, three-race veteran and with an incurable fascination for all that life can throw, to take on this 'mission impossible'.

Co-skipper Alexei Grischenko, for so long separated from his family and thrust into the Western limelight, committed suicide during the leg-one stopover in Punta del Este. There too, popular Swedish crew member Janne Gustavsson, from *The Card*, was killed in a motorbike accident. On leg two, Tony Phillips was killed on the cruising entry *Creighton's Naturally*. He was recovered from overboard (one of seven occurrences in the race) but could not be revived. The race also saw the participation of the first all-women's crew led by Tracy Edwards aboard *Maiden*, previously raced by Pierre Fehlmann as *Disque d'Or*.

Dalton got his win in the sixth race of 1993/4 with *NZ Endeavour*. Here a profound choice was made. The IOR rating rule was entering its final days, and the boats it encouraged were no longer fast for their length or sweet handling.

Because hulls had become so much lighter over the 30 years' life of the IOR, moving from wood and aluminium to advanced composites, designers were forced to weigh the boats down with lots of internal lead ballast to hit the designed displacement. It was a self-defeating madness of a rating rule past its time.

There were two responses. Bruce Farr designed the ultimate expression of the IOR maxi, which Grant Dalton took to victory in the Maxi class with *NZ Endeavour*. Handicap honours had been dropped, but a second winner was possible amongst the brand-new Whitbread 60 class. These boats were specially created for the race, designed to be fast for their length and with internal water tanks so that their weight and trim could be varied to maximize performance in any given conditions. Cheaper to build and equip and with fewer crew, the Whitbread 60s also aimed to curb spiralling competition costs.

It proved to be a double Kiwi win for Ross Field, who had been one of *Steinlager 2*'s watch captains, who won with *Yamaha*. This was the second of two boats that the Japanese sponsor had built and showed more development than her rivals.

The 1997/8 and 2001/2 races were exclusively for the Whitbread 60 class. They also witnessed the dominance of skippers whose forte was inshore racing. Americans Paul Cayard won in the Swedish-backed *EF Language* and John Kostecki in the German-sponsored *illbruck*. With a US$20 million budget and a full three years' preparation testing keels, rudders and sails, *illbruck* was the model modern professional campaign in 2001/2.

In the same race, Neal McDonald replaced Roy Heiner as skipper of *Assa Abloy* after leg one, completing the first husband-and-wife skipper rivalry in the race. Lisa McDonald headed the women's crew on *Amer Sports Two*.

On *Amer Sports One*, Grant Dalton was the butt of many a joke. He'd claimed that if the women on *Amer Sports Two* ever beat him, he'd 'run down the streets of Auckland with a pineapple stuffed up his a***'. It so nearly happened. On the stage to Miami, *Amer Sports Two* briefly got her bow in front. It actually occurred on the final short leg from Gothenburg to Kiel. Dalton duly stuffed a pineapple down his shorts, though no further.

▽ *Amer Sport One* nearing Sydney during the Volvo Ocean Race, 4 December 2001.

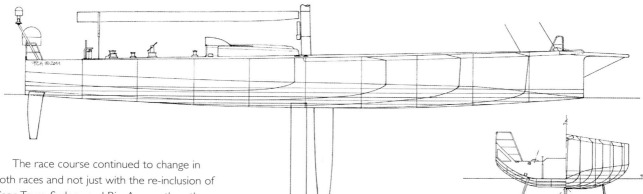

The race course continued to change in both races and not just with the re-inclusion of Cape Town, Sydney and Rio. Among the other ports tried out in various permutations were São Sebastião (Brazil), Miami, Baltimore (USA), La Rochelle (France), Gothenburg (Sweden) and Kiel (Germany).

## The Volvo Ocean Race

It was in Baltimore that Swedish automobile-maker Volvo bought the race from Whitbread. It triggered a change far more profound than a renaming. Whitbread had ceased to be a beer brewer and become a hotel, restaurant and coffee-bar operator. It had never put its own brands in front of those supporting entries. It had been an easy co-existence with beer, banking, insurance, cigarette, chocolate, clothing and other brands. Volvo, however, made the race central to its global marketing strategy.

It heralded a new class of boat, too, the Volvo 70 replacing the Whitbread 60s for the 2005/6 edition. Longer and faster, the key difference was that the new boat used keels that could be canted up to windward to boost sail-carrying power, instead of the Whitbread 60's fixed keel and water ballast configuration.

Points now replaced the clock, with points earned at scoring gates as well as at the finish of ocean legs, and additional ones up for grabs for round-the-buoys races in the host ports.

**'As far as I can remember, there aren't a lot of points of land named after people who sat at home and criticized Christopher Columbus.'**

**Paul Cayard** | Skipper of *Pirates of the Caribbean*

Just as Yamaha had done the first time the Whitbread 60s were used, Dutch entry ABN Amro built two boats ahead of the start to jump straight from first-generation design to second generation. Kiwi Mike Sanderson sailed the newest of the Juan Kouyoumdjian-designed pair, called *ABN Amro One*, while Sébastien Josse helmed *ABN Amro Two*.

## The disaster-prone 2005/6 edition

The new boats were no lookers. Straight ends, slab sides, narrow bows, wide sterns, daggerboards and boxy coachroofs made them more machine than yacht. With so many new systems and technologies employed, what happened on the first leg shouldn't have been a surprise. Kouyoumdjian had given his boats twin rudders, accepting that a little more drag was a good trade-off in such a beamy, powerful boat.

From a new start port of Vigo, Spain, the fleet sailed into a first-night Bay of Biscay gale. Paul Cayard's *Pirates of the Caribbean* broke a bulkhead and had a keel leak and headed for port. So did the Spanish yacht *movistar*, with damage to keel, rudder and daggerboard. Both had to be transported to Cape Town after extensive repairs. Still sailing, the Swedish boat *Ericsson 3* had her keel come loose, though she limped gingerly into Cape Town.

Controversy raged over the canting-keel systems. Kouyoumdjian recessed the big pivot in the hull's surface. Farr Yacht Design, believing that this contravened the 'fair surface' language of the Volvo 70 design rule, hid their pivot

△ The 2005 Volvo Open 70 class using a new and slightly controversial canting keel capable of canting transversely up to an angle of 40 degrees. The class quickly proved itself to be the fastest distance monohull class ever built.

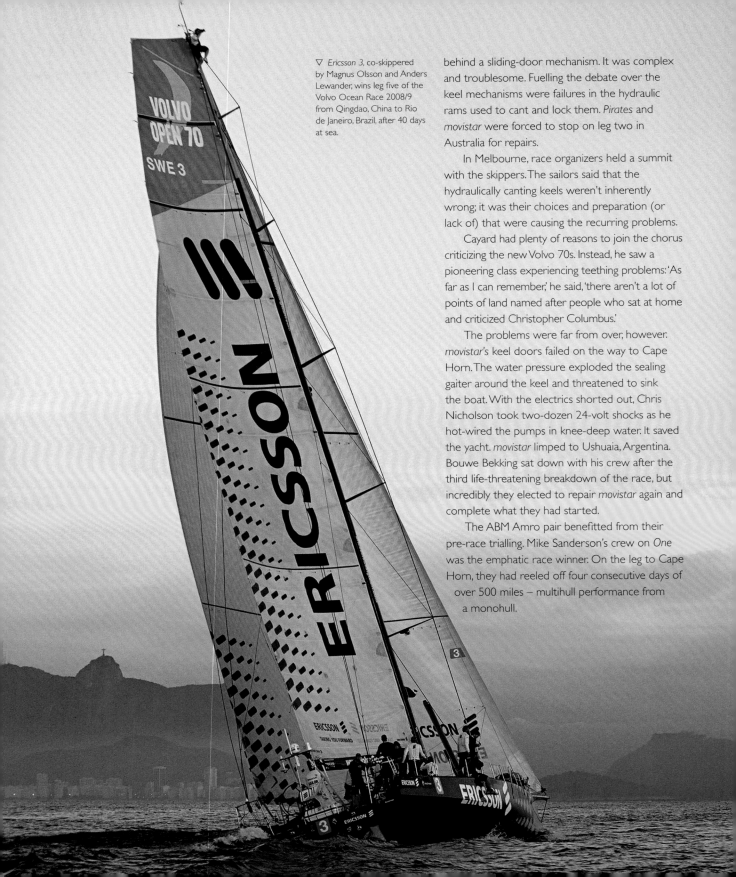

▽ *Ericsson 3*, co-skippered by Magnus Olsson and Anders Lewander, wins leg five of the Volvo Ocean Race 2008/9 from Qingdao, China to Rio de Janeiro, Brazil, after 40 days at sea.

behind a sliding-door mechanism. It was complex and troublesome. Fuelling the debate over the keel mechanisms were failures in the hydraulic rams used to cant and lock them. *Pirates* and *movistar* were forced to stop on leg two in Australia for repairs.

In Melbourne, race organizers held a summit with the skippers. The sailors said that the hydraulically canting keels weren't inherently wrong; it was their choices and preparation (or lack of) that were causing the recurring problems.

Cayard had plenty of reasons to join the chorus criticizing the new Volvo 70s. Instead, he saw a pioneering class experiencing teething problems: 'As far as I can remember,' he said, 'there aren't a lot of points of land named after people who sat at home and criticized Christopher Columbus.'

The problems were far from over, however. *movistar*'s keel doors failed on the way to Cape Horn. The water pressure exploded the sealing gaiter around the keel and threatened to sink the boat. With the electrics shorted out, Chris Nicholson took two-dozen 24-volt shocks as he hot-wired the pumps in knee-deep water. It saved the yacht. *movistar* limped to Ushuaia, Argentina. Bouwe Bekking sat down with his crew after the third life-threatening breakdown of the race, but incredibly they elected to repair *movistar* again and complete what they had started.

The ABM Amro pair benefitted from their pre-race trialling. Mike Sanderson's crew on *One* was the emphatic race winner. On the leg to Cape Horn, they had reeled off four consecutive days of over 500 miles – multihull performance from a monohull.

Sébastien Josse's crew on *Two*, all younger than 25, revelled in their boat's potential to set a 24-hour record of 527 miles in the Southern Ocean. Their race, however, will always be remembered for the penultimate leg across the Atlantic, when Hans Horrevoets was swept overboard in a big nose dive. His drowned body was recovered after 40 minutes and his crewmates brought him home.

Also onboard were the *movistar* crew. The Spanish boat suffered its fourth major failure of the race. Again it was the hull floor around the keel, fractured when the boat landed off a big wave. Bekking's crew abandoned their broken boat. Seb Josse and the *ABM Amro Two* crew put their grief for Horrevoets to one side for a moment, to rescue the ten men from *movistar*.

And so the Volvo Race reached the stage where it is today. The Swedish organizers took the bold step of completely changing the nature of the race. True, the Cape of Good Hope and Cape Horn remained in the course, but for commercial reasons, the course now had stops in the Middle East, the Indian subcontinent and Asia.

The Southern Ocean, the defining part of the race since 1973/4, was now a bit player. There were new threats of a different kind. The activities of Somalian pirates off the east coast of Africa prompted Volvo to route the fleet to an undisclosed location in 2011/2, where they were embarked on a ship and transported for the two legs in and out of the Abu Dhabi stopover.

These changes were made for the 2008/9, 2011/2 and 2014/5 races and still split opinion amongst race fans. The winners certainly earned their laurels: Brazil's great Olympian Torben Grael in *Ericsson 4*, France's multihull hero Franck Cammas in *Groupama 4* and

British double Olympic medallist Ian Walker in Abu Dhabi's *Azzam*.

In 2011/2, the distance climbed to 38,000 miles, although the tally that mattered to the organizers was 11 countries in five continents. With even more stops added, critics say that the race feels more like a tour-format league than the ultimate round-the-world race. Those who defend it point to the commercial returns of the big audience, and the need to serve sponsors by visiting these non-traditional parts of the world.

There is no question that it is a tricky balance for Volvo to achieve. The number of teams has declined markedly to just five in 2011/2. The Volvo 70 was dropped in favour of cheaper, identical Volvo 65s designed by Farr Yacht Design. Entries rose to seven in 2014/5.

What is irrefutable is the truth that the race is just as hard to win as ever, and any weakness in preparation or execution will be cruelly exposed.

△ The Dutch Volvo 70 yacht *ABN Amro Two* rescues the crew of the Spanish yacht *movistar* during leg seven of the Volvo Ocean Race on 22 May 2006 in the English Channel. The crew of *movistar* had to abandon their yacht when the keel detached. In the distance, the Dutch frigate HNLMS *Van Galen* approaches to collect the body of *ABN Amro Two* crew member Hans Horrevoets, who died when he was washed overboard four days earlier.

# Round-the-World Races
# Vendée Globe

*'I don't think we can send another race into the Southern Ocean with very wide craft that won't right themselves. There is a limit to what we can ask the rescue authorities to undertake.'*

Robin Knox-Johnson | Winner of *The Sunday Times* Golden Globe Race (predecessor of the Vendée Globe)

## Route tracker

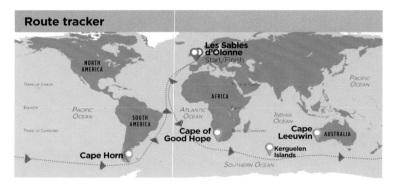

## Vital stats

**What:** 28,000-mile round-the-world race

**Where:** Start and finish in Les Sables d'Olonne (France)

**How often:** Quadrennial

**Boat type:** Open 60 monohulls

**Crew:** Singlehanded

▷ Séb Josse on the bow of his IMOCA 60. The Frenchman is a multiple circumnavigator, racing in the Vendée Globe, Barcelona World Race, Volvo Ocean Race and Jules Verne Trophy.

2012/13 saw the Vendée Globe in its full pomp. The seventh edition cemented its reputation as the toughest solo race of all. It also celebrated the fact that François Gabart, the youngest-ever winner, had set the fastest time achieved in the closest-fought race to date.

Gabart's time in *MACIF* of 78d 2h 16m shows how far the race has come since Tituoan Lamazou, in *Ecurieul d'Aquitaine II*, won the first edition back in 1989/90 in 109d 8h 47m: a gain of 29 per cent.

It is not only in France that this race is big. There, media coverage tops that of the Tour de France cycle race and the French tennis open at Roland Garros. Elsewhere, the Vendée Globe is known as the race that seems to create an inexhaustible supply of drama, especially in the Southern Ocean.

### Not for the fainthearted

An upturned white hull and a sailor facing the bleakest of alternatives – rescue or death – in the brutal wasteland of the Southern Ocean is an image seen on TV and newspaper front pages from a number of rescues. It is enough to send a chill down the spine. Some 2,000 miles from Africa, Australasia or South America, the nearest land can be two miles down under waves that can be as big as houses. The Vendée Globe is one of the hardest sailing races going, and definitely not something for the faint of heart.

The data tells the story. In the first seven races, the attrition rates (through retirement or disqualification for receiving help with repairs) show that only 54 per cent, 47 per cent, 40 per cent, 62 per cent, 67 per cent, 37 per cent and 45 per cent of starters were ranked as finishers.

It's not hard to pinpoint why the more extreme circumnavigations pull in the public interest. From being a rarity in the 1970s, round-the-world racing has become relatively commonplace. There are even races such as the defunct BT Global Challenge and the Clipper Race where a non-sailor can buy a berth on a round-the-world race yacht and receive the training to take part as easily as booking a weekend break.

Other races continue to prosper, but those taking nine months, with multiple stops, struggle to hold the non-sailing public's attention for such an extended period. Thus it is the more extreme events that prosper – the Vendée Globe, with its one person racing-alone-around-the-world narrative, and the Jules Verne Trophy for the fastest round-the-world record.

### Non-stop around the world

The 'Vendée' in the title comes from the Atlantic coast region of La Vendée. Long before city and regional support for sporting events became a recognized business tool, this French department chose to support the race from the outset.

The event was the brainchild of Philippe Jeantot, who had already won the four-stage BOC Challenge solo round-the-world race twice. Three 1986/7 BOC competitors, Jeantot, fellow Frenchman Guy Bernadin and South African Bertie Reed, had chewed over the idea of creating a non-stop race during the Sydney stopover.

Jeantot felt that a new race was needed so that sailors 'could reach their utmost limits', and he secured Les Sables d'Olonne on the Vendée coast as the race host.

Jeantot entered and bet Reed and Bernadin that he'd win by a week. He was joined by a long line of BOC competitors, including Reed, Jean-Yves Terlain, Jean-Luc Van Den Heede, Tituoan Lamazou, transatlantic heroes such as Loïck Peyron and Philippe Poupon and up-and-coming stars from the Figaro Race such as Alain Gautier.

Validating the concept of the non-stop race was that no less a person than Eric Tabarly fired the starting canon on 26 November 1989.

'During the BOC I was aware of the limitations on this human adventure by the stopovers,' recalled Jeantot. 'The bonds that a sailor makes with his boat day after day are brutally broken coming back to land. After each stopover you had to re-establish the relationship that had been forged between the man, his boat and the sea.'

Romantic? Certainly; and this is another reason why, although British clubs and organizations pioneered trans-ocean racing, it was the French who turned it into an art form and a working business model. They never lost the man-and-woman-against-the-sea narrative, no matter how commercially sophisticated the races became. It is

▽ François Gabart skippering his IMOCA 60 *Macif* during the 2012/13 Vendée Globe.

telling that, if you go to the race village or host port at the start of a major French trans-ocean race, most visitors are not dressed in sailing gear. There is a complete cross-section of the general public.

Just as Jeantot turned up in the first BOC Challenge with a boat whose concept was more advanced than anyone else's, so Gautier's *Generali Concorde* was probably the first landmark Open 60 monohull. Designer Jean-Marie Finot made her very wide on deck but much narrower on the waterline. With fine bows and broad stern, the hull was a powerful delta shape to exploit the vast sail area. The boat wasn't developed enough for the race and eventually finished sixth, but as a template for future Open 60s, *Generali Concorde* was one of the most influential monohulls in solo sailing.

## Off to a dangerous start

The first serious incident occurred before the fleet had left the South Atlantic. Philippe Poupon capsized in *Fleury Michon X* (see box). The first Vendée Globe was free from rules in other areas, too. One was no limit as to how far south competitors could go in the Southern Ocean.

Below the Roaring Forties, there's the latitude of the Furious Fifties. Beyond that, the Screaming Sixties. The distance is shorter as the fleet loops around Antarctica, as they sail between the Cape of Good Hope to Cape Horn, but the conditions are more extreme. There is an increased chance of hitting growlers, semi-submerged masses of ice that have broken off icebergs.

For the second race in 1992/3, a waypoint was added to the course in a bid to keep competitors away from the worst of the ice threat. 'The object of the Vendée Globe is to be a beautiful and difficult race – not a dangerous race,' explained Jeantot.

But dangerous it was, even before the start. The question of the stability of the new, wide, Open 60s, which were often a quarter as wide as their overall length, continued to be a talking point – more especially following the loss of American BOC veteran, Mike Plant. The keel bulb of his *Coyote* had snapped off in the Atlantic on the way to Les Sables d'Olonne. *Coyote* remained inverted on her big, flat deck. An extensive search failed to find Plant.

△ The Open 60 *Generali*, skippered by Frenchman Yann Eliès, ploughs through Southern Ocean rollers in December 2008. Yann had to abandon the yacht soon after when he suffered a badly broken leg when a huge wave smashed into his yacht 800 miles from Australia. He was rescued by an Australian navy vessel, but his yacht was lost at sea.

### Philippe Poupon's rescue

At this early stage in the Open 60 class, there were few limits or rules other than length, and no checks made on stability. Poupon had modified the boat with an additional mizzen mast to boost sail area. When *Fleury Michon X* capsized while still in the South Atlantic, there wasn't enough weight in the fixed keel to overcome the forces pressing the boat down on her side.

Loïck Peyron was the first of three competitors diverted to Poupon's aid. Although he looked nonchalant, it was nothing less than a supreme piece of seamanship that enabled Peyron to sail close enough to throw Poupon a long rope and allow him time to make it very secure, before trimming his sails and getting under way again. Not only did Peyron pull *Fleury Michon X* upright, but he captured it all on video, as well.

△ (Left to right) From the moment Loïck Peyron threw Philippe Poupon the line until Peyron managed to pull *Fleury Michon X* upright, Poupon captured all of it on video amongst exultant shouts of jubilation.

Soon after the start, there was further tragic news. British yacht-broker Nigel Burgess issued a Mayday as gale-force winds ravaged the 13 starters in the Bay of Biscay. Burgess's yacht was found drifting and, some time later, the Briton's body was also found. As he was wearing a survival suit and had two emergency beacons tethered to him, it's thought that Burgess was abandoning his yacht when he had some sort of accident.

Six of the 13 starters were forced back in the first week. Yves Parlier's *Cacolac d'Aquitaine* was dismasted. Les Sables d'Olonne was the only place that the singlehanders could pit-stop and

be allowed assistance for repairs. Graphic proof that the solo sailors had to deal with whatever the race threw at them, alone and unaided, came from Bertrand de Broc. He'd been thrown violently by a wave and almost bit his tongue clean through. With advice from the race doctor, de Broc used a mirror and needle and thread to sew some sutures in by himself.

Gautier won the race in *Baggages Superior*. Compared to his previous boat, *Baggages Superior* was built from light composites and carried more sail, with a powerful mizzen mast. But the conditions were not in Gautier's favour; he took

## The rescue of Rafael Dinelli

On Christmas Day, 1996 in the Southern Ocean, it was blowing storm-force 60 knots, gusting 75 knots. 'Apocalyptic conditions,' Rafael Dinelli called them. Unchecked by land for thousands of miles, the waves towered above the Vendée Globe yachts. Dinelli was trying to steer *Algimouss* (ex-*Crédit Agricole IV*) from inside. He had no sail set, but was still surfing down the cliff-face waves.

△ Raphael Dinelli, standing up to his knees in water on the deck of his yacht *Algimouss*, shortly before it sank.

*Algimouss* had been knocked down repeatedly and then, on one wave, the boat accelerated. 25 knots under bare poles, 30 knots... 'Then we fell, like a lift whose cables had been cut.'

*Algimouss* capsized completely. The mast broke, punctured the deck and the Southern Ocean flooded in. The compartmentalization of the hull by watertight bulkheads should have stopped the yacht from foundering, but the forward deck hatch had gone and the mast continued to impale the hull. Australia was 1,100 miles away, to the northeast.

Dinelli triggered his emergency beacon and,

up to his knees in water, found his survival suit. After three hours, the mast finally came free and *Algimouss* came upright. Dinelli spent time tied to the remaining stump of mast or below on top of the galley, which was just above the level of the water. He tried bailing to keep warm. On deck, the breaking crests threatened to choke him.

After 48 hours, Dinelli felt '...not far from death. I could feel its presence. I had passed the first threshold of descent beyond which would lie clinical death, beyond which, what?'

Then he heard a noise. A Royal Australian Air Force P3 Orion maritime patrol aircraft. Making several passes, they pinpointed the yacht and dropped liferafts, which drifted down to Dinelli. Struggling in his weakened state, Dinelli managed to get in a raft as *Algimouss* settled even lower in the water. Two containers were also dropped. One containing drinking water smashed on impact, although it did contain a note: 'Pete Goss, ten hours south.' The second, with food, couldn't be reached.

Mercifully, Goss was closer already. After two days of sailing his *Aqua Quorum* back into the same horrendous seas, the yellow hull of Goss's boat appeared just metres from Dinelli's raft.

The hero's work was not yet done. Goss's Royal Marine experience and paramedic training meant that he knew how to support an emotionally shattered Dinelli. He nursed him – Dinelli's eyes were salt-burnt, his hands and feet frostbitten.

'Best possible Christmas present,' was Goss's summary of having saved another competitor's life.

one day longer than Lamazou, the only winner not to set a new record.

Christophe Auguin triumphed in the third race in 1996/7 in *Geodis*, to become the first person to win the solo circumnavigation double. He'd won the BOC Challenge in 1990/1 and 1994/5.

## Vendée Globe carnage

That third race will be remembered primarily for its epic rescues and its step-change in boat development. The pace of progression was evident in Parlier's *Aquitaine Innovations*. She had a rotating wing mast, supported by shrouds anchored to big outriggers sprouting from the sides of the hulls. What's more, carbon-fibre construction and a displacement of 7.6 tons made her a third lighter than some of the first-generation Open 60s.

Parlier's furious pace at the front of the pack was first checked with forestay damage and later stopped entirely when ice damage to his rudders forced him out.

The spate of capsizes escalated the debate of the stability and safety of the early iterations of the

Open 60 type from criticism to raging controversy. Thierry Dubois' *Pour Amnesty International* had one of the newly developed canting keels thought to be able to right an inverted boat. But it didn't. The huge, flat decks of this generation of Open 60s seemed only to have excellent stability when they were upside down.

It was a turning point in singlehanded racing. No less a voice than that of Sir Robin Knox-Johnston said, 'I don't think we can send another race into the Southern Ocean with very wide craft that won't right themselves. There is a limit to what we can ask the rescue authorities to undertake.' Additional stability rules were imposed for the fourth edition in 2000/1.

## La Petite Anglaise

Perversely, the scares of the previous race did not deter either competitors or sponsors and 24 entered, including Ellen MacArthur. The young Briton wanted to emulate Catherine Chabaud, whose sixth place in the third edition made her the first woman to complete a non-stop, solo, round-the-world race.

△ After his boat, the *VM Matériaux*, capsized 200 miles from Cape Horn in the Southern Ocean, French skipper Jean Le Cam held out for 30 hours in the hull of his boat during the Vendée Globe 2009, hoping against all hope that someone might come and find him. To his utter disbelief he was eventually rescued by fellow competitor Vincent Riou on *PRB*, who had been over 100 miles astern at the time of the capsize.

△ Ellen MacArthur on her Open 60 *Kingfisher* during the Vendée Globe, 2000/1.

France had taken *La Petite Anglaise* to its heart. But no one was expecting a first-timer in the Vendée Globe to brush the biggest, strongest field to one side and chase Michel Desjoyeaux up the Atlantic to Les Sables d'Olonne. Her second place seemed like a win.

It was Yves Parlier who, in 13th place, wrote the most extraordinary storyline of the race. His *Aquitaine Innovations* hit trouble in the Southern Ocean. 'I have dismasted. I am going on. I do not need assistance,' he told Race HQ in a terse email.

What followed was the most extraordinary episode of endeavour, resourcefulness and determination. For three weeks and 3,000 miles, Parlier nursed his boat to the remote Stewart Island off New Zealand. There, he used survival blankets and electric bulbs to cocoon and heat the repairs he'd made to the mast. The cold ambient temperatures made it essential to generate enough heat for the epoxy resins to cure.

Somehow, he managed to raise the repaired mast. Parlier's food supplies were running perilously low, so he harvested seaweed to eat. Seriously weak and completely drained, Parlier completed the race. He took 127 days compared to Desjoyeaux's new record of 97 days, but it was a Herculean and heroic effort.

Mercifully, the next three races of 2004/5, 2008/9 and 2012/13 were relatively uneventful. In 2004/5, Vincent Riou took Desjoyeaux's *PRB* for a second lap of the planet and a back-to-back victory. Mike Golding lost the keel of *Ecover* 250 miles from the finish, but remained upright and sailed home in third place. Desjoyeaux returned in 2008/9 to become the only two-time winner, whilst the 2012/13 story was Gabert's glory.

Underlying the Vendée Globe's growth into one of the sport's majors were the numbers. They worked for the sponsors. Les Sables d'Olonne Race Village had 1.2, 1.5 and 1.8 million visitors during the 2004/5, 2008/9 and 2012/13 editions. In that last race, the Vendée Globe ranked 14th amongst all websites in France. The virtual-race game, in which those ashore could race against the skippers, had a total of 490,000 subscribers. Over 700 hours of television was carried by broadcasters around the world.

By any measure, the Vendée Globe is an exceptional event, with an impact far beyond the sailing world.

## The rescue of Tony Bullimore

On 6 January 1997, the Australian Maritime Rescue Coordination Centre received two alerts from the emergency EPIRB beacons belonging to Thierry Dubois' *Pour Amnesty International* and Tony Bullimore's *Exide Challenger*. Both were 1,400 miles southwest of Perth.

Only two years previously, another Australian navy ship had rescued Isabelle Autissier, 750 miles south of Adelaide in the BOC Challenge. This time, HMAS *Adelaide* was dispatched from Western Australia to carry out another search-and-rescue mission for imperilled singlehanded racers. International conventions oblige governments to save life at sea. Because of its location, it falls to Australia to cover 53 million square kilometres (21 million square miles) of ocean, some of which round-the-world racers regularly pass.

A RAAF P3 Orion located Dubois the same day and air-dropped a survival pack to him. A few hours later, another Orion found *Exide Challenger*. Of Bullimore, there was no sign.

For the next three days, five different Orions flew a total of 158 hours to keep vigil above the two yachts. On 9 January, HMAS *Adelaide* was close enough for her helicopter to fly off and winch Dubois off his upturned hull. The helicopter flew the next day and located *Exide Challenger*. It hovered for ten minutes looking for indications of life. When HMAS *Adelaide* reached the upturned boat herself, her captain sounded her horn and siren. Again, there was no sign of Bullimore.

HMAS *Adelaide* launched a small boat, its crew ready to cut through the hull. To their surprise, when they knocked on the side, Bullimore responded.

'I started shouting: "I'm coming, I'm coming,"' Bullimore recounted. 'It took a few seconds to get from one end of the boat to the other. Then I took a few deep breaths and I dived out of the boat. When I saw the ship standing there and the plane going overhead and a couple of guys peering over the top of the upturned hull, it was heaven, absolute heaven.'

Bullimore's body had started to shut down as it fought hypothermia, dehydration, the onset of frostbite and the partial amputation of one of his fingers. Surviving his five-day ordeal left Bullimore 'Absolutely ecstatic. I thought it would never happen.'

◁ The Royal Australian Navy frigate HMAS *Adelaide* on her search for Tony Bullimore.

△ After diving out of the boat in the freezing ocean, Bullimore is pulled into the rescue boat, barely coherent and suffering from severe hypothermia.

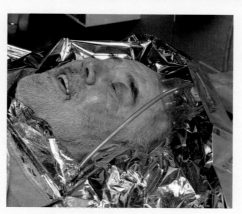

△ Before being hoisted up onto the frigate HMAS *Adelaide*, Bullimore is wrapped up in survival blankets as he recounts his tale of survival to the rescue crew.

# Round-the-World Races
# BT Global Challenge/ Clipper Race

*'As we pull into Albany, Australia, all of us on Henri Lloyd are rubbing our bloodshot eyes and giving each other hugs. And as I think back to the last three weeks, and everything we put into this race, I have no regrets. We laid it all on the line and pushed every last ounce of speed out of our boat.'*

Tasha Hacker | Clipper Race 2014, leg three, *Henri Lloyd*

Chay Blyth and Robin Knox-Johnston both took on the unthinkable and triumphed. In 1968/9 Knox-Johnston became the first person to sail around the world non-stop. He took the traditional eastabout route, maximizing use of the prevailing winds and current.

Blyth took the contrary path two years later in 1971/2, taking the westabout route where he pushed against the currents and bashed his way to windward against the prevailing winds.

Both were the first to undertake the feat and the first to succeed. And as with Knox-Johnston's voyage, the perceived wisdom was that it couldn't be done.

### 'It's only wind and water'

Advance the calendar 30 years, with many other achievements under their belts and knighthoods having been bestowed on each man, and both broke down convention again by organizing races around the world for amateur crews, some of whom had never even sailed before.

'Foolhardy' was a typical reaction, something Blyth encouraged when he launched his British Steel Challenge in 1992/3 with his throwaway line that the oceans of the world didn't constitute any

◁ The crew on the Clipper 70 yacht *Henri Lloyd*, skippered by Canadian Eric Holden, enjoy the infamous Southern Ocean 'sleigh rides' during the 2013/14 edition of the Clipper Race. *Henri Lloyd* claimed first place after 11 months, just ahead of *Great Britain*.

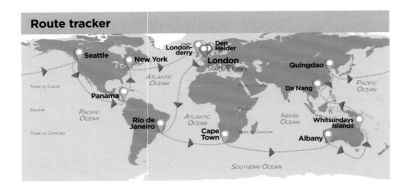

## Route tracker

Seattle · London-derry · Den Helder · London Start/Finish · Quingdao · New York · Da Nang · Panama · Rio de Janeiro · Cape Town · Whitsundays Islands · Albany

ATLANTIC OCEAN · PACIFIC OCEAN · PACIFIC OCEAN · ATLANTIC OCEAN · INDIAN OCEAN · SOUTHERN OCEAN

TROPIC OF CANCER · EQUATOR · TROPIC OF CAPRICORN

▷ Battling a fierce Southern Ocean storm on the yacht *GREAT Britain* during the Clipper Round 2013/14.

## Vital stats

**What:** 40,000-mile multi-stage, round-the-world race

**Where:** Start and finish in London (UK)

**How often:** Biennial

**Boat type:** Clipper 70s

**Crew:** Fully crewed

particular danger: 'It's only wind and water.'

By 1992, round-the-world racing had become the preserve of the professional. The amateur adventurers of the 1960s and 1970s had had their time, but it was in their spirit that the means for ordinary people to experience their own voyages of personal discovery and fulfilment were created.

Blyth was first out of the blocks, persuading British Steel, who had backed his 1970/1 solo voyage, to come aboard as title sponsor. A purpose-built fleet of 21-m (67-ft) David Thomas-designed yachts was built for the 1992/3 British Steel Challenge.

Knox-Johnston followed up with his Clipper Race, built on the same business model of charging crews a fee for their berths, and raising revenue from boat-name sponsors, stopovers and others affiliated with the race.

The Clipper Race was first staged in 1996, the same year as Blyth's second race, but Knox-Johnston chose the so-called warm-water route, the yachts pushed along by tradewinds and passing through the Panama Canal to avoid having to route south and around Cape Horn and its infamous fierce conditions.

Blyth's second race saw telecoms giant BT take over the title sponsorship from British Steel and in the third, a new fleet of Rob Humphreys-designed 22-m (72-ft) boats was launched. Again, they were steel built, cutter rigged and featured simple hanked-on headsails, but they were similarly ruggedly built for their task. The longest legs stretched as far as 5,000 miles, the course taking in the great Capes – Cape Horn, Cape Leeuwin

and the Cape of Good Hope – and with stages over 40 days for each of the Southern Ocean legs. It was tagged 'the world's toughest race', and it certainly subjected yachts and crew to a true test of endurance.

The BT Global Challenge folded after 2004/5, when a backer could not be found for the 2008/9 event. Knox-Johnston's Clipper Race has continued, however, going from strength to strength and proving that the demand for pay-per-berth races is undimmed. Both races incorporated intensive pre-race training.

### Clipper Round The World Race

The less arduous route of the Clipper Race allows it to be run on a two-year cycle rather than the four years of the Global Challenge. The fleet is now using its third generation of yachts, the original David Pedrick-designed 18-m (58-ft) and successor Ed Dubois-designed 21-m (68-ft) boats now replaced by Tony Castro-designed 22-m (70-ft) yachts. The organizers of the race, Clipper Ventures, also run the four-yearly, single-handed Velux 5 Oceans Race, which comprises five ocean sprints. It is still the longest race of any kind in the world today.

Both Sir Chay Blyth and Sir Robin Knox-Johnston share considerable kudos for their races. Not only have firemen, bakers, midwives, teachers and the like achieved the unachievable by competing in the races, but the careers of some high-profile racing skippers have taken off from these launch pads. Among the notables are Mike Golding, Alex Thomson, Dee Caffari and Pete Goss.

△ The Clipper 68 yacht *Uniquely Singapore* on her way from Humber to La Rochelle during the first leg of the 2009/10 Clipper Race.

## A change of life

Beyond the lure of adventure, the crews who have taken part have had a chance to revise their perspective of the world and their lives. Some took career or relationship breaks to take part, while others sold their homes. Many without the means to pay for their berths undertook inventive fundraising campaigns, and significant funds for charity have been raised off the back of the races.

One relationship that is particularly noteworthy is that of Alex Thomson, who skippered the 1998/9 winner of the Clipper Race, and Keith Mills, one of his crew. A loyalty card entrepreneur, Mills caught the sailing bug and went on to back Thomson's solo career and British America's Cup teams, as well playing a key role in the London 2012 Olympic Games.

## Andrew Taylor's lucky escape

Accidents happen, but on the Clipper Round the World Race they have been very rare. Having someone go overboard is always frightening, and when Londoner Andrew Taylor, who sailed the trans-Pacific leg on the clipper *Derry-Londonderry-Doire* in 2014 went overboard in rough seas, he was lucky to survive.

He went over the side in rough weather and was only sighted again over an hour later.

The incident happened in rough weather with 35 knots of wind. Skipper Sean McCarter was working with Andrew on a sail change near the bow when he went over the side. Sean immediately went back to the helm, stopped the yacht and initiated the MOB (man overboard) procedure.

Race director Justin Taylor later explained that, 'In these conditions, a man overboard is swept away from the boat very quickly and visual contact can be lost in the swell. We have a well-rehearsed procedure to mark the position, stop racing and engage the engine to search for and recover the crew member as quickly as possible.

'An hour and a half is a very long time to be in the water in these conditions, but a combination of his sea survival training and seven months at sea as well as wearing a life jacket and dry suit will have contributed enormously to his survival.'

Andrew later said, 'It all happened so quickly, I was literally gone, like that. I didn't know if the crew were looking for me or not, I didn't know if they had seen me, I couldn't hear anything. I tried to stay so I could see the boat, I kept moving round, swimming round so I could see the boat thinking it'd be back really quickly, but it just got further and further away. I was holding the spray vest up trying to make myself a bit bigger, but after a while I thought the wind might be pushing it and pushing me further away, so I put it back down again. I kept watching the boat and then I saw

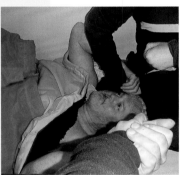

the side of the boat and thought that was a good thing – I thought it was turning around. Then I saw the back of the boat again and that's not a good thing. Then I just heard a noise and got wiped out by a really big wave. That's when the storm started. The storm was bad, that was horrible – hailstones, my hands were so cold.'

Andrew was rescued after one-and-a-half hours in the freezing ocean, suffering from severe shock and hypothermia. He subsequently made a full recovery and says he feels incredibly lucky to be alive.

△ Andrew Taylor floating in the Pacific Ocean as a tiny speck, after the yacht had turned around and made it back to his position. In the rough sea, it took over 15 minutes from the time the boat reached Andrew until the crew members finally managed to haul him back on board.

# Round-the-World Races
# Velux 5 Oceans

'One minute, I was trying to win a race that meant a great deal to me. Then one telephone call changed the whole situation. Winning a race isn't comparable to attempting to save a man's life.'

**Mike Golding** | Skipper of *Ecover*

The 1960 OSTAR transatlantic race and the 1968 Golden Globe circumnavigation busted the myth of solo long-distance racing as something unachievable.

It was proven possible and had put fire in the belly of singlehanded sailors, so what next?

In the Marina Pub on Goat Island in Newport, Rhode Island, a bunch of singlehanded racers downed some beers after the 1976 OSTAR. The consensus was that a new round-the-world race was needed. As the first and original solo race, the OSTAR was already spawning similar events such as the Route du Rhum, the Solo Transpac, the Solo Trans Tasman and the Bermuda One-Two.

## Around Alone

By logical extension, the purest and toughest test was to race around the world. The Around Alone was born, in idea at least. The objective was for it to be the ultimate test for the lone racer. And for the best part of three decades, that's exactly what it was. First staged in1982/3, it ran until 2010/11. But with just five entries in its final edition, all a shadow of the glory days of the first three races, it was plain that a major rethink was necessary. Surprisingly there was not one French sailor in the 2010/11 line-up, and given that solo racing has had a French heartbeat for so long, this was a vital sign that all was not well.

Partly, the Around Alone was a victim of its own success. While it was a multi-stage race, the Vendée Globe, launched by the French as direct rival in 1989/9, then surpassed it as the new ultimate challenge; non-stop around the planet.

The question facing the British organizers of the Around Alone, latterly called the 5 Oceans, was whether it was its best days or *all* its days that were behind it. It was being squeezed by the new boats, hot sailors and sponsors' dollars being pitched at the French races, while the lower-budget adventurer types were moving increasingly to the Open 40 class. A calendar clash with the Route du Rhum certainly sucked the air out of the Around Alone/5 Oceans as well.

Back at the end of the 1970s, these concerns were not even on the horizon. Helping to launch the new event was American David White, who took on the lion's share of the race organization. The rules were relatively simple, in keeping with the ethos of singlehanded sailing, which was the antithesis of the complex and codified world of grand-prix ocean racing. White was also planning to enter the race, and so had his own boat to build and finance as well as securing a race sponsor. Who said singlehanded sailors aren't resourceful?

Potential entrants registered from South Africa, Czechoslovakia, Britain, France, the USA, Japan, Australia and New Zealand, so the interest was encouraging. By 1981, the event was still without financial backing, until British entrant Richard Broadhead approached the UK industrial gases group, BOC, looking for sponsorship.

Sorry, Broadhead was told, individual sponsorship did not meet BOC's objectives – but an event that could be used to tie in its disparate worldwide interests just might. Broadhead's loss was the event's gain, and the Around Alone became the BOC Challenge.

## The BOC Challenge

Fittingly, Newport, Rhode Island was selected as the race start and finish, and in August 1982, 17 sailors from eight countries set off on the first leg to Cape Town. All eyes were on former French deep-sea diver Philippe Jeantot, not because of his evident fitness, but because he had a specially conceived boat.

Jeantot's *Crédit Agricole* was, in the words of race chairman Robin Knox-Johnston, 'As if a fighter jet joined a competition for piston-engine aircraft.' Designed by Guy Ribadeau Dumas, it was already two generations ahead of its conventional rivals. *Crédit Agricole* had an unfashionably beamy hull, with twin rudders to steer it when heeled. There was a cloud of sail on a tall rig, with three different-sized headsails permanently set up on furlers. To generate additional stability to carry maximum sail power, the hull had internal water-ballast tanks that could be filled and emptied as the boat sailed. The mainsail boom was attached to the deck rather than the mast, a far stronger arrangement, and it was angled up in the air as opposed to being horizontal. This meant that it would stay clear of the water if the boat was overpowered and heeled over.

The race was run in four stages, with stops in Cape Town (South Africa), Sydney (Australia) and Rio de Janeiro (Brazil), and Jeantot ran away with it. He beat South African Bertie Reed's *Voortrekker* by 11 days. There was drama aplenty. Four yachts pulled out on leg one, David White amongst them, and on leg two, Tony Lush had to be rescued by fellow entrant Frances Stokes after *Lady Pepperell* lost her keel. It drove home the truth that in the empty wastes of the Southern Ocean, the only likely help was from another competitor.

Then, close to the finish in Sydney, Desmond Hampton wrecked Sir Francis Chichester's famous

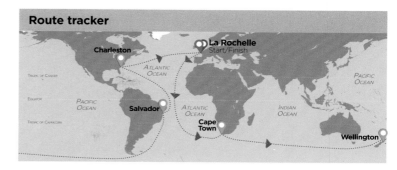

### Vital stats

**What:** 28,000-mile round-the-world race

**Where:** Start and finish in Newport, Charleston (USA) and Bilbao (Spain)

**How often:** Quadrennial

**Boat type:** Monohulls

**Crew:** Singlehanded

◁ French skipper Philippe Jeantot on *Crédit Agricole*, gutting flying fish on board during the 1982/3 Around Alone Race.

*Gipsy Moth V* ashore on Gabo Island. The wind had shifted while he was asleep. It was the yacht Sir Francis had retired from in the 1980 OSTAR, as his health deteriorated.

On the next stage, France's Jacques de Roux was pitchpoled in winds of 60 knots. His *Skoiern III* was dismasted, and the broken spar punched a hole in the hull below the waterline. De Roux was 3,000 miles from the nearest land. For more than two days, de Roux bailed. Richard Broadhead turned his *Perseverance of Medina* around and sailed 300 miles back, upwind and against the current, and somehow managed to find the Frenchman.

'Do you want to come on board *Perseverance*?'

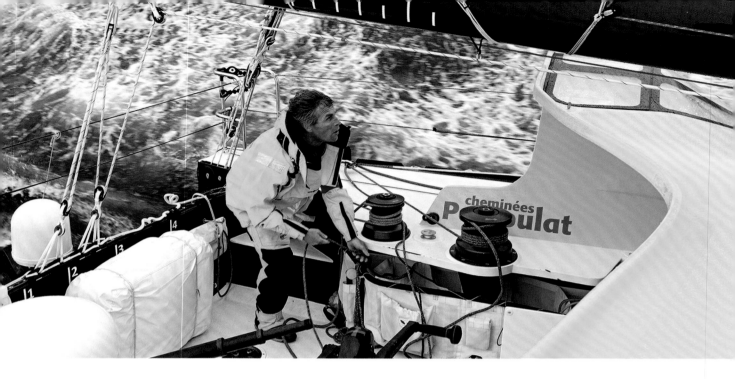

△ Bernard Stamm, the Swiss skipper of *Cheminées Poujoulat*, in the Bay of Biscay on 23 October 2006, the day after the Bilbao start of the Velux 5 Oceans. Stamm went on to win the race in April 2007.

Broadhead bellowed across the tumult. De Roux gave him a crazed-eye look and answered, 'Yes, of course I do. I'm sinking.'

## Bigger, faster, better

Where the first race was split into two classes, 32–44ft and 45–56ft, the second race in 1986/7 saw a more logical split: 40–50ft and 50–60ft. The impact of *Crédit Agricole* was evident in that not only were the 11 class-one boats based on similar concepts, but so were some of the 14 smaller class-two boats, as well. Now the boats featured fully battened mainsails. Wind-vane self-steering was consigned to history, replaced by electronic autopilots and powered by wind- and water-driven generators or solar panels. All in all, the fleet had speeded up by as much as 20 per cent.

Jeantot proved again that the man/machine combination of his new *Crédit Agricole II* was still the benchmark. He defended his title, taking 134 days in place of his earlier 159. The winning margin over Tituoan Lamazou's *Ecureuil d'Aquitaine* was three days. The future of the two men remained entwined, as Jeantot was to later found the Vendée Globe in 1989 and Lamazou was its first winner.

Before he created the Vendée Globe, Jeantot

had a third crack at the BOC Challenge, but this time the pursuing pack didn't just close up but passed him altogether. The 1990/1 winner was fellow Frenchman Christophe Auguin in *Groupe Sceta*. The ever-more quickening pace of the race was reflected in his 120-day winning time over Alain Gautier's *Generali Concorde*, two days behind.

For the third stop in the third race, Uruguay's Punta del Este was swapped for Rio. In recognition that sponsored boats were always going to dominate, another class was added for Corinthian amateurs. Among them was Jacques de Roux, the careful, consummate sailor who once lectured on navigation in the French navy. Rescued in the previous race, he went missing in the 1986/7 race. His *Skoiern IV* was found sailing under self-steering. There was no sign of de Roux other than a meticulously maintained plot on his chart and a half-finished meal in the cabin. It was presumed that he'd left the cabin to attend to something urgent on deck and had fallen overboard.

Indirectly, another life was lost in the third race. Yukoh Tada was a Tokyo taxi driver who'd won class 11 in the first race. His *Koden Okera V* was a clever yacht brimming with electronic systems. Tada also carried a saxophone and paintbrushes and easel. He was a popular member of the race family. He designed his own boat for the third race, but suffered five knockdowns in the southern Indian Ocean and retired mid-race in Sydney. After the fleet set off again, he took his own life.

The course changed again in 1994/5, with Charleston, South Carolina, replacing Newport, Rhode Island, as the start/finish port. This was the last race with BOC as title sponsor. Auguin became a double winner like Jeantot, although his time didn't improve on his previous mark.

In third place was Jean-Luc Van Den Heede, whose *Vendée Entreprises* bucked the wide, beamy hull type and was unfashionably narrow. She stood out for another reason, as Van Den Heede, like Hampton before him, ran aground on the Australian shore approaching Sydney. The Frenchman refloated the boat on the next tide and finished second into Sydney. Less lucky was Isabelle Autissier. She had already been dismasted in the previous race, some 500 miles from Sydney. This time she'd won leg one into Cape Town, two days faster than Alain Gautier's time in 1990/1. Then, six days after leaving Cape Town, mast trouble struck her *Ecureuil Poitou-Charentes* again. She was now 1,300 miles from Cape Town. Turning back was out of the question. She rigged a spinnaker pole as a mast and limped to the remote Kerguelen Islands, where a spare mast was shipped to meet her.

Autissier's bad luck wasn't done yet. Two weeks after leaving Kerguelan with the temporary mast, her yacht was rolled 360 degrees. It tore the replacement spar out and holed the cabin top. In 60-knot winds and huge Southern Ocean seas, Autissier tried plug the gap and pump out the water below. She fired her EPIRB emergency position-reporting beacon. Because she was out of sync with the fleet following her stop, no competitors were near enough or free of their own difficulties to help her. From 1,600 miles away, the Australian navy sent HMAS *Darwin* to her rescue, achieved three days later.

Later, on leg three, Briton Harry Mitchell, a three-times competitor, triggered his EPIRB 1,500 miles from Cape Horn. An exhaustive search failed to find Mitchell or his yacht, *Henry Hornblower*.

## 1998/9 Around Alone

Another grounding proved to be story of the fifth race of 1998/9, which reverted to its original working name, the Around Alone. Having won leg one, Briton Mike Golding was leading leg two to the new stop of Auckland, New Zealand (replacing Sydney), when he ran aground on the shoals off Cape Reinga at the top of New Zealand.

Golding's *Team Group 4* was one of the new generation 60-footers with a keel that could be canted to windward. This added to the sail-carrying power of the boat, but added righting moment without adding weight, as the previous generation water-ballast boats had. Running aground with such a complex keel system knocked Golding out of the race.

This had the effect of putting Isabelle Autissier in the lead. But come leg three, the unthinkable happened. She was pushing hard and making 375-mile 24-hour runs when she was knocked down and capsized. Like *Team Group 4*, her *PRB* had a canting keel. But with a wide beam and flat decks, *PRB* proved to have excellent inverted stability and could not be righted. Autissier was 2,000 miles from land.

Few could believe that Autissier's torrid run of bad luck in the race could have struck a third time. Italy's Giovanni Soldini turned back 100 miles and, the next day, managed to find Autissier on her upturned hull in just half-mile visibility.

Soldini's *Fila* went on to win in a new best time of 116 days. He was the first non-French winner of a solo round-the-world race since Knox-Johnston. The famous Briton took on the organization of the 2002/3 edition through his Clipper organization. The race was revamped, with a start in New York and a 'reverse' first leg to Torquay, England. The New Zealand stop moved from Auckland to the relatively remote port of Tauranga.

Swiss sailor Bernard Stamm recorded the first of two successive wins, repeating the feat of Jeantot and Auguin before him. But the organization changes had failed to revitalize the race. Entries dropped to 13 in 2002/3, to seven in 2006/7 and five in 2010/11. The calibre of boats fell away, too. The 2006/7 saw another significant revision, with the race being moved to Europe for the first time. This meant that when the fleet left Bilbao, Spain, in November, they headed straight into the teeth of a savage Bay of Biscay gale in the first 48 hours.

Three boats, including favourites Mike Golding and Alex Thomson, were forced into port for repairs. The pair were to meet again in an epic rescue. The last two events were called the 5 Oceans, but no amount of renaming and remixing of the formula could arrest the decline in entries. It seemed that in its own race with the Vendée Globe, the Around Alone, the one-time leader, had become distinctly second place.

## 2006/7: Mike Golding rescues Alex Thomson

Mike Golding was the former fireman who'd become Britain's most successful singlehanded racer. He'd risen through the ranks as winning skipper of Sir Chay Blyth's BT Global Challenge. A string of top finishes in solo races was crowned with winning the 2004 Transat.

Alex Thomson's career was launched by being the winning skipper in Sir Robin Knox-Johnston's first Clipper Race, before becoming skipper of a string of Open 60s called *Hugo Boss*. Thomson set a string of 24-hour solo speed records.

The contest between the two Britons was keenly anticipated. Both had proven, fast boats. Golding, 46, was the established star; Thomson, 33, the coming man. The pre-race jostling between them was brittle and unfriendly.

Thomson was lying third, 1,500 miles east of Cape Town, when in a matter of seconds there was an explosive breaking sound and *Hugo Boss* was lying on her side, rig in the water in 30-knot Southern Ocean conditions. Thomson was thrown out of his bunk. Both men, racing hard, had been getting four hours sleep in 24, napping in 20-minute bites.

The hydraulic ram controlling *Hugo Boss*'s canting keel had sheared off the hull's internal structure. Thomson got the sails down, but realized that the violent motion could lead to the keel tearing out of the bottom of the boat. He made a distress call. The wind was forecast to increase to 50 knots.

Golding had been 80 miles behind, but his *Ecover* had passed *Hugo Boss* as Thomson dealt with the chaos. Golding turned back into the wind to attempt a rescue reminiscent of fellow Briton Pete Goss, who'd successfully rescued France's Rafael Dinelli in the 1996/7 Vendée Globe in the depths of the Southern Ocean.

Golding said later that his fire-service training kicked in immediately. 'One minute I was trying to win a race that meant a great deal to me,' he said. 'Then one telephone call changed the whole situation. Winning a race isn't comparable to attempting to save a man's life.'

Battling a rising sea, Golding waited for daylight to reduce the risk in trying to pick up Thomson. Battling an engine with a sticking throttle and a troublesome fuel supply, Golding managed to pick up Thomson from his swamped liferaft on the fourth or fifth attempt. Thomson had injured his hand, making the grab and transfer even more difficult. 'It was the happiest and saddest day of the race,' said Thomson. Thanks to the yachts' onboard satcom, the rescue was streamed live via video link. The drama and extraordinary seamanship was witnessed by millions.

That should have been the end of the story. A life saved, two men's chances of victory gone.

Then, in the cruelest twist of fate, *Ecover's* mast broke six hours later, shattering in two places. Thomson and Golding, pre-race foes, worked together to create a jury rig, forming a bond of kinship between them never likely to be broken.

▷ Mike Golding and Alex Thomson on their way to Cape Town on Golding's damaged boat *Ecover*.

◁ Mike Golding, skipper of *Ecover*, chases *Hugo Boss*'s skipper Alex Thomson at the start of the Velux 5 Oceans solo round-the-world yacht race. From being frosty rivals, they became firm friends after Golding's daring rescue.

*'What can I say about Mike? He saved my life. What we went through out there in the Southern Ocean will never leave us. It's a common bond we will share for the rest of our lives. I owe him one, big time.'*
Alex Thomson

# Barcelona World Race

## Vital stats

**What:** 23,000-mile round-the-world race

**Where:** Start and finish in Barcelona (Spain)

**How often:** Quadrennial

**Boat type:** IMOCA Open 60 monohulls

**Crew:** Twohanded

After solo round-the-world by stages (the Around Alone/BOC race) and solo round-the-world non-stop (the Vendée Globe), the logical progression in the burgeoning competitive circumnavigations arena was a two-handed, non-stop race.

Thus the Barcelona World Race was born, first run in 2007/8. But it was far more than an addition to the calendar. Being twohanded, it had a distinct dynamic of its own and an even more unrelenting rhythm of racing than the solo races. It also saw the critical mass of shorthanded racing shift from its traditional roots in England and France to Spain. Here, the number of sailors, the media profile of yachting, the availability of sponsors and the willingness of cities and regions to use events as a business enterprise were validating factors.

The concept of the race was created by OC Sport, the company started by Mark Turner and Ellen MacArthur as Offshore Challenges to manage Ellen's projects. Through mergers and acquisitions, it has since become a significant force in marketing and managing high-tempo and endurance sports.

After the first race, the Spanish co-organizers of the Barcelona World Race took over its management, though OC Sport has maintained its interest in the intellectual property rights.

From the outset, the Barcelona World Race attracted a high quality of entry, no mean achievement given that the majority of IMOCA race campaigns are planned on a four-year cycle with the Vendée Globe as their primary focus.

Sponsors recognized that the Barcelona World Race provided additional value and visibility and gave skippers the chance to shake down a new boat or maximize a proven boat. Another facet was that it brought some of Spain's best-known sailors to the international stage – Whitbread/Volvo Ocean race veteran Guillermo Altadill and 49er-class Olympic

medallists Iker Martínez and Xabier Fernandez.

Barcelona is an excellent venue, thanks to a well-connected airport and an extensive waterfront close to some of the city's most popular areas. It also allows the fleet to sail out of the Mediterranean in the northern hemisphere autumn/winter and pick up the tradewinds, thereby avoiding the potentially destructive conditions that have affected races starting from northern France.

Nine boats contested the first race, which quickly settled into a duel between Jean-Pierre Dick (France) and Damian Foxall (Ireland) on *Paprec-Virbac* and Vincent Riou and Sébastien Josse (France) on *PRB*. Four boats had technical problems in the southern Indian Ocean, including *PRB*. Alex Thomson (UK) and Andrew Cape (Australia) on *Hugo Boss* set a record-breaking 501-mile 24-hour run and pursued *Paprec-Virbac* all the way to the finish.

The winning time was 92d 9h, a time that Dick, this time sailing with Loïck Peyron (France) could not better in the second edition of 2010/11. However, on that occasion the fleet had to pass through the Cook Strait, bisecting New Zealand, as a media-pleasing, mid-race fly-by of civilization.

Even so, a new *Paprec-Virbac* held off 13 rivals. Any thoughts that the Mediterranean start was an unremarkable part of a race around the planet were proven false by the light and shifty winds that held the fleet in their grip. *Paprec-Virbac* wriggled through the Straits of Gibraltar and into the Atlantic a full 330 miles ahead of *Hugo Boss*, the last boat out.

**Route tracker**

This was an incident-full race, with three dismastings (Jean Le Cam and Bruno Garcia's *President*; Michel Desjoyeaux and François Gabart's *Foncia*; and Dominique Wavre and Michel Paret's *Mirabaud*). Two more boats retired with keel damage and structural problems.

The fleet dropped in size to seven for the third edition in 2014/15. Many potential entrants were focusing on constructing their new generation of the IMOCA 60s, which were launched in 2015.

The winners in 2014/15 were the most experienced duo in the fleet, Bernard Stamm (Switzerland) and Jean Le Cam (France) in *Cheminées Poujoulat*. Stamm is a two-time winner of the Around Alone/Five Oceans solo round-the-world race, while this was Le Cam's first win in five circumnavigations. The Barcelona World Race triumph, however, followed hot on the keels of the 2013 Transat Jacques Vabre, meaning Le Cam had won the two biggest two-handed races back to back.

▽ Part formation lap, part early exchange of blows, the competitors race off the Barcelona shore before heading to open water.

# Jules Verne Trophy

*'The new watch has just taken over and I honestly feel like we are out of control... We are deep in the Southern Ocean in strong winds and steep waves. We are sailing at a boat speed continually in excess of 30 knots. We are now losing the moon and heading straight for an ice field.'*

**Nick Maloney** | Crewman aboard Jules Verne Trophy winner *Orange*, 2002

### Route tracker

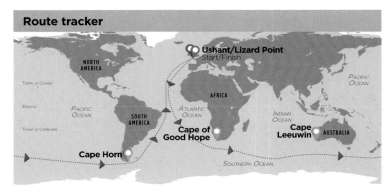

### Vital stats

**What:** 25,000-mile round-the-world record attempt

**Where:** Start and finish through a line connecting The Lizard (UK) and Ushant (France)

**How often:** Variable

**Boat type:** Multihulls

**Crew:** Fully crewed

Like all the best ideas, the Jules Verne Trophy was simplicity itself: a prize for the fastest, non-stop lap of the planet under sail. No limits. No rules. Except for a designated start/finish point and a ban on powered sail-handling systems.

Success or failure would be the result of the blood, sweat and tears of the humans harnessing the forces of nature. The only assistance the crews could rely on was the advice relayed by an onshore router, effectively another member of crew who studied meteorological data and advised the timings and angles of course changes to keep the boat's performance boiling. The secret of record setting is not so much about peak speeds, but about consistent, day-in, day-out, high average speeds.

And then in a nice twist, a dash of romance was added to the idea, drawing inspiration from Jules Verne's famous 1873 novel *Around the World in 80 Days*. In it, Phileas Fogg accepted a wager from fellow members of the Reform Club in London's Pall Mall of £20,000 (over £1 million in today's money) if he could travel around the world in under 80 days.

In Fogg's time he was reliant on road, rail, steamship and assorted four-legged animals, but the allure of the Jules Verne Trophy was that, in the 1980s when it was dreamt up, sailing around the world in 80 days was considered a far from easily attainable target.

Yves le Cornec was credited with the 80-day concept and soon established an organizing committee of fellow French notables including Tituoan Lamazou, Florence Arthaud, Jean-François Coste, Yvon Fauconnier, Gabriel Guilly, Bruno Peyron, Olivier de Kersauson, Yves Le Cornec, and Didier Ragot, plus New Zealander Peter Blake and Briton Robin Knox-Johnston.

The agreed start/finish was to pass through a line connecting The Lizard in southwest England and the Creac'h Lighthouse on Ushant on France's northwestern corner. The course was simply south, then east, then north, passing the great capes: Good Hope, Leeuwin and Horn.

In 1983 three boats, all considered the fastest

▷ The 40-m (130-ft) offshore racing trimaran *Banque Populaire V* has been the record holder since 2011, when she successfully circumnavigated in 45d 13h 43m.

at the time, took up the challenge, setting off at reasonably close but different times. Their crews chose what they believed to be the best time to pull the trigger for a slingshot start down the Atlantic towards the equator.

Peter Blake and Robin Knox-Johnston joined forces with *ENZA*, the former *Formule TAG* catamaran, and played up to the script by visiting the Reform Club prior to departure. Bruno Peyron set off in *Commodore Explorer*, the former *Jet Services V*, and like *ENZA* another cat, whilst Olivier de Kersauson set off in the trimaran *Charal*, ex *Poulain*.

When *ENZA* and *Charal* were both knocked out with hull damage, *Commodore Explorer* had things far from easy. She too suffered damage, and required some virtuoso helming from American Cam Lewis to keep the hull flying above the seas to allow repairs to be made. It was the first of many tremendous stories to stem from attempts on the record. Ultimately Peyron's crew were successful, breaking the 80-day barrier with a time of 79d 6h 15m.

It was the first of three Jules Verne records set by Peyron, his third slashing the record by an astonishing 13 days. He also had an equal number of aborted attempts. The record shows a 50 per cent failure rate by those who try to crack it. Only two of the 16 failed attempts made by the close of 2015 were successfully completed circumnavigations, but that failed to set a new record.

The rest were aborted. As proof of how humbling the Jules Verne record can be for even the best sailors and fastest boats, consider that Oliver de Kersauson achieved two successes and seven failures; Bruno Peyron has been knocked out three times with hull or mast failure; Ellen MacArthur has been dismasted; and Franck Cammas capsized.

Bit by bit, the fastest lap of the planet has come down dramatically to half of where it was in 1983, testament to higher skill, better equipment and smarter routing, allowing ever more powerful multihulls to be red-lined around the world.

## Jules Verne Trophy records

— 74d 22h 17m (1994, Peter Blake and Robin Knox-Johnston, *ENZA*)
— 71d 14h 22m (1997, Olivier de Kersauson, *Sport-Elec*)
— 64d 8h 25m (2002, Bruno Peyron, *Orange*)
— 63d 13h 49m (2004, Olivier de Kersauson, *Geronimo*)
— 50d 16h 20m (2005, Bruno Peyron, *Orange II*)
— 48d 7h 44m (2010, Franck Cammas, *Groupama 3*)
— 45d 13h 42m (2012, Loïck Peyron, *Banque Populaire V*)

# Coastal/
# Inshore Races

# Chicago–Mackinac

## Lake Michigan

*'The distance of the Mackinac Cup Yacht Race makes the
fixture compare favorably with the long ocean cruises
which recently have been attracting the attention of the
yachting world.'*

**Godfrey H. Atkin** | Donor to fund the Mackinac Cup

▽  The picturesque start of
the Chicago–Mackinac race on
Lake Michigan, with the boats
crossing the start line in front
of the Chicago skyline.

The Chicago Yacht Club (CYC) was formed
in 1875 as the city flourished, not just as the
centre of the midwest, but the centre of
America. Some 30 railroad lines ran into the city, and
canals and the Great Lakes linked it with New York
to the east and the Gulf of Mexico via the Mississippi.
Rebuilt after the 1871 Great Fire, the yacht club and
its race reflected the city's rebirth and its industrial
and commercial prominence.

The 'Mac' was first won in 1898 by
William Cameron's 20-m (64-ft) sloop
*Vanenna* against four rivals in a 51-hour
race. Today, the 333-mile race regularly
attracts 3,000 crew and a fleet of
300 boats. Strictly speaking, the
race is not all threes. The 333-mile
distance between Chicago's
Navy Pier, Illinois, and Mackinac
Island, Michigan, is 289
nautical miles.

The second race
wasn't held until
1904 but it has
continued virtually

uninterrupted since, two world wars included, with the years 1917–20 an exception. The pause after the Great War was due to many owners being absent and their yachts having been laid up.

To consider a freshwater race on an inland body of water any less of a test of sailing would be a mistake. The foundering of the schooner *Vancedor* on the rocks of Fisherman's Island, west of Charlevoix, triggered a re-evaluation of the route. A slender majority of the CYC voted to reroute the race to Harbour Springs, where it finished in 1912 and 1913. Past Commodore William L. Baum, the remaining surviving donor of the Mackinac Cup, decreed that until the Mac ended at its original finish the trophy would not be awarded. The traditional destination thus reinstated in 1914.

Chicago is known for its wind, and there have been many blustery Macs. In 1970, northerly gales saw only 79 of 169 starters complete the course. In 1937, it was eight out of 32; eight out of 21 in 1911. Tragically, 2011 saw the first and only fatalities in the race when *Wing Nuts*, a Kiwi 35 sportsboat, capsized. The deck extensions beyond the hull side meant that when *Wing Nuts* inverted in very high winds, she remained upside down.

A 40–60-hour duration is typical for the course that, with prevailing winds, often sees a start under spinnaker off the downtown Chicago waterfront. Crews then have to elect between the west and east shores of Lake Michigan to hold the breeze, with a coming together as the fleet passes Manitou Island and the Grays Reef channel. The course just reaches into Lake Huron, with the finish line set off Mackinac Island, Michigan.

A multitude of rating systems has been used over the decades to calculate the handicap winner. Multihulls as well as monohulls are eligible to enter. There are also first-to-finish honours.

*Pyewacket*, owned by the late Roy Disney – nephew of Walt – set the monohull record in 2002 with 23h 30m 34s. The late Steve Fossett, who made his fortune on the Chicago Futures Exchange before embarking on an unquenchable thirst for sailing, ballooning and aviation records, set the 18h 50m 32s multihull record in 1988, racing one of Dennis Conner's *Stars & Stripes* America's Cup catamarans.

Veterans of 25 races become known as 'Island Goats', after the Island Goat Society that was formed in 1959 with ten founder members.

## Vital stats

**What:** 287-mile inshore race

**Where:** Chicago, Illinois to Mackinac Island, Michigan (USA)

**How often:** Annual

**Boat type:** Monohulls

**Crew:** Fully crewed

## Route tracker

# Coastal Classic

New Zealand

*'What's remarkable is that Split Enz's record has stood for 13 years. Sailing technology has changed drastically since then, yet so far our record is untouched. It goes to show how incredible the 1996 race was in terms of serving up exactly the right conditions.'*

**Jon Vincent** | Spokesperson of HSBC Premier Coastal Classic

## Vital stats

**What:** 124-mile coastal race

**Where:** Auckland to Russell (New Zealand)

**How often:** Annual

**Boat type:** Multihulls and monohulls

**Crew:** Fully crewed

## Route tracker

Just as Boxing Day sees Sydney Harbour animated by the departure of the fleet racing to Hobart, so across the Tasman Sea, Auckland's Waitemata Harbour comes to life every Labour Day holiday for the Coastal Classic.

It is New Zealand's premier offshore race and still relatively young, having been first staged in 1982. The timing, however, was perfect, as New Zealand was spreading its wings in terms of yacht racing's ascendency in national importance.

Boating has always been a mass-participation recreation in New Zealand. Its long, narrow land mass and deeply indented coastline mean that the sea is never far away. But it was New Zealander Chris Bouzaid's 1969 victory in the One Ton Cup in Helgoland, Germany, with *Rainbow II,* that propelled top-level yachting into the national consciousness.

*Rainbow II* was the boat that wrote the first chapter in the Kiwi rise to the top flight of international yacht racing. The 1964 and 1984 Olympic gold medals for Helmer Pedersen, Earle Wells, Russell Coutts, Rex Sellers and Chris Timms were significant parts of the second chapter.

Roger Dilley of the Auckland Multihull Sailing Association came up with the idea of racing from Davenport Wharf in New Zealand's largest city to Russell Wharf in the Bay of Islands, location of the country's first national capital.

Instead of plain old Auckland–Russell for the race's name, Dilley dreamt up the catchier Coastal Classic. Coastal it most certainly was, the fleet sailing up the Hauraki Gulf, inside the Barrier islands, past Whangareri Heads, around Cape Brett and into the Bay Islands.

Given that Dilley was a multihull sailor, it is no surprise that his idea was for a first-to-finish sprint, the first fleet of 12 yachts split into multihulls and monohulls, or 'keelers' in the Kiwi vernacular. All that mattered was elapsed time. Handicapped corrected time results were introduced in later editions.

Peter Williams' 19.2-m (62-ft) *Fidelis* was the largest of the starters, with Mathew Flynn's 7.4-m (24-ft) tri *Gulf Chariot* the smallest. The first-ever bragging rights went to Duncan Stewart's *Krisis* in a time of 18 hours, which was not bettered for four years.

Then *Split Enz*, a Ron Given-designed catamaran, was first home in a fleet now grown to 100 boats. The 12.4-m (40-ft) cat was Given's first big multihull design and enjoyed a long and successful career. She set the Coastal Classic

record again in 1996 with a time of 7h 26m.

1988 saw the big guns take part in the shape of Grant Dalton's 24.8-m (80-ft) maxi ketch *Fisher & Paykel*, using the race as a shake-down ahead of the 1989/90 Whitbread Round the World Race.

The following year, the fleet got pounded. Coastal maybe, but New Zealand is isolated in the open ocean, and carries the full fetch of the Pacific on its eastern shore. Only 65 yachts from 155 finished, thanks to northeasterly gale-force winds. The seas off Cape Brett were especially agitated.

The appropriately named *Emotional Rescue*, a Davidson 56 owned by noted sailor Graeme Woodroffe, was a rare monohull first-to-finish after a 19-hour upwind battle.

By 1995, entries were topping over 200 and *Split Enz*'s domination was finally ended by an Australian catamaran, *XS*, designed and skippered by Robin Chamberlain.

In 1996 when *Split Enz* reasserted her dominance with a new race record, entries had climbed to 248, as divisions were added for classic and vintage yachts. The restoration of old yachts, many of which were key players in New Zealand's racing heritage, was a growing phenomenon.

1994 was a banner year for Steve Trevurza.

Sailing solo, he won handicap honours racing *Phonak*, the smallest boat in the fleet, a 6.5-m (21.3-ft) Murray Ross design. Trevurza won first overall on handicap, and was first on handicap in division four.

2009 saw Sydney-based New Zealander Neville Crichton set a new race record in his 29.8-m (96-ft) maxi *Alfa Romeo* with a time of 6h 43m 32s. Crichton is one of his country's most ardent competitors and supporters of yachting. A multihull claimed race-record honours once again in 2011, with Simon Hull's former ORMA trimaran *Team Vodafone Sailing* zipping up the course in 5h 44m 31s.

Firing the starting gun has become something of an institution. Amongst those sharing the honour have been Sir Peter Blake, Americans Dennis Conner and Ed Baird, Kiwi windsurfing multi-medallist Barbara Kendall and Dean Barker.

Despite the race having grown into New Zealand's premier event, and despite being open to monos as well as multis, it remains organized by the NZ Multihull Club, which grew out of the Auckland Multihull Sailing Association. Nowadays, the Royal New Zealand Yacht Squadron plays a full supporting role in the race management.

△ Auckland's Sky Tower dominates the Waitemata Harbour as the fleet count down to the start and head out into the Hauraki Gulf.

# Coastal/Inshore Races
# **Kiel Week**
## Germany

## Vital stats

**What:** Nine-day inshore regatta

**Where:** Kiel (Germany)

**How often:** Annual

**Boat type:** Multi-classes

**Crew:** Fully crewed and singlehanded dinghies

## Route tracker

Kiel Week shares a lot with Cowes Week. They are both long-established, week-long regattas with a wide variety of competing classes and a strong sense of tradition.

You would almost think they were related, and in one sense they are. In the years before the First World War, both regattas were distinguished by their royal patronage by King Edward VII, his nephew Kaiser Wilhelm II and nephew-by-marriage Tsar Nicholas II. Their racing yachts *Britannia* and *Meteor*, and the Russian steam yacht *Standart*, were familiar sights lying in Cowes Roads or Kiel Fjord.

### Much more than a regatta

Considering Kiel Week as only a regatta, though, is to mistake what it has grown into. It is as much a festival ashore as a racing event afloat. There is a full array of bands playing on free stages throughout the city, as well as a food market, street entertainment, conventions, a discussion forum and family attractions.

Kiel Week's proud proclamation is that it is one of the biggest sailing events in the world, and northern Europe's largest summer festival. Certainly the numbers are impressive: 2,000 events spread over nine days, attracting three million visitors.

Out on the water, some 5,000 sailors from upwards of 50 countries come to race at Kiel Week. The country count is high because Kiel Week is a fixture for Olympic-class competition, and frequently includes a particular European or world championship within the regatta. From yachts to windsurfers the entry list runs to 2,000, requiring 11 course areas to accommodate the 400 individual race starts.

Afloat, the action is mainly based out of Schilksee. Today, this large, purpose-built marina and accommodation development does not look so extraordinary, but when it was constructed for the 1972 Olympics, its sheer scale was unlike anything seen before.

1972 featured a Tall Ships Parade as part of the Olympic celebrations, and the town has retained strong links with the tall ships ever since, frequently coinciding their programme with Kiel Week. A highlight of the week is the Parade of Sail, now traditionally headed by the *Gorch Fock*, an 82-m (266-ft), three-masted, sail-training barque. Vessels from the German navy and other visiting navies also hold open days and onboard visits.

## Kaiserlicher Yacht Club

Kiel Week can be traced back to 1871, when the German Imperial Navy made its home in the Baltic seaport. Sailors with free time have turned to the sea throughout the ages, and in 1882 some 20 yachts sparred with each other in a series of races; the regatta was born.

Some of the officers who raced formed the Marine Regatta Verein in 1887, the direct antecedent of the Kiel Yacht Club. In 1891, Wilhelm II became commodore of the fledgling club and visited the regatta the following year for the first time. In one of the more convoluted courses of history, the KYC was renamed the Kaiserlicher Yacht Club in his honour. After the 1936 Berlin Olympics, the Nazis deemed the 'Yacht Club von Deutschland' their preferred name. After the Second World War, it reverted back to the KYC, although this time 'Kieler' replaced 'Kaiserlicher'.

After twice hosting the Olympic regatta at Kiel, nearby Hamburg was well advanced in considering a bid to host the 2026 Olympics, which would have brought the sports elite back to Kiel for a third time. However, the bid plan was dropped in 2015.

Today the racing in Kiel Week is organized by the KYC along with the Hamburger Segel Club, the Nordeutscher Regatta Verein and the Verein Seglerhaus am Wannsee. The Olympic and Paralympic classes are all represented, but there is also racing for another dozen dinghy classes such as the Europe, Flying Dutchman, International 505 and Laser Radial. One-design keel boats such as the J/80, J/70 and Melges 24 have their own starts, whilst also on the keelboat roster are the J2-24, Albin Express, Ballad, Folkboat and H-Boat. Bigger boats can race under ORC handicap rules.

Such a well-oiled machine is the Kiel Week organization that there's a valet service for boat trailers at the launch and recovery sites. Another stand-out characteristic of Kiel Week that has developed over the years is the annual poster. First introduced in 1948, the series represents the graphic design zeitgeist captured over the years. An invitation to create the poster is a feather in the cap, and some of them have been recognized by national and international prizes.

Not many sailing events have reached their 100th birthday. Kiel Week did that in 1982, and thoughts are already starting to turn towards the 150th anniversary.

△ The ILC 40 held its 1998 World Championship in Kiel. The big Kiel Week regatta draws in additional events.

▽ The German tall ship *Gorch Fock* leads the parade of sails for the opening of the Kiel Week in 2014.

# Hamilton Island Race Week

Australia

▷ Hamilton Island is one of the Whitsunday Islands that lie off the Queensland coast and inside the Great Barrier Reef.

*'I still can't believe we're fortunate enough to own a piece of paradise, and it's a big responsibility to develop it in a responsible manner.'*

**Robert Oatley** | Scion of Hamilton Island's owners

## Vital stats

**What:** Week-long race series

**Where:** Hamilton Island (Australia)

**How often:** Annual

**Boat type:** Monohulls and multihulls

**Crew:** Fully crewed

## Route tracker

In 1983 Australia conquered the sailing world, ending the longest winning streak in sport by becoming the first challenger in 132 years to win the America's Cup. Amongst those in Newport, Rhode Island, as a witness to history, was Keith Williams, developer of the Hamilton Island resort in the Whitsunday Islands on the Great Barrier Reef.

Why not, he mused, run a yachting regatta on the island? Palm-thronged beaches, balmy breezes, sunshine… all the ingredients were there except for boats. Back in Australia, Williams gathered kindred spirits in the shape of Melbourne yachtsman David Hutchen, yachting journalist Rob Mundle and Jock Sturrock, skipper of the first two America's Cup challengers from Australia in 1962 and 1967.

### The Wetsundays

Six months later, in April 1984, the first Hamilton Island Race Week was held and, remarkably, 94 yachts entered. Given the distances involved – 1,000 miles – to Sydney, it was a strong response.

Some yachts even came from Perth, Western Australia. However, a perfect start it was not, as the tropical weather refused to shift out of the wet season and rain fell for almost the entire week. Yachting humour being what it is, the Whitsundays were promptly renamed the 'Wetsundays', and the mid-regatta, Mardi Gras-style party was christened the 'Muddy Gras'.

Undaunted, the organizers kept the April slot in the diary for the next eight years before bowing to nature. 1989's cyclone Aviu was the clincher. A shift was made to August, the start of the southern summer, and the race has generally been blessed with tropical sunshine and tradewinds ever since.

A regular competitor has been the Oatley family, led by the founder of a wine-producing empire, Robert Oatley. 2003 was a headline year, as Oatley's son Sandy won the grand-prix division with his *Another Duchess* and Oatley was offered the opportunity to buy the island out of receivership. Having founded Rosemount Wines in 1969, Oatley sold it in 2001 and was in a position to move smartly on the deal.

Hamilton Island has been central to the Oatley family ever since, with continual investment to upgrade the facilities. It is a considerable operation, with an airport, four hotels, 11 restaurants and an 18-hole golf course. Instead of a property developer running a regatta, from 2003 onwards, sailing enthusiasts were now managing a holiday destination. A sure sign of the Oatleys' intent to hit new high notes with the regatta was the appointing in 2008 of Glen Bourke as CEO of the island. Bourke is a former Laser triple world champion, America's Cup competitor and chief executive of the Volvo Ocean Race.

## A very Australian regatta

Hamilton Island Race Week is now an Australian regatta with an international reputation. Overseas visiting yachts remain uncommon, because travelling to Australia's east coast would take them away from their home waters for much of the sailing season. That said, however, the likes of Hong Kong's Karl Kwok have contested the regatta. His TP52 *Beau Geste* won the IRC top prize in 2015 as part of a world-girdling campaign that including

competing in Auckland (New Zealand) and Copenhagen (Denmark) in 2016.

Grand-prix boats are taken care of in IRC classes as well as racer/cruiser classes. The bulk of the fleet is made up of the cruiser–racer divisions, comprised almost exclusively of production boats. There are also non-spinnaker classes for the less racy, as well as divisions for trailer boats and multihulls.

The programme is a full one, combining a round-the-islands race with several days of as many as four windward/leeward courses. However, the tone of the regatta is evident from the mid-event day off, when there is a poolside beach party. There is a full range of lunches and dinners, and hole-in-one golf competitions.

One 'Hamo' institution that has been pulled from the programme after 25 years is the Whitehaven Beach Party. It was a victim of its own success, with word spreading far and wide. Instead of being a party for competitors and their families, revellers came across from the Queensland coast especially for it. The party might be over, but the regatta remains an enormously fun institution. Long may it continue.

▽ The best in Australian ocean racing, including big names like *Wild Oats X*, *Ichi Ban* and Sydney Hobart overall winner *Wild Rose*, gather for the six-day showdown open to cruising and sports boats, cruising and racing multihulls, trailer-sailers and grand-prix racers.

## Coastal/Inshore Races
# The Admiral's Cup
## United Kingdom

*'Okay boys, we're over now; let the damn boat sink!'*

**Dick Nye** | Skipper of *Carina*

### Vital stats

**What:** Inshore and offshore race series, including the Fastnet

**Where:** Cowes, UK

**How often:** Biennial (from 1957 to 2003)

**Boat type:** Monohulls

**Crew:** Fully crewed

### Route tracker

Myles Wyatt returned to the UK having competed in the 1951 Bermuda Race with his famous yawl *Bloodhound*. How, he wondered, could American yachtsmen be persuaded to come and race in Britain and Europe?

The answer lay in the Admiral's Cup. Slowly, yacht racing was getting back on its feet after the ravages of the Second World War. The US was thinking of restarting the America's Cup. In Britain, Wyatt and senior figures of the Royal Ocean Racing Club (RORC) were brimming with ideas.

'As our night-time talks grew longer and the level of the Plymouth Gin bottle fell ever lower, the more expansive our thinking became,' said senior RORC man, Peter Green. Why not a series linking the RORC's own Fastnet Race with the Bermuda and Sydney–Hobart races? Or how about a Round Britain Race, leaving the choice open to skippers which way round they went?

Eventually Sir Peter Green, who was to become chairman of Lloyd's of London, Sir Myles Wyatt, admiral of the RORC, Captain John Illingworth, who'd helped create the Sydney–Hobart, and Geoffrey Pattinson donated a gold gilt cup for a new series in 1957. It was Selwyn Slater who actually sourced the twin-handled, lipped-bowl trophy through a friend in the silverware trade. It was a gold cup from the 1830s that had originally been a prize for horse racing.

**It started with a private challenge**

A 'Private Challenge' was duly issued 'from a group of English yacht owners to the Americans' for between three and five yachts to contest a series made up of the RORC's 220-mile Channel Race and 605-mile Fastnet Race, plus premier races within Cowes Week – the Britannia Cup and the New York Yacht Club Cup.

The Channel Race would score double points and the Fastnet Race triple, and by dint of the Cowes Week races, the Royal Yacht Squadron was an integral part of the Admiral's Cup from the outset.

The Americans accepted and were keen. Ironically, though, where the challenge called for

between three and five yachts, the US could not field a yacht to match Myles Wyatt's own 19.5-m (63-ft) yawl *Bloodhound*. So Wyatt stood down and could not compete for the trophy to which his office, as RORC admiral, had given its name.

Representing the hosts were Peter Green's own *Myth of Malham*, which he co-owned with the redoubtable John Illingworth, Selwyn Slater's *Uomie* and *Jocasta*, owned by fruit farmer Geoffrey Pattinson.

Illingworth had heavily influenced Jack Laurent Giles in *Myth*'s design. She was to become a seminal yacht in the progress of ocean-racer design, and she was a genuine rule beater. The RORC rating rule taxed headsails in its calculation up to a maximum of 85 per cent, so Illingworth used 150 per cent jibs with a tiny mainsail, instead. The hull was given short bow and stern overhangs to trick the rule into thinking *Myth* was shorter than she actually was. Eventually *Myth of Malham* competed in five Admiral's Cups, a record.

### The first Admiral's Cup

The Americans sent over Blunt White's *White Mist*, William Snaith's *Figaro* and Dick Nye's *Carina*.

Cowes was only partly home to the new event. Until the end of the Channel Race, the yachts were based further east at Gosport. It remained this way until 1971, when the new Groves & Guttridge marina was built and the biennial Admiral's Cup moved in.

When *Myth* and *Uomie* scored first and second in the Channel Race and *Uomie* won the Britannia Cup, Britain looked in excellent shape. America came back, with *Figaro* winning the NYYC Challenge Cup.

The Fastnet Race finale was one of the heavy-air affairs on which the race's reputation is based. Through the filthy weather, Dick Nye drove *Carina*, who averaged 8.3 knots for the race. Nye drove his crew as hard as he had his yacht. 'Is every man a tiger?' he bellowed. 'Grrrrr!' they replied. When *Carina* passed the Plymouth breakwater to take the

△ The American yacht *Sidewinder* battles through heavy seas at the start of the Channel Race in the 1985 Admiral's Cup.

△ The Farr-designed British yacht *Oracle* punches through rough seas during the 1991 Admiral's Cup.

less well in the Solent where lack of knowledge almost unseated them. Sweden joined in to boost the line-up to five teams, but the well-prepared Americans showed that Britain could be beaten on home turf.

The host nation's response was to hold selection trials for the first time in 1963. The USA posed the strongest threat, and that's how they finished. Britain regained the trophy with America the runners-up. Germany participated for the first time to make six teams. Amongst their three boats was Hans-Otto Schümann's *Rubin*. He was to become the Admiral's Cup's most ardent competitor, entering ten times and winning in 1973, 1985 and 1993. The physics of racing yachts was a lifelong passion of Schümann's. In 1963, for instance, *Rubin* carried spinnakers with four rows of slots sewn in from side to side. They were meant to manage the airflow of the wind in the sail.

### The Cup goes global

Australia and Ireland joined the ranks in 1965; Spain and Finland in 1967. Inexorably the series was growing, as was the potency of the foreign teams. Bill Psaltis of the Cruising Yacht Club of Australia downplayed his team's chances on their second visit. 'We've come over here to race, to learn and to find out what our standard is.'

*The Financial Times* read the runes right: 'None of the Australian helmsman has ever raced in the Fastnet. Two of their boats are two years old and the other is 15; the average age of the crews is 41. If such a challenge came from anywhere but Australia, it would be treated as a pleasant piece of sporting eccentricity.'

Australia not only won but by a huge margin. However, the competition was a winner, too. The 1967 series really carved out the Admiral's Cup's identity and set it up to become one of the most influential events for more than five decades. Owners of ocean racers around the world increasingly factored the series into their plans. Yacht designers, boatbuilders, mastmakers and sailmakers all saw it as a proving ground where reputations could be won and lost.

This significance was captured by J.R.L.

winner's finish gun, he uttered the memorable words: 'Okay boys, we're over now; let the damn boat sink!'

Britain's three yachts garnered enough points to win the first Admiral's Cup. Interestingly, on the other side of the Atlantic when *Rudder* magazine reported *Carina's* Fastnet win, plus the transatlantic race that had preceded it and their 'unique place in yachting history', it made no mention whatsoever of the Admiral's Cup. Even in the RORC's own main committee minutes, the Admiral's Cup was recorded only as a footnote to the 1957 Fastnet Race.

It seemed the private challenge had remained a little too private. In truth, the seeds had been sown for one of the great ocean-racing events of all time, one that ran every two years until 2003.

The Americans would not be drawn back across the Atlantic a second time in 1959, when the Admiral's Cup was staged again.

France and the Netherlands did come, however, with three boats apiece. The Dutch very nearly won.

Britain led before the Fastnet Race, which this time was an exasperating light-wind affair until a gale sped the fleet home in the later stages. The French yachts pulled out and Britain scraped home.

By 1961, *Rudder* has shifted its indifference of 1957, largely because the Americans were back and they won. The US trio took a big lead from the outset in the Channel Race, but fared

Anderson in *The Guardian*. 'To my mind, and I am sure many yachtsmen agree with me, the Admiral's Cup is a trophy far more worth winning than the America's Cup. The America's Cup has simply become a contest of racing machines sailing around buoys. And the machines are now so expensive, that to build and race them almost demands syndicates of millionaires. Victory in the Admiral's Cup calls for seaworthiness in a yacht and seamanship in a crew over days and nights at sea in all sorts of conditions. It is a test of men and boats rather than of sailing machines.'

Reading this 50 years later, it's clear that Anderson's words contained many valid observations. Ocean racing continues to improve the breed of ocean-capable racing yachts, although the sea is as great a leveller as ever. The America's Cup has spiralled away even more from the mainstream, becoming super-specialized once again, like it was in the glory days before and after the First World War when exceptional yachts were created for it.

However, for an extended period from the 1970s to the 2000s, the very best sailors in the world competed in both the Admiral's Cup and the America's Cup. Men such as Ted Turner, Lowell North, Dennis Conner, Rod Davis, Tom Blackaller, Jochen Schümann, Russell Coutts, Brad Butterworth, Tom Schnackenberg, Peter Lester, Bruno Trouble, Bertrand Pacé, Harold Cudmore, Lawrie Smith and Phil Crebbin, to name a small number of the elite cadre.

## The winning prime minister

In the Admiral's Cup, British prime minister Sir Edward Heath did something no other head of government had done: lead a team to victory in a major international competition whilst still in office, in 1971. He counted this, and his Sydney–Hobart win in *Morning Cloud*, as achievements he was immensely proud of.

The Admiral's Cup reached its high-water mark in the 1980s. The 1981, 1983, 1985, 1987, and 1989 series attracted an extraordinary run of 16, 15, 18, 14 and 14 teams.

It's instructive to list the countries involved,

because racing a three boat was a phenomenal undertaking and the vast majority were bona-fide teams, not another country's 'B' team. Those competing included Australia, Austria, Argentina, Belgium, Bermuda, Brazil, Canada, Denmark, France, Germany, Hong Kong, Ireland, Italy, Japan, the Netherlands, Papua New Guinea, Portugal, Spain, Sweden, Switzerland and the USA. The winner's circle expanded from Britain, the USA and Australia to include Germany, New Zealand and France.

Each Admiral's Cup series provides a snapshot of the grand-prix racing at the time, highlighting trends in rating rules, sail technology, boat construction, paid professional crew, advances in boat construction, sponsorship, advertising, performance instrumentation and so forth.

What is sad is that the Admiral's Cup's glory faded and died. Today, the famous trophy resides in Australia as the last country to win it in 2003, in a sparsely attended series that followed 2001's cancellation.

It declined for a number of reasons, including the end of the IOR rule, rising competition from other events and a lack of leadership from the RORC. They vacillated over the rating rules and types of boat to succeed the IOR, whether to relocate the regatta and, believe it or not, whether to keep the Fastnet Race as part of the series. It was a sad end for a magnificent event.

> '*To my mind the Admiral's Cup is a trophy far more worth winning than the America's Cup (which) has simply become a contest of racing machines sailing around buoys.*'
>
> **J.R.L. Anderson** | *The Guardian*

▽ Sir Edward Heath (centre) skippers his yacht *Morning Cloud IV* to victory in the 1971 Admiral's Cup – Heath's sailing master Owen Parker to the left and seasoned sailor Peter Nicholson at the helm.

# Coastal/Inshore Races
# **Antigua Sailing Week**
## Caribbean

*'It could be Cowes Week after you have died and gone to heaven.'*

**Jack Knights** | Journalist

## Vital stats

**What:** Day-race regatta

**Where:** English Harbour, Antigua

**How often:** Annual

**Boat type:** Monohulls and multihulls

**Crew:** Fully crewed

## Route tracker

The late British yachting journalist Jack Knights summed up the attractions of racing in Antigua: 'It could be Cowes Week after you have died and gone to heaven.'

Those words were written at the end of the 1970s, when Antigua Sailing Week had just got under way. It was the original hedonistic regatta. Sublime sailing by day; Caribbean vacation by late afternoon, through the evening and into the small hours.

No wonder the format has been repeated by other start-up regattas around the world.

Antigua lies in the necklace of the Lesser Antilles islands, with the Atlantic to the east and the Caribbean Sea to the west. Think of sunshine, palm trees, ranks of tropical cumulus overhead, rum punches and steel bands and you've set the scene.

The Arawaks paddled from Venezuela to discover the island, followed by the Caribs, and then by the various navies of Europe. Horatio Nelson liked the cut of Antigua's hurricane-proof harbour, and English Harbour was developed. Where the wharfs and buildings once serviced, succoured and victualled the Royal Navy, so today it makes a great yachting centre.

The regatta started in 1968 through the efforts of Antigua-based yachtsmen and local hoteliers. Its timing at the end of May and early June sought to extend the tourist season, and it was no accident that it was sponsored by the Hotel Association, or that the locals originally dubbed it 'Antigua T-shirt Week'. That name didn't last long. For one thing, it seemed that both male and female sailors liked a well-distributed sun tan and didn't wear t-shirts too often...

The beauty of the regatta being a tourism initiative was that the word was spread fast and effectively via the travel trade. Yachts came from the US, Canada and Europe. A race up from Guadeloupe served as a feeder race for yachts down in the south. And Nelson's Dockyard in English Harbour made the perfect venue for parties, prizegivings and balls.

From the word go, the ethos was to embrace all visitors to Antigua. For non-sailors there were beach and veranda parties, while sailors without boats could sign up for a crew spot. A mid-week lay day remains an institution in the regatta, though it results in only a partial slowing of the pace.

In the early days the fleet was not so racy, comprising sturdier, slower-cruising boats, some classics and other types that, like their owners and crews, had kicked back and were enjoying the easy life in the Caribbean. That didn't last for long. The word spread, and soon Antigua Sailing Week had become a big draw for the growing ranks of sailing photographers. The yachting magazines then played their part, as they made the transition from black-and-white printing. If you wanted colour in your colour-print pages, what could be better than bikinis, spinnakers and cocktails?

Over the years the dates have moved, but the start date is generally the last Sunday in April. Entries soon blossomed to more than 250, a number that swamped the island, with plenty of hot boats and top crews lining up. As bareboat yacht chartering in the Caribbean grew, so the swifter of these boats also joined in.

In 1988 the classic boats were split off with the creation of the Antigua Classic Yacht Regatta,

and this has grown to become equally famous. Typically entries for Antigua Sailing Week now number around 100, a sign that there is more competition from other racing events in the calendar.

Racing is held under the auspices of the Caribbean Sailing Association, using the CSA handicap rule. This is a simple-to-obtain and simple-to-use rating system based on in-water measurement of yachts in sailing trim and measurement of sails.

There are usually five main races, while the race up from Guadeloupe continues to feed boats into Antigua. Like the Lord Nelson's Ball, the legend of the regatta continues to prosper.

▽ Having popped the kite, the bowman fastens it at the end of the spinnaker pole aboard the ZX86 *Morning Glory* during the 2004 edition of the Antigua Sailing Week.

# Coastal/Inshore Races
# Cowes Week
## United Kingdom

*'After two days I was hooked. It is a fantastic regatta but to do well, learning about the Solent tides is essential.'*

**Alex Downer** | At 13 the youngest skipper competing at Cowes Week in 2015

## Vital stats

**What:** Eight-day regatta

**Where:** Cowes (UK)

**How often:** Annual

**Boat type:** Dayboat and keelboat classes

**Crew:** Fully crewed

## Route tracker

NORTH SEA

IRISH SEA

UNITED KINGDOM

**Cowes**

Isle of Wight

ENGLISH CHANNEL

FRANCE

It can be timed to the minute, the moment that the modern yachting regatta was born: 9.30am on Thursday 10 August 1826.

This was when the first Cowes Week was staged, so commencing a run that now sees it sitting at the head of the table as the longest-running regularly staged regatta in the world. There had been many other races and events before then, but they were not strictly sporting, including racing in Cowes amongst the local pilot cutters.

### The mecca of yachting

Longevity is what sets Cowes Week apart today. There probably isn't a sailor in the world who hasn't heard of it. And those outside of the UK routinely refer to Cowes as the 'mecca of yachting', such is its aura.

That 1826 race was uncannily similar to the origin of the America's Cup in 1851. The prize put up was a 'gold cup of the value of £100' (seemingly a far from uncommon prize at the time) and it was organized by the Royal Yacht Club, which had yet to change its name to the Royal Yacht Squadron.

The race was from Cowes, west to Yarmouth, east to Southsea and then back to Cowes. The next day there was another race, an Annual Sailing Match, to be sailed around buoys in the mid-Solent, this time for a winner's purse of £30 and a second-place prize of £20. On the evening of the first day there was a ball and on Friday evening there were fireworks. Go to Cowes Week today and you will find exactly the same thing. Of the many balls and parties, Thursday's RYS ball remains matchless in terms of prestige.

So well received were those first races in August 1826 that the residents of Cowes – 'sensible of the pleasure and advantages they derive from their port having become the rendezvous of the Royal Yacht Club' – subscribed for another trophy for a second regatta that same year in September. Between the two events a total of 17 different yachts participated.

At the time, yachting was in its infancy. The RYS was founded as the Yacht Club in London in 1815. Cowes, a fishing and ship-building town on the Medina river on the Isle of Wight, was a popular location for gentlemen to own homes and keep their yachts. In 1814 some had joined in the pilot-cutters parade, but mainly they cruised in company or performed manoeuvres as a squadron, much like the Royal Navy.

This dressage at sea was codified in a Signals Book. Some of the more unusual standard messages between vessels include, 'Can you lend me your band?' and 'Have you any ladies aboard?'. And to shore: 'Send me 300 oysters'.

After 1826's initiation of bona-fide yacht racing, the custom of reigning monarchs presenting trophies began with George IV. The Queen's Cup remains one of the principal trophies of Cowes Week, presented by Queen Victoria in her diamond jubilee year of 1897. The Britannia Cup was first contested in 1851 and later named after the 1893 cutter raced by Edward, Prince of Wales (later King Edward VII) and his son, King George V, for nearly 40 years until 1935.

This ardent support from the royal family brought much lustre to the regatta over three centuries. In more recent times, HRH Prince Philip was a keen competitor for many years. Prince Charles and Princess Anne competed, too, sometimes with legendary yacht designer Uffa Fox in the Flying 15 keelboat Coweslip or the Dragon Bluebottle. The ebullient, eccentric Fox was famous for his salty language and repertoire of sea shanties.

For many years, between 1954 and her retirement in 1997, the Royal Yacht Britannia was a fixture in Cowes Roads. Prince Philip would embark at Portsmouth after attending the horse racing at 'Glorious' Goodwood and race at Cowes, before Britannia took the queen and other members of the royal family to Scotland for their August break at Balmoral. Competitors and visitors to the Solent alike were saddened when Britannia sailed away from Cowes for the last time.

In earlier times, the presence of the court at Queen Victoria and Prince Albert's preferred summer home of Osborne House on the Isle of Wight did much to establish the reputation of Cowes Week. An 1845 account noted: 'Cowes presented a magnificent scene, upwards of 80 vessels being under sail.' Yachting was still very much a pursuit of Corinthian gentlemen, with their professional crews frequently being fishermen outside of the summer months. This 1894 report also captures the flavour well: 'The Cowes Week has always been an assemblage of aristocrats, but the year 1894 has eclipsed all previous gatherings. Never have so many yachts graced the beautiful waters of the Solent. A profusion of craft was anchored ... and flew every national ensign, American, French and German predominating.'

△ Left: King George V was an avid racer aboard the gaff-rigged cutter Britannia, as his father Edward VII had been before him. Their presence boosted the allure of Cowes Week.

Right: The Royal Yacht Britannia was a familiar sight in Cowes Roads for four decades, as HRH Prince Philip competed in Cowes Week, until her emotional farewell in 1997.

◁ Cowes Week is one of the great occasions on the British sporting calendar, and the RAF's Red Arrows aerobatic team are regular visitors.

▽ Quintessentially Cowes Week: the Royal Yacht Squadron is centre stage as the Victory and Squib day-boat classes race westwards from the start line.

The flag of the recently unified Imperial Germany, that is. The Edwardian era, led by King Edward VII, was a vast contrast to that of his mother's, Queen Victoria. It was noted for its lavishness. At Cowes Week it was also marked by the unrelenting competitiveness displayed by the king's nephew, Kaiser Wilhelm II, through his determination to beat the king's racing cutter *Britannia*. There being no German yards or designers at the time comparable to Britain's, the kaiser bought the Scottish cutter *Thistle*. Then, through a succession of ever larger and more powerful yachts called *Meteor*, he sought superiority over *Britannia*.

While still Prince of Wales, Edward told of his ire at the kaiser's desire to beat him. He remarked to Baron von Eckardstein that the Cowes Regatta, 'Used to be a pleasant relaxation for me; since the kaiser takes command, it is a vexation.'

The parties and balls were elevated to an epic scale in Edwardian Cowes. Lying off was the Royal Yacht *Victoria & Albert*, guarded by a battleship, plus the kaiser's sea-going palace *Hohenzollern*

supporting his racing yacht *Meteor*, plus other head-of-state yachts: the king of Spain's *Hispania* and Tsar Nicholas II's *Standardt*.

Edward VII's death in 1910 and the advent of the First World War meant that the likes of this were not seen again. The heyday of the 'big boat' racing yachts was not over, however. George V brought his father's *Britannia* back to competition in 1920 and, updated, kept her competitive and tempted other owners to compete. Post-First World War, the owners were less aristocracy and more giants of industry, men such as Sir Thomas Lipton (tea), Sir Thomas Sopwith (aircraft), Pierpont Morgan (banking) and W.L. Stephenson (Woolworth's stores). The schooners had given way to the huge but elegant 23-, 19- and 15-Metre yachts, and then the J-Class.

After the Second World War, the Cowes Regatta expanded either side of its original three days, with other yacht clubs on the island as well as the mainland taking their turn to organize a day's racing. Come 1953, the regatta was utilizing both weekends, and Cowes 'Week' had grown to nine days. With expansion came consolidation, necessary to bring order to the hectic and confusing array of multiple dayboat and keelboat classes, sailing multiple courses organized by different yacht clubs. Starting and finishing was brought to a central location, the Royal Yacht Squadron.

1957 saw the birth of the Admiral's Cup, a three-boat team event. It mixed offshore races (the Fastnet and Channel races) with intense inshore racing when they joined in Cowes racing in the Solent amongst the ocean racers of Class 1 and Class 2. With an eye on the competition, Prince Philip suggested further streamlining of the organization of Cowes Week. In 1964 Cowes Combined Clubs (CCC) was created to forge direct links between the Royal Yacht Squadron, Royal Thames YC, Royal London YC, Royal Southern YC, Royal Southampton YC, Island Sailing Club and Cowes Town Regatta Committee. Later, the Royal Ocean Racing Club, Cowes Corinthian SC and Royal Corinthian YC joined the CCC.

Today, Cowes Week has

effectively settled back to seven days. There is no racing on the second Sunday, and entries tail off on the second Saturday. But there is still racing for 1,000 yachts. They range from venerable dayboat one-designs such as the 1911 vintage XODs to a full range of racer-cruisers, racing under the IRC rating rule across 40 different classes. This equates to 8,000 sailors. The spectacle attracts some 100,000 people, lining vantage points on the mainland such as Lepe Point or Cowes itself, where the sight of yachts sailing along the seafront towards the finish is pure spectacle.

The regatta is far more modern today. Granted, the balls remain a vital part of yacht-club life, but the main marina in Cowes now has a proper events centre and sound stage for music acts. And, of course, on Friday night at 9pm sharp, there is still the famous fireworks display.

'The thrill of Les Voiles de Saint Tropez lies in the diversity of the fleet. It's a sight for sore eyes and clearly Les Voiles is essentially a state of mind!'

**Jean-Pierre Mannetstatter** | Race director, Modern round

## Coastal/Inshore Races
# Les Voiles de St Tropez

The cocktail of one part alcohol, two parts yachtsmen and one part off-lying seamark is best avoided – unless you want a new yachting challenge created, that is.

So it was that two prominent Tropezienne figures savoured a glass of Provençal wine and made a sporting bet. The loser would buy dinner for the winner of a race from St Tropez to the Nioulargue shoal off the Bay of Pamplonne. The protagonists were Dick Jayson, who owned a Swan 44 called *Pride*, and Jean Lorrain, who skippered a venerable 12-metre class yacht, *Ikra*, owned by Jean Redele, the motorsport pioneer who created the French car-maker Alpine.

The year was 1981 and La Nioulargue was born. Scheduled in the first week of October, it slotted comfortably alongside established Mediterranean regattas such as Cannes' Régates Royales, the Imperia Regatta and events in Monaco and Porto Cervo in Sardinia. From an impulsive sporting bet, the event blossomed into such a famous event that a limit of 200 boats had to be imposed.

Some said that the origin of the regatta was spurious, and that a 12-metre that had been part of an unsuccessful British America's Cup effort from the 1960s racing against a comfortably fitted out and able offshore cruiser-racer was no race at all. And yet that first race between *Ikra* and *Pride* epitomized what was to become the ethos of the regatta – all types, all lengths and all ages of yachts could compete. From a start off the Tour de Portalet standing on St Tropez's harbour wall, the pair set off around La Nioulargue and finished at the beach near Club 55.

Patrice de Colmont created this casual beach club way back in 1955, when filmmaker Roger Vadim shot a bikini-clad Brigitte Bardot there in the film *And God Created Woman*. Club 55 has been cool ever since. A yacht race in St Tropez seemed like the perfect way to add another week to the beach season before winter set in, so de Colmont embraced the idea of La Nioulargue enthusiastically.

**Going public**

In its second year, Jean Lorrain and Dick Jayson had to share their 'private' regatta with 12 other owners, although this was clearly no hardship given that amongst them was the world-famous German conductor Herbert von Karajan, who brought his Germàn Frers-designed 23.6-m (76-ft) IOR maxi *Helisara*.

From two to 12 to 200 entrants, the regatta grew exponentially. The vibe of the 1970s was to wriggle out of the straightjacket of the sport at a time when racing was regimented by an inflexible structure of this-type-of-yacht for that-type-of-event. La Nioulargue was more informal, more fun and more like the Caribbean than Europe.

The yachting photographers were amongst the early adopters of the regatta. The juxtaposition of yachts against the pastel backdrop of the old former fishing port, the hard autumnal Mediterranean light and the sheer variety of stunning yachts made it a must-see fixture. Through their images in magazines, the pull of the regatta was spread around the world.

This growth was not without the odd foot-fault. De Colmont headed to Porto Cervo, Sardinia, in 1982, armed with t-shirts and bottles of Provençal rosé hoping to lobby other owners

◁ *SFS*, the former Volvo 70 *Abu Dhabi*, powered up in the Gulf of St Tropez.

## Vital stats

**What:** Day races

**Where:** St Tropez (France)

**How often:** Annual

**Boat type:** Monohulls

**Crew:** Fully crewed

### Route tracker

▽ The 50-m (164-ft) schooner *Eleonora*, a 2000 recreation of one of Nathanael Herreshoff's most famous yachts, *Westward*, launched in 1910.

of maxi yachts to come over for the second event. He arrived late for his appointment and found the owners formally dressed and equally formal in attitude. Instead of a stilted meeting, the French beach-owner reverted to what he knew best and threw a wine tasting on the docks the next morning before racing. The late Briton Bill Whitehouse-Vaux caught the vibe and promised to take his *Mistress Quickly* to St Tropez. Others were to follow.

### A collective holding of breath

However, the regatta's runaway success was stopped in its tracks by tragic events in 1995, when the famous 42-m (138-ft) *Mariette,* a two-masted schooner built in 1915 and owned by fabled Silicon Valley venture capitalist Tom Perkins, ran over the smaller 6-Metre *Taos Brett IV* in a frightening collision. Jacques Bourry, crew on the smaller yacht, lost his life and the tragedy morphed into a criminal investigation and lengthy litigation. The prosecuting authorities launched actions against not just the regatta organizers, but also the owners and skippers of both yachts. This caused a collective holding of breath by event hosts and sailors worldwide, as the ramifications could have had a profound effect on the sport. Eventually fines were imposed, but the way was clear for racing in St Tropez to continue after a five-year hiatus.

A successor regatta picked up the mantle of La Nioulargue and Les Voiles de St Tropez was born. The elements were the same, although the organization was completely different. In place of the International Yacht Club de Pamplonne was the Société Nautique de St Tropez. The essential essence of the regatta remained unchanged – a glamorous and picture-perfect location with an equally glamorous and picture-perfect collection of eclectic yachts.

The roster of exceptional yachts that have competed over the years is breathtaking. Baron Edmund de Rothschild's *Gitana*; the three-masted, 63-m (207-ft) *Creole*, owned variously by Stavros Niarchos and the Gucci family; the three-masted schooner *Shenandoah*; HSH Prince Albert's gaff cutter *Tuiga*, often described as the finest classic yacht sailing; *Kentra*; a full-house of J-class yachts such as *Endeavour* and *Velsheda*; and the avant-garde Wally-class yachts;

### The stunning clash of new and old

If you want to see a wonderful culture clash between yachts fashioned from teak, oak, pitch-pine and bronze, and who have already celebrated their 100th birthday, and those that are oven-baked and vacuum-compressed from the latest high-modulus carbon fibre and epoxy laminates, St Tropez is the place and Les Voiles is the regatta.

Nowadays there are three course areas for modern, classic and Wally yachts, and a multitude of classes racing on them. There are just as many yachts from the hot contemporary design offices of Frers, Farr, Judel/Vrolijk, Reichel/Pugh, Briand, Ker, Kouyoumdjian, Tripp, etc. as there are from those now considered legends: Fife, S&S, Rhodes, Illingworth, Herreshoff, Sangermani, Mylne, Crane, Gardener and others of their ilk.

The crowds flock to St Tropez for the spectacle, and, yes, for people-watching. Sailing enthusiasts continue to be enthralled by seeing how technology and materials have progressed through a timeline from the 100-plus classics to the latest café-racers. The differences between the European and American schools of yacht design from the last century are evident, as are the influences of class and rating rules. By setting go-fast factors (primarily sail area) against go-slow factors (such as weight), rating rules through the ages have attempted a theoretical assessment of speed in order to create handicaps.

Although there are yachts thunderously large in length, displacement and sail area, there is also a class of comparative minnows in the shape of the Tofinu 9.5. This Joubert/Nivelt dayboat from master builders of the modern/retro yachts, Latitude 46 on Brittany's Île de Ré, marry dark hull colours and deep-gloss varnish work with sleek hull lines, spindly, high-lift keels and towering carbon-fibre rigs. Mind you, at 9.5m (31ft) long, the Tofinu is a dayboat the same length and cost as many a production cruising boat. There's no denying that they and Les Voile de St Tropez were made for each other.

A day at Les Voiles is a thing of great joy. One can start with breakfast at Senequier's on the port, a café famous for being famous. While there, it would be hard to be indifferent to the superlative yachts moored stern-to in the port. It is one of the hardest in which to secure a spot in the entire Mediterranean, and the harbour master knows how to judge the most suitable yachts.

Coffee and croissant done, there is no racing before midday, so an agreeably gentle start to the day is possible. With finishes by late afternoon, there's time for aperitifs and beers in the cockpit before heading ashore. Those in the know can beat the odds and secure a restaurant table. Despite its less than ritzy reputation, you can still find *pétanque* (boules) played in the dusty squares of the old town if you want a more gentle pursuit than a late night in the discothèques.

The early 200 limit to entries was dispensed with. Nothing breeds success like success, after all, and in 2015, some 330 yachts competed. The organizers know that keeping true to the event's roots is no easy task. The risk of Les Voiles becoming too much of a catwalk is something they are aware of.

André Beaufils, president of the SNST, is steering a course back towards an 'owners and friends' spirit to the regatta. 'Owners, skippers and sailors jump at the prospect because of the adrenalin hit it gives them and with it the ensuing celebration on shore,' is how he sees the regatta's enduring appeal.

△ The American yacht *Rambler 88*, owned by George David, is typical of the international cast drawn to Les Voiles de St Tropez.

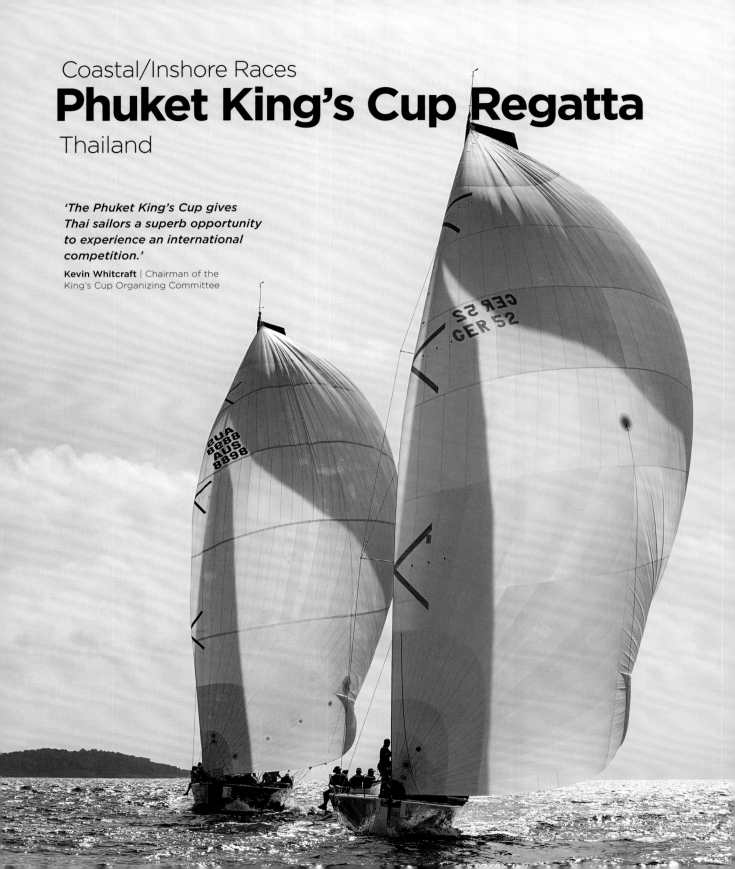

Coastal/Inshore Races

# Phuket King's Cup Regatta

Thailand

*'The Phuket King's Cup gives Thai sailors a superb opportunity to experience an international competition.'*

**Kevin Whitcraft** | Chairman of the King's Cup Organizing Committee

T hailand's King's Cup Regatta, held on the island of Phuket, has grown into Asia's largest and best-known regatta. Not that Phuket feels like an island – since the 1970s, the 30-mile long island has morphed from a remote rainforest region of Thailand to a holiday destination of worldwide renown. It now attracts four million tourists a year.

For a time its reputation was somewhat unsavoury, but today it is known for its top-drawer hotels, excellent dining, upmarket spas and, of course, for its exceptional beaches. Other attractions include good diving and the necklace of small, mushroom-like islands in the Andaman Sea, whose trailing vegetation and soft rock are undercut by marine erosion.

Where tourism led, yachting followed, and Phuket was one of the first destinations in southeast Asia for bareboat yacht charter to be marketed to Europeans. In 1987 the first King's Cup was staged, and today it is run with the full support of the Royal Varuna Yacht Club, in conjunction with the Yacht Racing Association of Thailand, the Royal Thai Navy and the province of Phuket.

The first event was staged to mark the king's 60th birthday and the annual regatta, staged in December, has gone from strength to strength ever since. Today, a 100-boat fleet is typical, which means around 2,000 sailors coming to Phuket for five days of racing and social events.

Among those driving the regatta at its inception were Royal Varuna Yacht Club commodore Chris King, Dr Rachot Kanjanavanit, Al Chandler and Adolph Knees. It was architect M.L. Tridosyuth Devakul and developer Mom Tri who offered the newly opened Phuket Yacht Club Hotel, at Nai Harn Bay in Phuket. From day one, the regatta had royal patronage and it had a home. The portents were good.

If the first fleet wasn't chock-full of elite boats, it more than made up for it with enthusiastic competitors. Singlehanded Laser dinghies and windsurfers were in the mix. Famously, Scott McCook launched his small catamaran off a beach in Singapore, sailed up to Phuket, won five races and headed home again.

Recreational sailing in Thailand was given a big boost by one of the RVYC's co-founders, HSH Bhisatej Rajani. He answered a newspaper advertisement placed by Walter Meyer calling for like-minded sailors wishing to establish a yacht club. They met in a Bangkok restaurant and the idea took flight. Not only did Rajani help found the Varuna Marina Club, which became the Royal Varuna Yacht Club in 1967, but he also introduced the king to dinghy sailing. When the idea of creating a new regatta was proposed the king was happy to support the initiative, having become an avid sailor. In 1967, he and his eldest daughter, Princess Ubolratana, finished tied first in the OK singlehanded dinghy fleet at the fourth Southeast Asia Peninsula Games.

Dinghies are still raced at the King's Cup in an associated event, including the Laser and Topper singlehanders. By far the biggest class is the children's Optimist class, which in 2014 had more than 30 entrants, nearly all Thai.

The big boats are more international, split into racing classes competing under the IRC handicap rule, multihulls and cruising classes, plus a special division for skippered as well as bareboat-chartered yachts. The Firefly 850 sports catamaran has its own class start.

Bookended by the opening ceremony and prizegiving at the weekends, the format has settled into five days of round-the-buoys races up to a maximum of 12. The event has become truly international. Not only are noted Asian regatta regulars such as Neil Pryde, Frank Pong and Geoff Hill regular competitors, but entrants from China, Singapore, Russia, Switzerland, the UK, Turkey, Japan, Malaysia, the USA, Germany and other countries are the norm.

## Vital stats

**What:** Week-long regatta of inshore races

**Where:** Phuket (Thailand)

**How often:** Annual

**Boat type:** Monohulls, multihulls and dinghies

**Crew:** Fully crewed

## Route tracker

Look no further than the Extreme Sailing Series for a blueprint of how to create and stage a successful stadium sailing series.

Others have attempted it – in the 1980s, the Ultimate 30s and ProSail Formula 40s in the USA and Ultra 30s in the UK prospered and withered in short order. By contrast, the Extreme Sailing Series got its formula correct at the outset, with high-speed boats, top-level competitors, a slick programme of short races and, crucially, the realization that racing had to be put on in locations where the general public could not miss it.

And, boy, have some of the venues been challenging, such as one of Amsterdam's larger canal basins. It was the sailing equivalent of racing Formula One in a car park.

**Thrills, spills and plenty of action**

The series was the brainchild of Dutch two-time Tornado class Olympic sailor Herbert Dercksen. His Tornado Sports worked with Swedish boat/ mast builder Marstrom to create the Extreme 40 catamaran, a high-speed catamaran specifically designed to break into components that would fit into 12.4-m (40-ft) shipping containers.

OC Sports was brought in to run the racing, media, hospitality and management of a new series, which was launched in 2007 with events in Amsterdam (the Netherlands), Munich (Germany), Marseilles (France) and Cowes (UK).

The thrills-and-spills style of racing guarantees plenty of action and is ideal for publicity. A photograph of Ben Ainslie capsizing his JP

▽ Launched in 2005, the Extreme 40 catamaran was produced with the aim of providing an easy-access multihull that could be competitively raced in a variety of conditions. Here, Swiss boat *Alinghi* competes in the fleet race of the 2011 Extreme Sailing Series, Cowes.

## Vital stats

**What:** Four-day series inshore race

**Where:** Multi-stage world tour

**How often:** Annual

**Boat type:** Extreme 40 catamarans; from 2016 GC32 catamarans

**Crew:** Fully crewed

## Route tracker

**Worldwide**

▷ The Extreme Sailing Series promotes its thrills-and-spills appeal. And not without good reason.

Morgan-branded carbon-fibre Extreme 40 in 2008 was used around the world. The circuit that year was won by Switzerland's America's Cup winner, Ernesto Bertarelli. It also scooped up two prestigious sports sponsorship and business-to-business awards, thoroughly validating Dercksen's and OC Sport's concept and execution.

### Going global

Year by year, the Extreme Sailing Series has grown and developed new markets. In 2009 the Middle East and Asia were added to the tour, with stops in Oman, Singapore and Hong Kong. Oman, with its long-term plan to develop sailing, entered its own team, and from 2009 secured a string of successive annual series wins, all achieved with different British helmsmen: Peter Cumming, Paul Campbell-James and Leigh McMillan.

In some sort of reverse flattery, given that France has so long been the hotbed of racing multihull development rather than a Dutch/Swedish/British triad, 2009 was also the year when top French sailors Loïck Peyron, Franck Cammas and Yann Guichard competed in the

Extreme Sailing Series. Dercksen, a restless entrepreneur who had already been active in the watch industry, sold his interest in the Series to OC Sport in 2010 to move on to his next project, high-end super-yacht tenders.

By 2011, the Series had filled out to an 11-venue tour. Qingdao (China) and Boston (USA) hosted events for the first time, while the regatta in Turkey saw a national TV broadcaster carry live racing for the first time. Istanbul was also memorable for the busy Bosphorus waterway being closed at race time. The racing catamarans took priority.

By 2012, OC Sport reckoned that one million spectators had seen the Extreme 40s race in venues around the world, and by 2014 the number of competing teams had risen to 11. St Petersburg (Russia) and Sydney (Australia) had joined the tour. As locations with iconic backdrops, they set an ever-higher standard.

The 2013 America's Cup in San Francisco picked up two key themes best seen in the Extreme Sailing Series; racing off city fronts and high-speed

multihulls. However, the sheer speed of America's Cup boats – because of their ability to foil above the water, powered by their high-tech, hard-wing sails – undoubtedly made the Extreme 40s look like last decade's technology.

The response of the Extreme Sailing Series was to retire the Extreme 40s for the 2016 season and replace them with GC32 catamarans. Although lacking the wing sails, with the extra logistics they demand, the GC32s have the ability to foil in winds as low as eight knots and to hit speeds as high as 39 knots.

The Extreme Sailing Series shows no sign of slowing down.

# Coastal/Inshore Races
# Sail Indonesia
## Indonesia

### Vital stats

**What:** Three-month-long rally event for cruisers

**Where:** Darwin (Australia) to Langkawi (Malaysia)

**How often:** Annual

**Boat type:** Monohulls, multihulls

**Crew:** Fully crewed

### Route tracker

Think of a contemporary way to run a sailing event and there would probably be no yacht club, no permanent office space, no landline and no fax machine. It would be a 'virtual' organization – and that's exactly how Sail Indonesia is run. It is a rally that leaves Darwin in Australia's Northern Territory in July each year for three months of rally-style yachting, as the fleet sails in company.

Only for the month before departure in Australia is there a fixed phone line. For the rest of the time, the organization resides in the ether, run primarily via the Sail Indonesia website.

Unsurprisingly, the target for Sail Indonesia is the long-distance, blue-water sailor. Variously these are the permanent liveaboards, those undertaking a circumnavigation or others wanting to carry out some significant ocean voyaging.

The Indonesian archipelago is one of the world's largest and boasts a high reputation for the quality of its diving, tropical rainforests, culture and wildlife. It is also on well-trodden tradewind routes for long-distance voyagers, as they loop around the world from east to west on the tradewind route. However, byzantine local regulations can make

visiting a red-tape nightmare of permits, visas and import/export licences that foreign yachts and their crews are subject to.

Hence the attraction of taking part in an organized event in a fleet, as opposed to being an individual yacht. The involvement of the Indonesian Confederation of Marine Tour Companies, GAHAWISRI, did much to facilitate the bureaucracy in the early events.

Part of the attraction of rallies is the social side, especially when couples or small groups are cruising together for extended periods. Poker pals, rum buddies and all sorts of cruising mates can bring variety when sharing anchorages, experiences, tips and know-how.

With government support, Sail Indonesia participants are also able to experience a full array of welcome ceremonies and festivities in communities where overseas visitors (from

Norway and New Zealand to Japan and Canada) are still occasional rather than routine.

The origins of the event go back to 2000, when Indonesia's tourism and maritime affairs ministries sought to bring a number of disparate sailing events under one umbrella. These started from Darwin as well as Fremantle in Western Australia and concluded in Batam, south of Singapore, following stops in Bali and Palau Seribu near Jakarta.

The ethos of keeping costs down by running a lean management structure goes all the way back to the beginning. In 2001, the first event saw 16 yachts leave Darwin. The hoped-for participants from Fremantle didn't materialize. The big Australian boats *Helsal II* and *Australian Maid* took line honours (130h) and handicap honours respectively. The fleet increased to 20 in 2002, and with a pre-start party and a finishing banquet, the event was putting down roots.

The format of Sail Indonesia has morphed on a regular basis, so that the route visits different cruising grounds. Between 2009 and 2014, there were different themes to Sail Indonesia: Sail Bunaken, Sail Banda, Sail Wakatobi-Belitung, Sail Morotai, Sail Komodo and Sail Raja Ampat. This was designed to introduce visiting yachtsmen to different locations and give a welcome lift to tourism.

By 2010 the participating fleet was regularly hitting 100, with 2012 seeing a peak of 133 yachts.

There was a setback in 2014 when the Kapung authorities impounded the yachts on arrival, proof that the red tape of permits and paperwork can still entangle even an organized fleet.

A new rival event – Sail2Inodnesia – something many of the established cruising rallies have experienced over the years, also made an impact on the 2014 Sail Indonesia, with entries dropping to around 50.

△ The Indonesian archipelago is one the world's largest, and a draw for sailors seeking the less well-travelled route.

# Darwin to Ambon

## Australia/Indonesia

### Route tracker

Ambon Island
INDONESIA
Palau Buru — Maluku
Nusa Tenggara — Timor — Palau Jamdena
Darwin
NORTHERN TERRITORIES
AUSTRALIA

### Vital stats

**What:** 634-mile inshore race

**Where:** Darwin (Australia) to Ambon (Indonesia)

**How often:** Annual

**Boat type:** Monohulls and multihulls

**Crew:** Fully crewed

The Darwin to Ambon race is another signifier of the spread of sailboat racing and cruising beyond its traditional roots in Europe, North and South America and Australasia.

This race from the capital of Australia's Northern Territory pretty much follows the rhumb-line course through the Timor and Arafua Seas, past the Indonesian island of Sermata, which lies off East Timor, and into the Banda Sea. There lies the island of Ambon and the finish.

In centuries past, traders travelled down from southeast Asia to the continent of Australia; in recent times, it is Australian sailors who have headed north. The distances are so great, and the destinations so few, that sailing to Western Australia or Queensland is not a well-travelled route. Going north, however, opens up a plethora of cruising grounds and different countries.

That was the thinking of the Darwin yachtsmen who organized the first race, originating in Australia and heading to another international port. That first race in 1973 to Dili, the capital of East Timor, was contested by just six yachts. The event grew over the next couple of years to a fleet of 60, but the unstable political situation in East Timor saw the cancellation of the 1975 race. From necessity, those creative Darwin sailors raced instead around the Bathurst and Melville Islands, a detour that found its own place in the race calendar.

*'The annual Darwin to Ambon yacht race is one of the many ways we maintain and strengthen our relationship with Ambon.'*

**Katrina Fong Lim** | Lord Mayor of Darwin

But a yearning to 'go foreign' saw a new race to Ambon for the first time in 1976, with six yachts contesting the pioneering contest. The 600-mile downwind track ended in the archipelago known to European (particularly Dutch, Spanish and Portuguese) and Chinese explorers as the Spice Islands, famous for the production of mace, cloves and nutmeg. They are properly known as the Maluku Islands, and are located northeast of Timor and west of New Guinea.

There are some 13,000 islands in Indonesia, so Ambon made an excellent jumping-off point for cruising amongst them or heading to other sailing events in Malaysia. Darwin itself is an excellent base for sailors and port of call for transiting yachts. A full range of engineering, sailmaking, electrical and repair services is available there, as well as business services and flight connections.

As happened with the Dili race that had preceded it, political instability impacted on the Ambon race and the decision was made to cancel it in 1998. This was a real setback given that entries had reached 100 in the previous year. The Ambon race wasn't run for another eight years, when the political situation was again considered stable.

21 July 2007 saw the race resume, and it has gone from strength to strength since. This followed a visit to Darwin by representatives from Ambon, and the reconfigured race was launched under the auspices of the Dinah Beach Cruising Yacht Association after a return visit reported favourably on the situation in Ambon. Other partners in the event include the Indonesian Ministry of Culture and Tourism and the Ambon City Government, plus the Northern Territory Government and the city of Darwin.

The race distance is 634 miles, with the current race record set by Darwinian John Punch in his catamaran *Zuma*. His record was 53h 29m in the 1998 race. The monohull record was set in 2014 by Geoff Hill from Hong Kong, with a time of 61h 02m in his Santa Cruz 70 *Antipodes*. Besides the monohull and multihull divisions, there is a class for yachts using motor assistance.

Apart from the experience of downwind sailing and finish festivities in such an exotic location, the race also has a strong sense of community. This includes a schools programme that raises money and donates books and sporting equipment to local Indonesian schools.

▽ The Darwin–Ambon race is pitched at blue-water sailors heading north from Australia's Northern Territory.

# Coastal/Inshore Races
# **Raja Muda Selangor Regatta**
Malaysia

*'It is unique in that it is made up of a collection of offshore passages, interspersed with inshore "round the cans" races. This provides for constantly changing conditions for the participants.'*

**Sharafuddin Idris Shah** | Current Sultan of Selangor and founder of the Raja Muda Selangor International Regatta

The Royal Selangor Yacht Club is Malaysia's oldest, and also its most forward thinking. Located less than an hour from Kuala Lumpur, the RSYC is the engine room for the expansion of yachting in Malaysia – and the Raja Muda Selangor International Regatta is very much its flagship event.

The format uses the well-trodden path of mixing inshore day races with passage races. It is built around the coastal races between Port Klang, Pangkor, Penang and Langkawi, totalling some 260 miles, interspersed with one day's racing at Penang and concluded by a further two days' racing run out of Kuah Harbour, Langkawi.

The Raja Muda Selangor International Regatta takes the fleet northwest along the Malaysian coast on the west side of the Malay peninsula before reaching its destination at the island of Langkawi. This gives crews a constantly changing mix of locations, and with towns, hotels and marinas at all locations, their needs are well catered for. Regatta dinners in the ports visited are welcome and, perhaps, expected. A little more out of the ordinary is a rickshaw race run in Penang's Straits Quay.

The regatta owes its birth to the King's Cup in Phuket, which was launched in 1987 to mark the king of Thailand's 60th birthday. Seeing that a number of yachts were transiting through the Royal Selangor Yacht Club, the Raja Muda (Crown Prince) of Selangor at the time decided to inaugurate a regatta that would give crews additional racing while making their way to Phuket.

Royal patronage of both events certainly helped to cement their positions from the outset, and Sharafuddin Idris Shah, the Sultan of Selangor, remains a keen sailor and ardent supporter of the growth of water-based sport and industry in his country. He has seen the Raja Muda Selangor International Regatta become one of Asia's major yachting events. Another signifier of this is the fact that the regatta is run in conjunction with Britain's

Royal Ocean Racing Club, organizer of the world-famous Fastnet and ever keen to foster offshore racing wherever it is found in the world.

From beginning to end, the event lasts nine days. The fleet attracts a broad spectrum, from grand-prix boats (built in increasing numbers in southeast Asia) to charter yachts and venerable cruisers. Oddly, the latest racers feature bowsprits from which to fly Code-series asymmetric downwind sails, while some of the old cruising boats also have bowsprits from which headsails are flown, traditional-style.

Makes such as J/Boats, Swan, X Yachts, Santa Cruz, Beneteau and Hanse are well represented, as are current hot race boats as well as those enjoying life extensions under their second or third owners. Prominent regular competitors over the years have included Hong Kong-based sailmaker Neil Pryde and businessman Frank Pong.

Light airs mean that dropping the anchor to avoid being carried back on the tide is always an option during the passage races. Another challenge are the many fishing nets (not all of which are lit) ready to snag the keels and rudders of the unfortunate or less than keen-eyed. Race officers have been known to send the fleet motoring towards the next finish when the wind has been unco-operative at scheduled start times, as delays can impact on the progression of the regatta from venue to venue.

## Vital stats

**What:** Coastal passage races and day races

**Where:** Port Klang to Langkawi (Malaysia)

**How often:** Annual

**Boat type:** Monohulls and multihulls

**Crew:** Fully crewed

## Route tracker

# Copa del Rey

Mallorca, Spain

*'They have sailed their way out of spots that we would not have sailed out of, just the difference in hull shapes and so on, that makes them quite slippery.'*

**Terry Hutchinson** | Tactician, *Quantum Racing*

There's a 1903 Copa del Rey and also a 1982 Copa del Rey in Spain. Both are named in honour of the king, although one is Spain's premier knock-out football competition and the other is the pre-eminent multi-class regatta in the Mediterranean.

It was the Asociación Nacional de Cruceros (National Cruisers Association) and the Real Club Náutico de Palma that took the plunge with the first Copa del Rey in 1982, their initiative rewarded with more than 50 boats competing. Palma was an ideal yachting hub, bristling with berths, services and yacht clubs long before the tourism boom turned the biggest of the Balearic islands into one the best airline-connected destinations in Europe.

The Real (royal) Club Náutico had already grown from its 1948 origins into one of Spain's most important clubs, and the Marivent Palace just outside Palma in Cala Major had long been the Spanish royal family's summer residence for its August vacation. The Bourbon family has a distinguished record of sailing at the highest level. The former king, Juan Carlos, competed in the 1972 Olympics in the Dragon class. It was his patronage, most often racing one of the many grand-prix boats bearing the *Bribon* name, that cemented the Copa del Rey's reputation. His son Felipe, who succeeded him, has continued to support the event. He raced in the 1992 Barcelona Olympics to sixth place, while Felipe's sister Christina also sailed for Spain in the previous Olympics in Korea.

The second Copa del Rey, in 1983, was notable for being won by *Barracuda*, a one-tonner designed by talented Majorcan naval architect and boatbuilder Pepin Gonzales, tragically killed in a road accident just as his reputation was growing.

King Juan Carlos won the next two regattas in *Bribon*, something repeated in 1993 and 1994. The regular presence of the king, and the fact that Majorcan businessmen and tourist leaders covered the cost of the royal racing yachts rather than using public funds, created a virtual circle of extensive media coverage and a raft of sponsors supporting the regatta and competing boats. Scroll back through the list of past winners, and *Bribon*

excepted, the others are invariably named after a brand such as commercial insurance, a bank, an aftershave, a beer or a car.

This blossoming of Spanish grand-prix yachting, built around the likes of Pedro Campos, Luis Doreste and Jaime Yllera in the 1980s and 1990s, is still felt today. Spanish top-level sailing spread its wings with the first of several America's Cup challenges in 1992.

For a time, it seemed that the clash of dates in August with Cowes Week might hamper the growth of Copa del Rey, but nothing of the sort happened. Not only did it prove a magnet for racing boats from Portugal and the Mediterranean, but it also attracted owners wanting a warm-weather alternative to the northern European summer-time regattas.

If there were growing pains, then they were similar to ones felt by other grand-prix regattas following the collapse of the IOR (International Offshore Rule) as the worldwide common currency rating in the 1980s. The replacement rules had a less universal take-up, but Spain stuck strongly to the IMS and ORC rules over the years.

From 2008, the regatta ran a mix of elapsed-time classes, mainly one-designs and 'box-rule' boats such as Swan 42s and TP52s, and corrected-time handicap classes. It was a quite a year, too, for El Desafio, Spain's America's Cup team, as they entered the TP52 and GP42 classes and won both. Nowadays, J/80s and X Yachts feature amongst the popular one-make classes. 2011, the 30th anniversary, saw José Cusi, skipper of *Bribon*, retire from the competition. He was the only person to have competed in all 30 regattas to that time.

While Cowes Week might have the black-tie balls of the principal yacht clubs, the Copa de Rey social programme is distinctly Mediterranean in feel, adding to the event's popularity. By 2014, King Felipe VI assumed the royal patronage mantle, and competed for the first time as monarch. As guest of honour at the prizegiving, he was able to present the trophies and shake the hands of the winners. It would seem that the allure and the competitiveness of Copa de Rey continues with the next generation.

**Vital stats**

**What:** One-week day-race regatta

**Where:** Palma da Majorca (Spain)

**How often:** Annual

**Boat type:** Monohulls

**Crew:** Fully crewed

**Route tracker**

◁ The final leg of the Copa del Rey regatta in Palma de Majorca, Spain

# Inshore Races
# Bol d'Or
## Lake Geneva, Switzerland

## Vital stats

**What:** 66.5-mile inshore race

**Where:** Start and finish in Geneva (Switzerland)

**How often:** Annual

**Boat type:** Monohulls and multihulls

**Crew:** Fully crewed

## Route tracker

The Bol d'Or is a lap of Lac Léman. Or, put another way, a race from Geneva eastwards to Le Bouveret and back to Geneva, a distance of some 66.5 miles.

It is one of the great European races, attracting some 26 boats when it was first run in 1939, with some 500-plus boats being the norm today. In 1990 a record 680 boats came to the start. Progress is such that the fastest boats now travel four to five times faster than the first winner, *Ylliam IV*, and the number of participants has grown 20-fold.

From the very outset, skippers and crews have eyed the top prize, the elegant Bol d'Or. Over the years this has led to the development of highly specialized lake-racer boats at the elite level of the fleet, boats that would typically be unsuitable for sailing in more open conditions.

In the 1970s and 1980s, the most advanced monohulls in the world could be found in the Bol d'Or fleet. These boats combined the fastest ideas from dinghies (high power-to-weight ratios and high righting moment) with those from keel boats (low-resistance hull forms and slender, high-lift ballasted keels). These hybrids were narrow-hulled boats with spindly, adjustable rigs carrying a mass of sail, kept on their feet by crews trapezing off the gunwhales or racks on the hull sides.

However, for the past 30 years or so, monohulls have given way in the first-to-finish stakes to the inherent lighter weight and sail-carrying power of multihulls. Monohull interest has not been eclipsed, however, with an additional prize, the Bol d'Or Vermeil, put up for their top honour.

The Bol d'Or itself is a one-day race, but the event has become a four-day affair. It typically kicks off on the Thursday of the race weekend with the opening ceremony and a celebrity race, followed by a skippers' briefing on the Friday. The race itself takes place on the Saturday, with the prizegiving on the Sunday.

The organizer, the Société Nautique de Genève, characterizes the race as a 'lake party', with a full range of activities at the clubhouse on the southern side of Lac Léman in Geneva's elegant suburbs. Paella and breakfasts for the 2,500-strong participating crew feature in the club's hospitality, as Switzerland's top yacht club opens its doors to both sailors and the public alike.

The Bol d'Or's fame has spread far, and there is always a good contingent of visiting entrants from within Europe. In 1989, Dennis Conner, the famous US sailor, brought the wingsailed 19.2-m (62-ft) catamaran *Stars & Stripes* over to Switzerland, after having won the America's Cup with it the year before.

Because the lake racers are so specialized, the organizers keep three boats of their own available for charter by overseas crews, as well as a crew

register exchange. This is aimed to facilitate visitors to this unusual event. The bulk of the fleet is made up of more ordinary boats, though still those suited to lake racing.

### A very Swiss affair

For a long period, the Bol d'Or was dominated by 6-m (19.7-ft) and 8-m (26.2-ft) boats, which racked up 30 wins between 1939 and 1969. Then came the Toucan period, triggered by the 21-year-old helmsman Philippe Durr, who raced the very first boat, *Toucan VI*, in 1971. She was only completed the day before the race, but her narrow lines and big spinnaker were perfect for Lac Léman

In 2011, the Toucan class managed to muster an entry of 40 boats to mark the their 40th anniversary. Sailors will always push themselves and their boats and, famously, Alain Gliksman entered a Toucan in the 1972 OSTAR/Transat and was the eighth monohull to complete the Plymouth–Newport transatlantic course – a stupendous achievement.

From 1980 multihulls have held sway, with the G32 a popular class. 1991 saw one of the most radical boats ever, Philippe Stern's *Altair XI*, picked up on the solid-wing sail first seen with *Stars & Stripes*. And before the America's Cup catamarans went foil-borne in 2013, the extraordinary *Mirabaud IX* demonstrated, through a hull made of carbon tubes to carry the rig and foil loads, that a conventional hull shell was not necessary if you 'fly about the water'. It looked like a bedstead flying over the water.

Given its location, it is no surprise that the Bol d'Or has attracted the elite of Swiss yachtsmen. Philippe Stern, whose family own the watchmakers Patek Philippe, is a seven-time winner; bio-tech billionaire and two-time America's Cup victor Ernesto Bertarelli is a six-time winner; Toucan ace Philippe Durr is another seven-time winner; and Louis Noverraz, who won an Olympic silver medal in 1968 in the 5.5-metre class aged 66, triumphed six times between 1939 and 1958.

△ Predominant light winds and flat water fostered the development of the specialized lake racers with big sail plans that compete in the Bol d'Or on Lac Léman.

# Coastal/Inshore Races
# Round Texel Race
## Texel, the Netherlands

*'This is amazing. We just went for it. Finally a normal Round Texel Race. Last year we were already hit and broken before the start.'*

**Carolijn Brouwer** | First female overall winner in the 35-year history of the race

## Vital stats

**What:** 62-mile coastal race

**Where:** Texel (the Netherlands)

**How often:** Annual

**Boat type:** Catamarans

**Crew:** Fully crewed

## Route tracker

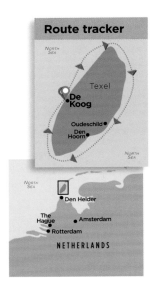

If we're talking numbers, the Round Texel Race is the clear winner for attracting the biggest catamaran fleet in the world.

The Romde um Texel loops around the island of Texel, one of the Frisian chain that arcs over the top of the Dutch and German North Sea coasts. They are low-lying and sandy, and the waters between them are so shallow that areas dry out between the tides. In short, they are perfect for racing small catamarans, launched off the beach.

The first Round Texel was in 1978. Germany's Sigi Lach won with a Hobie 14 ahead of 83 rivals. Since then, the race has gone on to attract a 600-plus field on a regular basis.

Catamarans have been raced at high levels for decades. Top-level cats had contested the 'Little America's Cup' – the International Catamaran Challenge Trophy – since 1961, and the Tornado had been an Olympic boat since 1976.

Then along came Californian Hobart 'Hobie' Alter. He had used his pioneering moulded foam and plastic manufacturing process – which had revolutionized the surfboard market in the 1960s – and applied it to turn out mass-market Hobie cats. These recreational boats were the opposite of the likes of the custom-built and costly Tornadoes. But, boy, did they succeed in turning on new generations of first timers to sailing and making

multihulls part of the mainstream. It was this wave that the Round Texel Race rode.

The Round Texel Race starts and finishes at Paal 17, a beach complete with bars, informal dining, pavilions and unobstructed views across the North Sea all the way to the sunset. The North Sea might not be California, but the Frisian Islands enjoy a similarly laidback lifestyle.

June is the fixed month for the race, although the particular Saturday on which it is staged depends on the tides in a particular year. The start is just ahead of high water, as to complete the 62-mile course, the boats have to sizzle over the extensive shallows to the northeast of the islands.

Shallow water and a holiday atmosphere make the race sound easy. It's not. Besides the high-energy competition, it's an exposed course and the wind can turn it on. 2005 is still remembered for being a wild and woolly race.

There is also the ever-present risk of collision with other boats, or the sudden deceleration as daggerboards and rudders run into mud or sand in the shallow water. This can fling crew forwards around the spindly wires supporting the rig, the forces even greater on the faster, bigger boats with both crew out on twin trapezes.

There is more water than a dewy field, but

not much. Informality reigns, although massed ranks of sailors are bound to be competitive and the fleet always includes some star names. That's part of the attraction for the weekend amateurs. Raced against and beat a world champion? Did it! Finished in front of an Olympic gold medallist? Yes!

Over the years, the stars have shone. First was Briton Reg White, the man who had built the Tornado prototype for the trials to select a catamaran for the Olympics. He went on to become the class's first world champion and first gold medallist in 1976. White won the Round Texel in 1994, aged 54.

Australia's Darren Bundock, a double Olympic silver medallist from 2000 and 2008, won the race in 2003 and again in 2007. Then he sailed with his current world-champion crew, Glenn Ashby. Both men went on to be America's Cup sailors, with Ashby also proving to be the world's best in the singlehanded, international A-class catamaran

category. To 2015, he'd won seven consecutive world titles.

Over the years, the bigger, faster and more complex cats such as the Hobie Tiger and F-18 have done well on handicap, largely because they are able to get free of the mêlée and sail more efficient and less tactically compromised races.

Bundock's wife, Carolijn Brouwer, is also part of the Round Texel's honour roll. A world champion in the Laser Radial and Europe women's singlehander class, Brouwer competed in three Olympics and was a helmsman in two Volvo Ocean Races on *Amer Sports Two* (2001/2) and *Team SCA* (2014/5).

In 2012 Brouwer and Wouter Samama (himself a former line-honours winner) won, the Dutch sailor becoming the first female helmsman to triumph on corrected time. The pair completed the course in 2h 51m with a big lead, and won the race with a corrected handicap time of 3h 10m.

△ The low-lying Friesian Islands mean plenty of winds for the world's biggest catamaran race.

## Coastal/Inshore Races
# Barcolana
Italy

*'Being at the starting line together with so many yachts is really challenging, even dangerous. Combined with light winds, which favoured the smaller yachts, it was a difficult race.'*

**Jochen Schümann** | Skipper of *Esmit Europa 2*

I n Trieste there is lighthouse – Farro della Vittoria – that's built on the foundations of a former Austrian fortress, designed to be higher than Berlin's 63-m (204-ft) Victory Column that sits at the opposite end of the Tiergarten to the Brandenburg Gate.

It commemorates Italy's dead from the Second World War. At the top of the 68-m (220-ft) tower is a bronze, winged Victory, carrying a torch in one hand and a laurel wreath in the other. To photographers covering the Barcolana regatta, the elevated Victory makes a perfect juxtaposition with the huge fleet of yachts on the water below.

'Huge' is the only suitable word. Entries have exceeded 2,000, with all the boats competing off a single start line. That equates to something like 25,000 sailors on the water and 250,000 spectators watching the show from the shore.

Standing sentinel across the Bay of Trieste at the other end of the long start line is the Miramare castle, built in the 1850s as a summer house for Archduke Ferdinand Maximilian of Austria. It is another irresistible attraction for photographers wanting the defining Barcolana image.

Curiously for such a big regatta, the Barcolana is not well known. Yet it is spectacular, due to the sheer numbers of yachts competing. It is the biggest Mediterranean regatta of all, and one of the largest regattas in the world. What separates the Barcolana is that the fleet races *en masse*. It's a thrilling, wonderful and nerve-wracking spectacle, one-part competition and one-part festival, and so much more than the sum of its parts.

There is a certain organized chaos that goes with the Barcolana. Understandably, the facilities are stretched to breaking point – try finding a hotel in Italy and Slovenia within 35 miles that's not been booked months in advance, or repeated year on year. Mooring typically sees yachts rafted up to ten deep on one berth or buoy, and yachts frequently go around turning marks 100 abreast.

◁ The massed start of the Barcolana fleet, under the watchful eye of Trieste's Farro della Vittoria.

All sorts of boats are eligible, from boats up to 6.5m (21ft) in length to giants, classed in increasing size from maxi and super maxi to mega yacht (above 24m/78.7ft). Feeder races from Split and Rijeka (Croatia) and Isola (Slovenia) help brings yachts to the head of the Adriatic Sea and Gulf of Trieste.

The Barcolana has blossomed into something that floods millions of euros into the local economy, a fact that is recognized by political figures. In 2011, the winner was *Esmit Europa 2*. Owned by Igor Simic, the crew was led by German Olympic gold-medallist Jochen Schümann, it carried the European Union flag, counted José Manuel Barroso, former president of the European Commission, as her patron and was sponsored by Russian energy giant Gazprom.

The October wind is not always co-operative, capable of being strong, the Bora that whistles down from the Alps, or completely absent. It vanished during the 2012 race, with only 20 yachts from 1,737 starters finishing inside the time limit.

This mad and magnificent event was started back in 1969 by the local yacht club Società Velica di Barcola e Grignano. The second Sunday in October has been the day of Barcolana from the outset. Over the years, the course has changed a little, including an excursion into nearby Slovenian waters, but generally it is a 13–17-mile rough square or triangle course. In recent years, it has been brought closer to the Piazza Unita d'Italia to maximize the link to the shoreside festival. This covers the whole gamut of food, wine, culture and music.

The Barcolana itself is augmented by preceding events such as historic wooden yacht races, a kids' Optimist-class regatta, kitesurfers, windsurfers and, in 2014, a round of the Extreme Sailing Series.

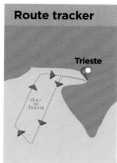

**Route tracker**

**Vital stats**

**What:** 15-mile coastal race

**Where:** Trieste (Italy)

**How often:** Annual

**Boat type:** Monohulls

**Crew:** Fully crewed

# The Sailors

## Ocean Greats
# Dame Ellen MacArthur

*'Francis has set us another very high benchmark – the chances of breaking it are very slim but if we don't try, we won't know.'*

**Ellen MacArthur** | On the solo round-the-world record held by Francis Joyon that she was about to smash

Some first meetings you don't forget, and your author's encounter with Ellen MacArthur was one such occasion. I met her when she called into *Yachting World* magazine's stand at the Southampton Boat Show as a 17-year-old full of ambition, infectious enthusiasm and the no-fear confidence of youth.

Definitely not a bright-eyed dreamer but a young woman going places, Ellen had already sailed around Britain on her own and become the youngest-ever person to be awarded a Yachtmaster qualification.

She was introduced to sailing by an aunt and famously saved her dinner money whilst at school to put towards buying a run-down 6-m (19-ft) Coribee in which she was to circumnavigate Britain. France was the hot-house of solo sailing in the 1990s, so she moved there and took on the 1997 Mini Transat race in *Le Poisson*, finishing 17th in the race from France to Brazil via the Canaries.

When Mike Golding, one of Britain's established sailing stars, was building a new Open 60 for the Vendée Globe round-the-world race, MacArthur lived in a shipping container in the same boatyard, doing odd jobs and immersing herself totally in seeing how a solo campaign ticked.

Others saw her determination to succeed and the rare ability to express herself in a way that connected with non-sailors, and she secured sponsorship for her own Open 60 to contest the gruelling solo Vendée Globe in 2000/1. In *Kingfisher*, she finished second and, aged 24, was the youngest-ever person to complete the race.

She was headline news in France and Britain, capturing perfectly the spirit of one person against the sea. By 2000, the power and time consumption of sending video back from a yacht via satellite communication was much more viable. MacArthur was one of its first stars, adept at taking followers thousands of miles away so that they felt her anguish, frustrations, anxieties and joys as if they were onboard *Kingfisher* too.

Two years later, she suffered a setback in her second round-the-world venture when dismasted in the Southern Ocean while attempting the fully crewed Trophee Jules Verne outright circumnavigation record.

However, in 2004/5 MacArthur achieved worldwide recognition in setting a new solo round-the-world record in her *B&Q/Castrama* trimaran. Her time of 71d 14h sliced 30 hours off the previous record, set by France's Francis Joyon.

Although obsessed with sailing ever since reading the books of Francis Chichester and Robin Knox-Johnston as a child, MacArthur was changed by her own sailing experiences in her appreciation of the world.

After planning another bid to win the Vendée Globe with another new boat, she chose to hang up her sea boots and create a foundation to focus on how we use the finite resources of our planet, advocating a more holistic approach to how we manage production and consumption.

In doing this, she left the Offshore Challenges/OC Group company that she'd formed with Mark Turner, a fellow competitor in the 1997 Mini Transat race. OC had grown into one of the most significant businesses, not just in yacht racing – project managing a stable of boats and sailors – but also in land-based adventure sports, all using the mass communication tools used so effectively during MacArthur's own solo circumnavigations.

△ Previous page:
Ellen MacArthur at the helm of her Open 60 Kingfisher during the 2000/1 Vendée Globe.

◁ Climbing to the end of the boom, Ellen MacArthur untangles the reefing lines.

## Vital stats

**Name:** Ellen MacArthur

**DoB:** 08/07/1976

**Nationality:** British

**Known for:** Fastest solo circumnavigation in 2005

# Ocean Greats
# Hilary Lister

*'On the water, I'm not just a body in a wheelchair.'*

Hilary Lister

The scale of Hilary Lister's achievement is staggering. Within two years of starting sailing for the first time, she crossed the English Channel alone from Dover to Calais.

The year was 2005, the time taken 6h 13m. Setting this voyage apart was the fact that Lister was so disabled, she could only handle the boat by 'suck and blow' commands into the straws controlling the electronic systems that adjusted the helm and trimmed the sails.

Lister was born able bodied but lost the use of her legs by her 15th birthday. Her condition progressively deteriorated so that when she crossed the Channel aged 33, she had no movement below her neck whatsoever.

Hilary Lister's story is all about what she is able to do, not what she can't. By the time she'd crossed the Channel, she had already completed her biochemistry degree at Oxford University, despite dictating her exam papers while being given epidural pain relief in her back, and was well into postgrad studies at the University of Kent. By 1999, the use of her arms was no longer possible.

Remarkably, the Dover–Calais crossing was not so much an ambition fulfilled, but the trigger to tackle even more difficult feats.

Two years later, she sailed around the Isle of Wight. The 50-mile voyage took 11 hours. And in 2008 and 2009, she sailed all the way around Britain in a stage-by-stage voyage. A dream to sail across the Atlantic still burns brightly.

Growing up, Hilary was sports-mad. Riding, swimming, hockey, netball, canoeing, fencing and rugby were her loves. She captained school teams and entered country-level competitions.

She was good enough to qualify for the British Paralympic team as a swimmer, but had to choose between her studies and training.

Ultimately, Lister determined that her degenerative condition was not going to define the limits of what she could do.

From a low point of feeling that everything she had cherished, from music to sport, was locked away forever, a day out sailing with a charity opportunity scheme reignited her dreams. 'Going sailing turned a light back on inside me,' she says. 'Sailing has given me a sense of freedom I never thought was possible.'

Lister is in no doubt that sailing saved her life. Of that first outing and subsequent ventures, she remembers: 'Going out of the front door that day was the hardest thing I'd ever done. It's hard to explain what it's like being stuck in a wheelchair. Here, I'm the boss. As well as steering, I can chose to sail flat, or go faster. It's wonderful to have choice again.'

Voice recognition and a switch activated by her forehead permitted Lister to carry out some simple tasks from her wheelchair at home, such as changing TV channels. Similar, but vastly more complex, control mechanisms were used to modify boats especially for her. The system of three straws connected to pressure-sensitive micro-switches was designed by Canadian Steve Alvey of Calgary and installed in *Me Too*, the Artemis 20 designed by Rogers Yacht Design and built especially for Hilary.

A chance meeting at the London Boat Show brought her together with the Royal Yachting Association, sailing benefactor Andrew Pindar and the UK Sailing Academy. They have all given her the training and support she needed.

▷ Only being able to move her head, Hilary Lister controls her boat with the help of three straws.

Creating the boat and the back-up team on land and water was a significant undertaking for the 3,000-mile Atlantic voyage that started and finished in Dover. In the first year, Lister was hospitalized in Plymouth after experiencing breathing difficulties, but remained undeterred.

Besides her Atlantic ambition, Lister works tirelessly for Hilary's Dream Trust to raise funds for other disabled sailors. In 2014 she sailed from Mumbai in India to Oman in the Gulf, with an Omani woman as her co-skipper as part of a commitment to increase opportunities for others facing challenges like hers. She is truly inspirational.

## Vital stats

**Name:** Hilary Lister

**DoB:** 03/03/1972

**Nationality:** British

**Known for:** Being a quadriplegic sailor

# Ocean Greats
# **Vinny Lauwers**

*'Through the marvels of modern technology, you are invited to climb aboard and set sail with me.'*
Vinny Lauwers

It took seven years to prepare for and seven months to complete. But on 12 August 2000, when Australian Vinny Lauwers sailed up Port Philip Bay and home to Melbourne, it was with the satisfaction of having been successful in what he'd set out to do: to become the first disabled person to sail non-stop around the world without assistance.

After a difficult childhood and troubled adolescence, Lauwers suffered a life-threatening accident when he was 22 years old. A car sped through a stop sign, struck him on his motorcycle and severed his spine in three places. He survived, only to face the new reality that he was no longer able to walk. Furthermore, his zest for life was extinguished. He was told he no longer had a job at the steelworks that employed him. Pain seemed ever present; a decent night's sleep ever elusive. His morale plummeted and his world closed in around him.

Lauwers picked himself up, shook off his despair and set about living the rest of his life in a stimulating and fulfilling way. Sailing was to prove his pathway back to recovery.

He rediscovered the sport having first experienced it when crewing on a yacht, aged 14, for the long passage from Melbourne to Sydney. The period after his injury was filled with pain and he underwent multiple bouts of surgery. But in that time, he'd had a dream of sailing around the world.

The trigger was renting a video that had a photograph of a yacht on its cover. It was about the Australian yachtswoman Kay Cottee, who in 1989 was the first woman to sail non-stop around the world. By 1993, a motivated Lauwers was rebuilding his strength having taken up wheelchair racing, and the circumnavigation dream, Lauwers likes to say, was then born with the help with a bottle or two of wine. Helping to get him back on the water was the Australian SWD charity – Sailors with disABILITIES – and they were intent on proving the naysayers wrong by competing in the 1994 Sydney–Hobart race. They completed the course, and SWD has continued to enter a crew every year since.

SWD founder David Pescud recalls that 1994 race to Hobart: 'Vinny came on board with some knowledge of boating and yachting. It was an absolute pleasure to help him reach the next level. Vinny was like a sponge – we couldn't feed him information fast enough. And throughout the steep learning curve and rough seas, Vinny was a wonderful shipmate and a great person to have in your team.'

His yacht, a van de Stadt-designed 14.6-m (47-ft) boat, was named *Vision Quest*. Lauwers managed its build from glassfibre himself, ploughing his AUS $400,000 accident compensation payout into the project, considering it a better investment than 'sitting back at home and watching TV for the rest of my life.'

Lauwers completed a solo Melbourne to Hobart passage in five days before his circumnavigation, although the return trip was far more taxing. Autopilot failure meant that he hand-steered for 12 of the 14 days. As preparation, it was exactly the sort of experience he needed.

In October 1999, he set off. Amongst those making their farewells was the then Victoria state premier Steve Bracks, who had become one of the many people inspired by what Lauwers was trying to do.

The 21,000-mile voyage threw plenty at Lauwers, and not just strong winds and big, breaking seas. Continuing autopilot problems persisted for much of the voyage. His radar failed. The wind generator self-destructed. The wear and tear list was long.

'I never thought I couldn't make it,' said Lauwers on his return. 'The sailing-round-the-world experience allowed me to come to terms with myself and put life into perspective. The troubles of the world and everyday life in society faded away.'

Accolades and awards recognized his astonishing achievement, and today he continues his work as an inspirational speaker.

## Vital stats

**Name:** Vinny Lauwers

**DoB:** 12/09/1967

**Nationality:** Australian

**Known for:** Being the first disabled person to sail non-stop and unassisted around the world

◁ Vinny Lauwers sailed the Van De Stadt-designed 14.6-m (47-ft) yacht *Vision Quest* around the world.

Ocean Greats
# Sir Peter Blake

> *'To win, you have to believe you can do it. You have to be passionate about it. You have to really "want" the result – even if this means years of work. The hardest part of any big project is to begin. We have begun – we are underway – we have a passion. We want to make a difference.'*

**Sir Peter Blake** | Last log-book entry in 2001

I f one man towers over New Zealand sailing, it is Sir Peter Blake.

He rode the wave that started in the 1960s when *Rainbow* won the One Ton Cup, as the Kiwis first stretched their muscles to the point where, within 20 years, New Zealand sailors, designers and boatbuilders were widely acknowledged as the world's best.

Blake was the skipper who captured the public imagination in the Whitbread Round the World Race, and he rewarded the sailing-mad Kiwi public with an emphatic win in 1989/90 with *Steinlager 2*. After three failed attempts at the America's Cup in 1987, 1988 and 1992, he led Team New Zealand to another emphatic victory in 1995.

The tragedy of the Blake story is that the man who enriched so many lives, and who was so respected around the world, met an untimely death – murdered in Brazil by armed criminals on the Amazon river in 2001. He was 53. Since his death, unsubstantiated reports suggest that his murder was linked to the illegal logging trade. Part of his Blakexpedition's brief was to sail to environmentally sensitive regions of the world and raise awareness of ecological issues.

It is difficult to overstate the impact of Blake's success and death on New Zealand. In a small country of four million people, he was known the length and breadth of the North and South Islands.

Winning the America's Cup was as significant for the country as Sir Edmund Hillary conquering Everest in 1953. Noted commentator Peter Montgomery, who broadcast to the world the moment Team New Zealand's *NZL 32* crossed the finish line – 'Now the America's Cup is New Zealand's cup!' – described the celebrations on the team's homecoming as something not seen since the Anzac troops returned home from the Second World War.

Then-Prime Minister Helen Clark had visited Blake on the Amazon three weeks before his murder to support his environmental project with the yacht *Seamaster*. She spoke at his funeral in England, and said these words at the memorial service at Auckland's Domain a few days later: 'Our small nation went into shock. Peter Blake was

## Vital stats

**Name:** Sir Peter Blake

**Dates:** 01/10/1948–06/12/2001

**Nationality:** New Zealand

**Known for:** Whitbread Round the World Race and America's Cup winner

◁ 'Big Red', as Peter Blake's all-conquering Whitbread Race-winning maxi *Steinlager 2* was known.

a living legend. As an outstanding sailor, he had brought great honour and fame to New Zealand. His death was unthinkable.'

What set Blake apart was leadership and charisma. He had an aura that could shift the atmosphere in a room full of people. He engendered unshakable loyalty amongst those who sailed with him, able to do any job on a boat himself, no matter how menial, but possessing unquestioned authority when called for. When he led Team New Zealand to its America's Cup win, Blake was the boss who had a boiler suit hanging in his office. He would routinely muck in and wet-sand the hull with the rest of the crew after racing.

Blake towered over the sport he graced. He never lost the tousled, Viking-blond hair of his teens, nor his moustache. As an itinerant crew member, his nicknames were `Six-Four' (his height) and `Blakey'. The latter stuck long after his achievements were recognized with honours: an MBE in 1983, an OBE in 1991 and a knighthood in 1995.

Blake grew up near the water in Bayswater, on Auckland's north shore. The Blakes were a sailing family, his father a Royal Navy gunboat captain during the Second World War. Peter was considered a natural on boats and with his brother Tony, a noted marine artist, was always afloat. The water was their playground. The family cruised north to Tonga and Tahiti, and the brothers raced in P- and Z-class dinghies in the Auckland Hauraki Gulf with boundless enthusiasm. Peter built his own cruising boat in a shed he'd put in front of his parents' bedroom window.

Like many Kiwis of his generation, he wanted to sample the world on an OE – overseas experience – and sailing was his ticket to do just that. Blake had studied at Auckland Tech and crewed on boats in New Zealand, but the notion of being able to make a career out of racing boats was then yet to become a reality.

A chance meeting in Malta with British yachtsmen Les Williams and Robin Knox-Johnston saw Blake join their 22-m (71-ft) *Ocean Life* in the Cape Town–Rio race. Cheerful, keen, strong and skilled, Blake was the dream crew.

Blake joined the British duo aboard *Condor* in the 1977/8 Whitbread Round the World race, suffering what was to become the first of two high-profile dismastings. The second, four years later, aboard the all-New Zealand designed/built/crewed *Ceramco*, of which Blake was the fully-fledged skipper, knocked the stuffing out of an epic duel with the eventual race winner, Cornelis van Rietschoten from the Netherlands.

However, the reports during this race, in which Blake communicated with Peter Montgomery through all sorts of atmospherics and interference on the radiotelephone, captivated New Zealand and brought the deep ocean into the homes, cars and offices of ordinary people.

In all, Blake went on to complete 600,000 miles of ocean racing, amongst them five Whitbread Round the World races including the all-conquering *Steinlager 2* victory in 1989/90. He set only the second sub-80-day round-the-world record on *ENZA* to claim the Jules Verne Trophy in 1994 with a time of 74d 22h 17m, and he headed Team New Zealand's America's Cup win in San Diego against Dennis Conner in 1995, plus the successful defence of the famous trophy in Auckland in 2000. It was the first time a challenger had held on to the Cup after winning it.

Blake described wining the America's Cup as the 'greatest gift a sportsman could give to his nation'. Certainly it brought about modernization of the Auckland city-front and a massive outpouring of national pride.

After the 2000 win, the forming of Blakexpeditions marked a new phase in his life. Blake had left competitive sailing behind and purchased *Seamaster*, a specially built expedition yacht with super-strong bows and lifting keel, in order to explore some of the world's most remote yet ecologically significant areas. Prior to the Amazon venture, *Seamaster* had already visited Antarctica.

'Good water; good life. Poor water; poor life. No water; no life,' was Blakexpeditions' guiding belief. Blake's plan was to travel to the source of the Amazon, taking *Seamaster* as far as possible into the heart of Amazonia and completing the voyage by canoe and on foot. Sadly, on 6 December 2001 at Macapa, Blake was shot, defending the lives of his crewmen from armed men who had boarded under the cover of darkness. It was the most terrible loss – to sailing, to New Zealand and to all who knew him.

*'I think Peter is to the waters what Sir Edmund Hillary has been to the mountains. He's just the most amazingly accomplished yachtsman. He is an inspiration to all New Zealanders.'*

**Helen Clark** | Former prime minister of New Zealand

▽ Peter Blake breaks the world record of the Race Around The World with his multihull *Enza* on 1 April, 1994.

# Ocean Greats
# Paul Larsen

## Vital stats

**Name:** Paul Larsen

**DoB:** 16/01/1970

**Nationality:**
Australian

**Known for:** Being a
world-record-setting
speed sailor

Imagine 120kph (75mph) speeds on the water.
Then imagine hitting this speed by wind power
alone…

This is the measure of Paul Larsen, who twice
set the fastest outright speed under sail recognized
by the World Sailing Speed Record Council. On
18 November 2012, Larsen piloted – it's the
appropriate word – Vestas *Sailrocket 2* to hit a
speed of 59.25 knots over a measured 500-m
(1,640-ft) run in Namibia.

It was the culmination of ten years of
dedicated development work in the design,
building and sailing of a speed sled specifically
aiming at becoming the fastest wind-propelled
vehicle on water. And there was more to come.
On 22 November, Larsen raised the world record
to a breathtaking 65.45 knots.

Rather like the race to break the sound barrier
in the aftermath of the Second World War, so the
50-knot barrier had long held sailors in its thrall.
But unlike the sound barrier, which attracted the
best of the British, American and Russian aircraft
manufacturers, speed sailing has rarely attracted
big factory teams.

When the World Sailing Speed Record
Council first adjudicated the record in 1972, Tim
Colman's *Crossbow* managed 26.3 knots. It took
until 1988 for 40 knots to be reached, and there
was a real sense that a barrier existed beyond
this level. It was not until 2008 that 50 knots was
passed for the first time by Sébastien Cattelan on
a kitesurfer.

The power–weight ratio favoured kitesurfers
until another Frenchman, Alain Thébault, set a new
record in 2009 of 51.56 knots in something that

could be called a boat — his *l'Hydroptère* was a
foiling trimaran.

Paul Larsen had sailed plenty of miles in big
multihulls with the likes of Skip Novak, Bruno
Peyron, Pete Goss, Tony Bullimore and Tracy
Edwards before creating a small, tight group of
enthusiasts to try and build the fastest boat on
the planet.

The team's first *Sailrocket* was self built in 2002,
with Malcolm Barnsley, a naval architect, working
with wind turbine-makers Vestas, the lead designer.
Larsen's team deconstructed the idea of a sailboat
and re-assembled their thinking in a way designed
to remove capsizing forces.

*Sailrocket 2* uses a wingsail to create the power,
but it flies on its own small skid float some 9.3m

> '*Most sailors think of a sailboat as something that reaches up to grab a bit of air, but why not build it like a plane that reaches down and grabs the water?*'
>
> **Paul Larsen** | Explaining the idea behind Vestas *Sailrocket*

(30ft) separate from the 12.4-m (40-ft), fuselage-like control pod in which Larsen pilots the vessel.

The key is the wing's location and inclination into the wind. The forces acting on it do not produce a capsizing effect. It is opposed by a hydrofoil, and the load on it and the wing cancel each other out. The net effect is that virtually all power translates into forward propulsion.

The forces the wing generates as *Sailrocket 2* speeds up are phenomenal. In *Sailrocket 1*, Larsen was launched 15.5m (50ft) into the air when a gust got underneath the boat. Larsen landed upside down and backwards, but avoided serious injury. Not for nothing does *Sailrocket 2* have a five-point safety harness for its driver.

Larsen has re-invented the sailboat with little

more than a school education and a free-roaming mind. Before settling in the UK, he had grown up in rural southeast Australia. 'We were thick in the bush – 30 acres, no phones, no TV, and stinking-hot summers. We grew up climbing trees and going down wombat holes.'

A seminal moment for Larsen was reading a book by American rocket engineer Bernard Smith, published in 1963, that proposed the aerohydrofoil concept for sailboats. 'Most sailors think of a sailboat as something that reaches up to grab a bit of air,' Larsen says, echoing Smith. 'But why not build it like a plane that reaches down and grabs the water?'

Larsen's next objective? 100 knots…

△ Paul Larsen aboard Vestas *Sailrocket* – the world's fastest sailboat.

# Ocean Greats
# Sir Francis Chichester

## Vital stats

**Name:** Sir Francis Chichester

**Dates:** 17/09/1901–26/08/1972

**Nationality:** British

**Known for:** Being a pioneering solo circumnavigator

△ In *Gipsy Moth IV*, Chichester kick-started modern solo circumnavigation in 1966/7.

F rancis Chichester epitomized the gentLéman adventurer, first in aviation and then in sailing, becoming famous for sailing around the world in 1966/7.

He was neither the first man to sail around the world nor the first to do it non-stop, but he did prove that the latter was possible and kickstart the huge interest in solo sailing that continues to this day.

American Joshua Slocum is credited as the pioneer solo circumnavigator. Between 1895 and 1898, Slocum spent more than three-and-a-half years threading his way around the world. He made frequent stops at anchor and in port. His book, *Sailing Around the World*, is considered a masterpiece of travel writing and has been an inspiration to countless sailors since.

Slocum's multi-stop voyage was due to the speed of his yacht *Spray* and the limitations of self-steering (a tied-off wheel and balanced sail trim), food and water capacity.

When Francis Chichester set off from Plymouth on 27 August 1966, he reached Sydney in 117 days. Departing again on 29 January 1967, he returned to Plymouth via Cape Horn in 119 days for total time of 226 days.

It was the longest solo voyage ever achieved, and his circumnavigation totally changed the perception of what was possible by one person in endurance passage-making. One key to his success was the development of a self-steering mechanism that linked a wind vane to a small servo rudder.

Chichester also created the template that those who followed in his wake strove to emulate: a yacht designed and equipped specifically to be sailed by one person; commercial backing (Chichester's *Gipsy Moth IV* carried the logo of the British Wool Council); and also recognition of the news value and public interest (albeit reluctantly on Chichester's part) in the 'one person against the sea' narrative.

Even if Chichester had not taken up sailing in 1953 when he was in his fifties, he would have been remembered for his flying feats and contributions to the advancement of air navigation.

Chichester came from a good family, emigrating after the First World War to New Zealand to make a mark in mining, farming and as a land agent. What wealth he amassed was partly wiped out in the Depression of the mid 1920s, but on returning to England he had enough funds to learn to fly at Brooklands in 1929, after which he bought a de Havilland Gipsy Moth biplane.

In flying back to New Zealand he was thwarted in his quest to beat Bert Hinckler's 1928 solo record from England to Australia, but Chichester went on to pioneer overwater flights to remote locations in the Pacific. He developed a concept of offset navigation, using sextant sun sights to fix his location at calculated distances from known landmarks. The previously hit-and-miss perils of finding islands in the ocean now had a mathematical solution.

His work for the Royal Air Force during the Second World War allowed single-engined fighter pilots to make long-range flights using knee-top calculations based on similar principles. Buying up surplus wartime maps, he then launched a successful mapping business in London that is still run by his son Giles today.

Prior to his circumnavigation, Chichester had already made his mark in the 1960 Transat/OSTAR singlehanded transatlantic race. He was among the five sailors to take up the challenge from war hero Lieutenant Colonel 'Blondie' Hasler for a race from Plymouth to the USA. At 12.4m (40ft), *Gipsy Moth III* was the largest yacht and romped home in 40 days, more than week ahead of Hasler himself. Chichester was second behind Eric Tabarly in the 1964 race, but already his mind was on *Gipsy Moth IV* and the round-the-world voyage.

On his return, Chichester was knighted at Greenwich, London. In a ceremony full of symbolism, Queen Elizabeth II used the same sword that Queen Elizabeth I had knighted Francis Drake with in the same place centuries before in 1581.

*Gipsy Moth IV* was preserved alongside the tea clipper *Cutty Sark*, but was freed from her concrete tomb at Greenwich when it was discovered that rainwater was rotting her from the inside out. She was restored from 2003–06 and sailed the world once again, marking the 40th anniversary of Chichester's epoch-defining voyage.

△ This image of *Gipsy Moth IV* rounding Cape Horn carrying only a storm jib painted a vivid picture to the non-sailing general public.

# Ocean Greats
# Sir Robin Knox-Johnston

## Vital stats

**Name:** Sir Robin Knox-Johnston

**DoB:** 17/03/1939

**Nationality:** British

**Known for:** Being the first person to sail solo, non-stop, around the world

△ Knox-Johnston entered the 1968/9 Golden Globe race having recently retired from the merchant navy. He went on to win in *Suhali*.

Few are the achievements that can never be surpassed, but such is Robin Knox-Johnston's feat of being the first person to sail around the world, alone and non-stop. He considered the objective as 'about the last thing there was left to do' in terms of exploring, discovering and conquering, and he may have been right.

In the 1960s, long-distance solo sailing was anything but routine. Following Francis Chichester's one-stop circumnavigation of 1966/7, and with the 1960s in Britain in full swing, *The Sunday Times* newspaper staged the Golden Globe race for a non-stop singlehanded race around the world.

Nine sailors started; only one finished. Knox-Johnston's 313 days (or 312 days, as he likes to claim, because of the International Date Line) earned his place in history. By contrast, Chichester spent 226 days at sea in his bigger, faster boat.

Knox-Johnston went on to have a full and varied sailing career and in 2014, aged 75, achieved a third-in-class finish in the Route du Rhum transatlantic.

He made the historic circumnavigation in the 10-m (32-ft), William Atkins-designed *Suhali*, which Knox-Johnston had built in India in the Mumbai docks while he was serving as second officer on a British India Line passenger ship working between Basra and Mumbai. Built from solid teak, and based on the Colin Archer style of double-ended sailing boats, *Suhali* had modest speed but good performance as a sea boat.

Rather like Francis Chichester's *Gipsy Moth IV*, *Suhali* had to be recovered from an existence as a museum exhibit. She is once again in Knox-Johnston's hands, being restored and refastened.

Fellow Britons John Ridgway and Chay Blyth set off ahead of Knox-Johnston in less suitable boats, and in Blyth's case sorely lacking experience. Both made stops to receive assistance and were already disqualified before they later quit.

Knox-Johnston had his own issues to contend with. Leaking keel fastenings forced him to dive under the boat and caulk the seams. His self-steering, a wind vane driving a servo rudder, caused repeated problems, as did the main rudder and continuing leaks.

He dropped mail off in South Australia and south New Zealand, was but not seen again until the north Atlantic where, as a merchant navy officer who had joined the Royal Navy Reserve at school (becoming a lieutenant commander by 1989), he used his Aldis lamp to signal his identity in Morse code.

Such was the scepticism and ignorance of what human beings could achieve after extended solitude at sea, he was given a thorough physical and psychological examination on his triumphant return to Falmouth. 'Distressingly normal', was the verdict.

As the first, only and fastest finisher, Knox-Johnston received the Golden Globe trophy and a £5,000 prize. What Knox-Johnston did with the rest of his life is quite remarkable. He had the audacity to sail the 22-m (71-ft) *Ocean Life*, a boat typically requiring a crew of at least a dozen, with Les Williams to win the two-handed 1970 Round Britain Race.

Somehow he crammed in competing in the Whitbread Round the World Race (1973/4) with *Condor*, the Round Britain Race with *British Oxygen*

(1974), the Weymouth Speed Trials with *Sea Falcon* (1974), racing in the Admiral's Cup on *More Opposition* and *Yeoman XX* (1975 and 1977) and joining forces with Peter Blake to break the Jules Verne record in *ENZA* (1994).

Standing out in 1970s were British *Oxygen* and the follow-up boats *Sea Falcon* and *British Airways.* These 18.6-m (60-ft) and 21.7-m (70-ft) catamarans foretold the interest in building big offshore multihulls, and their blue-chip sponsors were equally early adopters of what was to become the norm.

First and foremost, Knox-Johnston is a seaman who loves sailing. He has a long list of books to his credit, some based on unusual voyages. He cruised to Greenland with noted mountaineer Chris Bonington in 1991 so that each could learn the other's sport, and in 1989 undertook a transatlantic solo recreation of Columbus's voyage of discovery, using medieval technology – an astrolabe and Dutchman's log – to observe the sun and measure *Suhali*'s speed. He reached San Salvador in the Caribbean only eight miles out in latitude and 22 miles out in longitude after a 3,000-mile voyage.

Talk about a rich and full life. Knox-Johnston continues to enjoy it with an unquenchable *joie de vivre.* As creator of the Clipper Race, he has made it possible for thousands of others to sail around the world, and there is no better company than the man whose claim to fame is 303 days sailing alone.

△ The appropriately named Open 60 *Grey Power,* in which Knox-Johnston was still racing aged 75.

## Ocean Greats
# Sir Chay Blyth

### Vital stats

**Name:** Sir Chay Blyth

**DoB**: 14/05/1940

**Nationality:** British

**Known for:** Being the first person to sail westabout non-stop around the world

Chay Blyth has an infallible ability to boil things down to the essentials. When Francis Chichester sailed solo around the world, the next step was to do it non-stop. 'Only Robin Knox-Johnston had succeeded,' said Blyth, 'and I had to do the same. But in the opposite direction.'

So Blyth went in the westerly direction, which meant battling upwind against the prevailing winds and pushing against the regular currents. It was very much doing it the hard way.

Even so, his 1971/2 voyage took 292 days, three weeks faster than Robin Knox-Johnston's trip three years earlier. Blyth had a faster boat, the 18.3-m (59-ft) *British Steel*, and was sponsored.

It's improbable that such a feat would have happened if Chay Blyth hadn't met John Ridgway. Three years after leaving school, Blyth joined the army and ended up as platoon sergeant to Captain John Ridgway in the Parachute Regiment.

It was Ridgway, a resilient individual in the tradition of the Paras, who had the idea of rowing across the Atlantic in 1966. He and Blyth did this in the open, 6.2-m (20-ft) *English Rose III*, taking 92 days from Cape Cod (USA) to Aran Island (Ireland).

Two years later, Blyth entered the Golden Globe Race. Not only did he have negligible sailing experience, but he chose a wholly unsuitable boat. That Blyth retired only after passing the Cape of Good Hope spoke volumes about his robustness and determination. It also created an image that made writing the headline 'Boat of Steel; Man of Iron' inevitable when Blyth completed his solo circumnavigation in *British Steel*.

Blyth's profile went red hot as he was greeted in turn by Prince Philip, Prince Charles, Princess Anne

and Prime Minister Edward Heath. His no-nonsense approach to getting the job done earned him lifelong respect from Princess Anne, with Blyth especially supportive of the Save the Children charity that Princess Anne has been president of since 1970.

The voyage was a triumphant conclusion to a decade of firsts for Britain's sailing knights – Chichester, Knox-Johnston and Blyth.

Blyth's book, *The Impossible Voyage*, sealed his reputation as a never-flinching battler. This, together with Blyth's love of bucking convention and a sharp eye for publicity, attracted 'Union' Jack Hayward, a successful businessman who liked backing British endeavours. The 1970s were a happy association between the two men. Blyth proved the naysayers wrong by building the first foam-sandwich composite maxi yacht with unskilled labour, and then competing with the same crew of Paras in the inaugural 1973/4 Whitbread Round the World Race. *Great Britain II* set the lowest elapsed time.

The deals and headlines continued for another ten years. Blyth won the Round Britain Race (1978) in the 23-m (74-ft) trimaran *Great Britain IV*, the Two-handed Transatlantic Race in *Brittany Ferries II* with Rob James (1981) and achieved second place in the same trimaran in the Round Britain Race (1982).

Thanks to his extensive experience, Richard Branson brought Blyth aboard his two *Virgin Atlantic Challenger* transatlantic powerboat attempts in 1985 and 1986.

Yet how Blyth would want to, and should, be remembered is for opening up round-the-world racing to amateurs. His 1992 British Steel Challenge was a stroke of genius, and was copied by Robin Knox-Johnston's rival Clipper

Race. It enabled hundreds of ordinary people to undertake something extraordinary.

Anyone could compete. Blyth's Challenge Business built the fleet of boats, organized the event, trained the crews and ignored all the doubters who said 'foolhardy' and 'it can't be done'. In one exchange with the Royal Ocean Racing Club, who pondered the wisdom of sending individuals, some new to sailing, around the world, Blyth was at his most disarming, combative best.

'What experience do you think you need?' Blyth responded. 'There's nothing magic about sailing. It's only wind and water. Even at Cape Horn.' To the regret of many, the pressure to raise the money to pay for the huge overheads of running the fleet saw the business collapse after four races.

Chay Blyth moved back to Scotland after the Challenge Business was closed, returning to his home town of Hawick in the Borders. It was here that he'd started out aged 15, as an apprentice frameworker in a knitwear factory between school and signing up for the army. Today he indulges his love of horse riding, not least with the Hawick Common Riding, a celebration of the guarding by horsemen of the centuries-old disputed lands between the Scottish and English border.

Blyth holds a special place in sailing. He tells it best: 'Look at my roots, a working-class, secondary-modern Jack the Lad. After rowing the Atlantic and sailing solo around the world, I was projected to the highest echelons. I could hardly string three words together. What manners I had, I'd learned from the army. I had to alter the way I spoke, had to be couth. Sailing is another world, but people look at me and think, "If he can do it, I can".'

△ Blyth setting off to sail solo the 'wrong way' around the world, against the prevailing winds and currents, in 1971/2.

# Ocean Greats
# Dennis Conner

## Vital stats

**Name:** Dennis Conner

**DoB:** 16/09/1942

**Nationality:** American

**Known for:** Being the first American to lose the America's Cup – and then win it back

Between 26 September 1983 and 4 February 1987, Dennis Conner held the unwelcome sobriquet of the first American skipper ever to lose the America's Cup. For a sailor who redefined how to campaign for the sport's top prize, it was a burden that Conner felt compelled to shake off. He did so in emphatic style.

In 1983, his *Liberty* had lost narrowly in a tense and tight 3:4 series against *Australia II* in Newport, Rhode Island. Four years later, his *Stars & Stripes* absolutely trounced *Kookaburra IV* 4:0 off Fremantle. So superior was Conner's boat that *Kookaburra IV* only crossed ahead of *Stars & Stripes* on one tack in the entire series. Conner was the Comeback King, fully living up to his enduring nickname: Mr America's Cup. He made the cover of *Time* magazine and *Sports Illustrated*, holding the trophy he'd recaptured from Australia alongside President Reagan. An estimated 100,000 people lined Fifth Avenue when Conner and his crew were given a ticker-tape parade in New York City. Riding on Conner's float were mayor Ed Koch, San Diego mayor Maureen O'Connor and tycoon Donald Trump.

Trump paid for the parade (and gave Conner a huge fur coat). Two years earlier, Conner had cold-called Trump and refused to leave his HQ unless either the police removed him or Trump met him. Conner laid out his detailed plan to win back the Cup, intrigued Trump and sealed a deal. That plan was Conner's blueprint for the modern way to compete in the America's Cup; a skipper without a team owner, whose success or failure was entirely dependent on his own ability to raise corporate support. It was the zenith of Conner's 'No Excuse to Lose' approach, and it worked.

In winning the America's Cup four times, he surpassed the record of Scot-turned-American Charlie Barr, whose wins of 1899, 1901 and 1930 made him the first racing skipper of worldwide renown.

Before Conner rewrote the narrative, America's Cup campaigns since 1851 were east-coast dominated and privately funded. When he was invited over from San Diego to Newport to be part of Ted Turner's team on the terminally slow *Mariner* before moving teams to be starting helmsman for Ted Hood on *Courageous* in 1974, Conner was very much the outsider from the west coast. By then, he'd already forged a reputation in small sailboat classes.

Conner's success was all of his own making. He was a fisherman's son who grew up on San Diego's Point Loma, one block away from the smart set at the San Diego Yacht Club. He was the keen kid who hung around the club and got crewing chances. Assiduous in learning everything he could, Conner made himself a formidable sailor.

As an adult he lived to sail, starting his own drapery business to fund his endeavours. Conner became an in-demand sailor, and amongst the 28 world titles he racked up, he was frequently found steering the hottest grand-prix ocean racers. In the 1970s and 1980s, the US was still the critical mass of the sport in terms of designers, builders, sparmakers and sailmakers, and these industry pros served a big cohort of American yacht owners. Conner was the exception, the San Diego shop owner who got the best gigs because he was one of the very best at driving boats.

The 1988 America's Cup was an acrimonious mismatch between Conner's catamaran and Sir Michael Fay's giant monohull from New Zealand. For the first time, the America's Cup was dragged through the New York Supreme Court, and the prizegiving at the end of that series, won by the Americans, was boorish and unpleasant.

Conner was already 'Big Bad Dennis' for asking why you would build 12-Metre boats for the 1987 Cup in glassfibre, as the Kiwis had, 'unless you wanted to cheat'. This and other behaviour made Conner an easy target for justified criticism. But few saw what lay beneath: a sharp, personable, witty, sensitive and smart person. His closest friends and crew were unfailingly loyal. Conner was shrewd enough to call his Cup boats from 1987 onwards *Stars & Stripes*, creating a stylized logo. He was also smart enough to create his own yacht club, and appropriated another part of his country's identity for its USAYC name. Thus he assumed the mantle of national team for his private venture, and achieved complete control by doing away with the traditional yacht-club structure – yet more examples of Mr America's Cup creating a new template for how to compete in the event.

For all the success and the accolades, Conner remained passionate about sailing and passionate about his last Cup campaign in 2000. He bought and restored a string of classic yachts, breathing new life into a couple of 'last year's model' grand-prix boats to race in San Diego and down to Ensenada in Mexico. Perhaps what says more about Conner than anything else was competing in the Etchells 22 three-man keelboat class in 1998. It was an eye-catcher, as it brought together three America's Cup legends: John Bertrand, Russell Coutts and Dennis Conner. A man who had it all, Conner still thought nothing of towing his own boat coast to coast for a world championship in Marblehead, Massachusetts. He was, and remains, a giant of the sport.

△ *Stars & Stripes* (USA), skippered by Dennis Connor under full spinnaker in Fremantle, Australia, 1987.

# Sir Russell Coutts

## Vital stats

**Name:** Sir Russell Coutts

**DoB:** 01/03/1962

**Nationality:** New Zealand

**Known for:** Being the most successful America's Cup skipper ever; Olympic gold medallist

Meet 'Sir America's Cup', the man who surpassed 'Mr America's Cup' Dennis Conner as the most successful skipper in the history of the event.

From the point of winning an Olympic gold medal in the Finn singlehanded class in 1984, Russell Coutts has gone on to dominate those parts of sailing on which he's fixed his steely-eyed stare.

He has the talent shared by many others at the top of the sport, as well as the dedication and the focus. But what sets Coutts apart is the ability to systematically assemble everything that makes success possible on a specific target, and bring it to the boil under intense pressure at the right time.

So, five America's Cup wins to go with the Olympic gold, plus a slew of match-race titles. He was ranked number one in the world up against the likes of fellow Kiwi Chris Dickson and Australian Peter Gilmour and won the Worlds three times, in 1992, 1993 and 1996.

After Coutts' first America's Cup win in 1995, a new sponsorship of the match-race tour saw Faberge put up a US$1 million purse and one of their famous eggs for any crew who won five events in the season. Coutts called his key match-race crew Team Magic. They were fabulously competitive, racing hard and playing hard, earning them the rugby-based nickname the 'Tight Five'.

Ironically, given that the America's Cup would later end up in San Francisco, Coutts clinched the Faberge egg at the event run by St Francis Yacht Club and collected $400,000 in prize money, plus a $250,000 win bonus. He went on to become one of the biggest earners in sailing, regularly featured

in New Zealand's National Business Review Rich List.

Coutts may well have had another medal but for the fleet race qualifying format used in the 1992 Olympics. Many competitors were keen to stop his progress to the match race finale, where they expected him to sweep to the gold medal.

He did go on to become a multiple winner: the America's Cup five times (as helmsman in 1995, 2000 and 2003; as skipper/CEO in 2010 and CEO in 2013); World Sailor of the Year (1995 and 2003); Farr 40 World Championships (2001 and 2006); plus MBE, OBE and knighthood honours (1985, 1995 and 2009).

Coutts is the youngest of three brothers and comes from a sailing family. His grandparents raced, and his parents met at Napier Sailing Club on Hawkes Bay. His father built the boys a string of P-Class dinghies, the definitive youth trainer for budding Kiwi sailors. Coutts also raced Lasers and Z-Class. The family grew up near Wellington on the North Island. When Coutts was 11, the family relocated south to Dunedin, to a home right on the water's edge. Instead of having to be driven by his parents to go sailing, his boat was on his doorstep.

Coutts was ultra-competitive. Famously he confused left and right in his first race, aged nine, screaming 'starboard!' for right of way when he was on port. He was given the nickname 'Crash Coutts' before he buckled down and studied the rules and tactics in all the sailing books he could lay his hands on.

This dedication sowed the seeds of a thoroughness that became his hallmark, coupled with a structured thinking process that came from

> **'I don't care about records, I'm proud of what the team has achieved.'**
>
> **Russell Coutts** | America's Cup, 2013

excelling at maths at school and going on to take an engineering degree at Auckland University. It was a perfect grounding for the science of sailing, especially the modern America's Cup, which is about taking a small number of key strategic decisions at critical points coupled with the perfection of thousands of details.

Coutts burst onto the scene with a sixth place in the 1980 ISAF Youth Worlds, even though he was disqualified in two of the five races (in which controversial American sailor Russ Silvestri figured prominently). He achieved the title in Portugal a year later. Coutts was mature enough to convert these disqualifications into a resolve to research the facts, and when challenged, strip them of any emotion and present them clearly. Not many have got the better of Coutts in an argument since.

While still a student, Coutts thought hard about aiming for Olympic selection. It was a tall order, meaning switching from the Laser to the Finn class and taking on more experienced sailors within 18 months. Coutts won a tight trials series and headed to Long Beach, USA, where the Los Angeles Olympic regatta was being sailed.

He brought his full intensity to bear, withdrawing into what was known at the time as 'RussellWorld'. His father had instilled a powerful ethic of application to the task at hand. Going into the last race, Coutts was placed for a three-way fight for gold.

Having got this far, his legs and backside had become a minefield of saltwater boils from hiking out the Finn dinghy. The NZ team doctor had lanced them without anaesthetic, for fear of breaching drug codes. Coutts could scarcely walk down the beach for the last race, but gritted it out for gold.

In deciding to give sailing a go professionally, Coutts set about deciphering the match-racing code. And succeeded. Where Chris Dickson was the established star when New Zealand made its first America's Cup bid in 1987, he was recruited as back-up helmsman for 1992. Both campaigns fell short of their potential. When Peter Blake was persuaded to take over the leader, NZ Challenge was re-cast as Team New Zealand.

Blake made Coutts skipper as one of the first steps, and this cohesive, well-funded, tight and focused team won the America's Cup in San Diego 5:0. Coutts defended the Cup in 2000 and won 5:0, though his personal score was 4:0 as he handed the helm for the final race to understudy Dean Barker. It was a magnanimous gesture, as Coutts remembered that Barker's father had

△ Building a brand new America's Cup team from scratch and then winning a comprehensive victory in less than three years was a stunning achievement by Coutts in 2004 with *Alinghi*.

helped put some cash into his 1984 Olympic bid. It was typical of the thoughtful and caring side to Coutts that outsiders rarely appreciate.

From this high point, a woefully managed succession by the team's trustees from Blake to Coutts and Brad Butterworth as the new leaders of TNZ saw the team implode. American teams OneWorld and Oracle Racing hired away talent even as victory was celebrated. Coutts and his Tight Five followed later to a new team from Switzerland, Alinghi. Coutts was late into the hiring market, but he created a brand new team from

scratch, led it and skippered the boat to another 5:0 victory in 2003, all in the space of 33 months. It was a stunning achievement.

That he beat TNZ to do it generated strong feelings in New Zealand. The 'Blackheart' campaign whipped up unpleasant anti-Coutts and Butterworth sentiment, although why TNZ had fallen apart three years earlier was not properly understood by the general public.

Coutts' restoration to the highest standing of great Kiwis was complete, however, by 2009. The *New Zealand Herald* ran a front-page photo of his

knighthood ceremony flanked by All Black rugby great Sir Colin Meades and triple Olympic gold medal-winning middle distance runner Sir Peter Snell. All was forgiven.

Coutts sat out the 2007 America's Cup after a total breakdown with Alinghi team owner Ernesto Bertarelli. US software billionaire Larry Ellison phoned Coutts, the pair met, joined forces and went on to win the 2010 and 2013 America's Cups.

Coutts' beyond-the-horizon vision was seen in full effect in the 2013 event, in which he re-engineered the America's Cup. He brought it from out-of-sight on the ocean to easy-to-see off the city front, and turned two-hour-long races with few lead changes into 30-minute explosions of action. He did this by ending over 150 years of using monohulls, instead making foiling catamarans the Cup class of boats. He also championed the use of Emmy Award-winning graphics to make the critical but invisible parts of yacht racing (wind, current and advantage) illustrated on live TV images.

Coutts is the most successful skipper in America's Cup history. His influence is far-reaching, and his talent immense.

# Ocean Greats
# Fyodor Konyukhov

## Vital stats

**Name:** Fyodor Filippovich Konyukhov

**DoB:** 12/12/1951

**Nationality:** Russian

**Known for:** Being the first person to reach the five most remote places on Earth: Cape Horn, Mount Everest, the North Pole, the Arctic Pole and the South Pole

To say that Fyodor Konyukhov is something of a renaissance man would be an understatement. He is a sailor, rower, engineer, adventurer, climber, artist, author and priest. The list of his achievements is breathtaking in scope, variety and number.

He seems to have lived the life of three or four of the great adventurers and explorers rolled into one. Konyukhov has a weather-beaten face and beard that would not have been out of place on a 19th-century clipper ship, and in many ways his pursuit of the difficult and dangerous on land and water is resonant of the great explorers of that time.

Born the son of a fisherman, Konyukhov comes from the Sea of Azov, the arm of the Black Sea that's enclosed by Crimea. The signs of wanderlust were evident from an early age. At 15 he rowed across the Azov Sea before completing his education at Odessa's Navigation College and Leningrad's Arctic College. He then attended the Theological Seminary and Arts College in Bobruisk, Belarus.

Art has been a constant in his life. He has more than 3,000 paintings to his name, many showing scenes from his extreme adventures. In 1983 he became the youngest member of the USSR's Union of Artists. Nowadays he is an Honorary Academician (and gold medal winner) of the Russian Arts Academy.

His expeditions under sail go back to 1977, when he was part of a crew following the 1725–28 voyage of Danish-born Russian Vitus Bering, who mapped the coast of northeast Asia.

Konyukhov was first noticed outside of Russia in 1990/1, when he made a 224-day solo circumnavigation from Sydney, Australia. This was just before the USSR broke up and the Iron Curtain dropped, and it followed the first ever Russian boat (*Fazisi*) entering the Whitbread Round the World Race in 1989/90, part of Mikhail Gorbachev's policy of *glasnost*, or being more public and open.

Come 1992, Konyukhov was off again, this time making a westabout circumnavigation against the prevailing winds. His third solo round-the-world voyage was under the additional pressure of a race, taking part in the 1998/9 Around Alone race in the Open 60 *Modern University for the Humanities*.

A fourth solo circumnavigation was thwarted when he retired from the non-stop Vendée Globe in 2000/1 to stop in Sydney for medical attention and sail repairs. It says much about Konyukhov that he tried again for his fourth lap around the Earth after he'd taken up sailing a 26.4-m (85-ft) trimaran. He was successful in 2004/5, starting and finishing in Falmouth, England, with a halfway stop in Tasmania. In 2004, he crossed the Atlantic solo, one of 14 Atlantic crossings.

By 2010, Konyukhov was seeking a new purpose in life. He'd never completed his seminary studies, being told, 'You love life too much. Go live with the people.' So started his Odyssey-like lifestyle. By the age of 60, however, he completed his studies in the Russian Orthodox Church and was appointed a priest.

Konyukhov has said that in challenging and solitary times during his expeditions and adventures, he was able to see God. 'As an adult man, I understand that there is no solitude in this world. There are whales and dolphins accompanying you in the ocean, birds flying in the sky, and bears and seals meeting you on your way to the Pole. I know for sure that God and saints are always around when you pray. Nobody is available for help in the huge ocean, except them.'

Not that Konyukhov stopped putting his life on the line. In 2012 he reached the top of Mount Everest for the second time, having already reached the summit of the highest mountains in all seven continents. In 2014 he completed a five-month solo row across the Pacific, proving that age is truly no barrier for this particular adventurer.

▽ Konyukhov took this picture as he sailed his 26-m (84-ft) yacht *Trading Network Alye Parusa* through the Roaring Forties of the Southern Ocean, during the 2008 Antarctica Cup solo circumnavigation of Antarctica.

## Ocean Greats
# Bernard Moitessier

### Vital stats

**Name:** Bernard Moitessier

**Dates:** 10/04/1925–16/06/1995

**Nationality:** French

**Known for:** Being a circumnavigator, and a competitor in the 1968/9 Golden Globe Race

◁ Bernard Moitessier named his 12-m (39-ft) steel ketch *Joshua* in honour of Joshua Slocum, who voyaged alone around the world between 1895 and 1898.

As an example of being famous for failing to achieve what he'd set out to do, Frenchman Bernard Moitessier is without compare.

Yet in his eyes and those of his numerous admirers, Moitessier strove for and found a different, perhaps higher, level of success.

His seminal moment came in the Golden Globe race of 1968/69, the first ever non-stop, round-the-world event for solo sailors.

Having braved a number of setbacks, gear damage and the severe conditions of the Southern Ocean from the Cape of Good Hope and across the southern Indian Ocean, he passed south of Australia towards Cape Horn and the Atlantic.

But instead of completing the return leg of the race, he decided to head north into the Pacific. In a message written on paper and fired by catapult to a passing ship, Moitessier explained his reason: 'Because I am happy, and perhaps to save my soul.'

Instead of opprobium, the Frenchman was lauded for a decision that was as brave as carrying on. Moitessier, not Robin Knox-Johnston, the only finisher, would be recorded in history as the first person to sail around the world, alone, unassisted and non-stop. And Knox-Johnston was among the first to respect his rival's unusual and yet brave decision.

A restless vagabond, Moitessier was born in Hanoi, Vietnam, when it was part of French Indo-China. He grew up by the sea and worked his way as crew on sailing trading junks in southeast Asia before leaving for Europe as the Vietnam War loomed.

A book, *Vagabond of the Southern Seas*, about his nomadic travels helped to fund his 12-m (39-ft) centre cockpit, named in honour of American Joshua Slocum, whose 1895–98 multi-stop voyage around the world is credited as being the first solo circumnavigation and an inspiration to future generations.

The Frenchman and his wife (for part of the voyage) had already voyaged around the world via the Panama Canal before tacking on the Golden Globe. Voyaging rather than competing was his style, but at the time the event seemed like a

tremendous challenge rather than an out-and-out race.

He set off on 23 August 1968 behind Knox-Johnston (entrants were timed on departure rather than mustering for a combined start) and shaved nearly 25 per cent off the Briton's time to Cape Horn. Knox-Johnston generously suggests Moitessier would have caught and passed him in the Atlantic.

Despite not completing the Golden Globe, Moitessier did carry on with what became a voyage of personal discovery and finished his second circumnavigation. A self-portrait photo of him, sitting on *Joshua*'s deck, bearded and feet hooked over his thighs in the lotus position as he meditates, captured the enigma that was Moitessier.

His second book was appropriately titled *The Long Way*, a classic of the yacht-voyaging genre, complete with a contemplative and spiritual backstory.

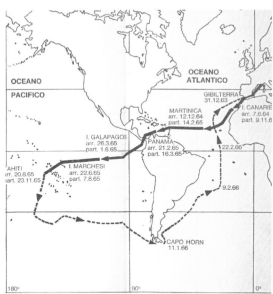

△ This map traces the journey of *Joshua*, named after Captain Joshua Slocum, the first man to circumnavigate the world between 1895 and 1898 on his oyster sloop *Spray*.

△ Moitessier meditating on board *Joshua*. The spiritual side of life at sea was so important to Moitessier that he stopped racing in the Golden Globe in order to circumnavigate the 'long way'.

# Ocean Greats
# Bruno and Loïck Peyron

## Vital stats

**Name:** Bruno Peyron and Loïck Peyron

**DoB:** 10/11/1955 and 01/12/1959

**Nationality:** French

**Known for:** Being multiple race-winning, record-setting, trend-setting brothers

▷ Loïck (left) and Bruno Peyron. Between them, they have a spectacular string of successes in winning races and setting records.

▷ Bruno Peyron's *Commodore Explorer* was the first to break the 80-day barrier for sailing non-stop around the world. 1993 was the first of three Jules Verne records.

If ever there were brothers entitled to be called the Sibling Champions, it is the Peyrons. Together as collaborators or apart in their own individual enterprises, France's Peyron brothers have held the sailing world in their thrall for much of the past 20 years.

Bruno is best known for being the first person to shatter the accepted sailing glass ceiling by circumnavigating the world in less than 80 days. As a co-creator of the Trophée Jules Verne, it was fitting that he was not just the first winner but also the only skipper to have set a new record for the fastest lap of the planet on three occasions.

Loïck, four years younger than Bruno, has a Jules Verne feather in his own cap, plus a string of titles inshore and offshore, in monohulls and multihulls, since his breakthrough win in 1985 of the Round Europe race in *Lada Poch*.

It requires a very special kind of person to carry on winning in the gruelling world of solo transocean sailing in both monos and multis, yet

△ Loïck Peyron skippers the giant trimaran *Banque Populaire* on his record-breaking 2014 Route du Rhum. He set a new record of 7d 15h 8m.

Loïck has done exactly that, scoring a standout victory in the 2014 Route du Rhum transatlantic.

Furthermore, there is a third Peyron brother who, in any other family, would not be outshone by his siblings. Born in 1960, Stéphane is the youngest of the three, but has carved out his own reputation by windsurfing across the Atlantic in 1986 from Dakar to Guadeloupe. More recently, he has become an acclaimed documentary maker.

Given that their father was a Shell supertanker captain and their uncle the famous sailor Jean-Yves

Terlain, the brothers were either going make their own mark at sea or stay firmly on dry land. In this case, their sailing ambition was fired by attending the launch of the famous yacht *Vendredi 13*, winner of the 1976 OSTAR singlehanded transatlantic race.

Just how repeatedly successful Bruno and Loïck have been is evidenced by this digest of their triumphs.

Loïck has won the ORMA Championship (which combines points from multiple events) four times

Bruno's career has focused more on record setting than contesting races. His tally is 39. Besides his three Jules Verne records (1993, 2002 and 2005), Bruno has set new fastest times across the Atlantic from west to east three times (1987, 1992 and 2006) and logged the greatest mileages in 24 hours on five occasions (1982, 1997, 2000, 2004 and 2006).

Little wonder that he has sailed more miles in maxi multihulls than anyone else.

In races, Bruno has managed a string of top three finishes, even if the big wins can't match those of his younger brother. But two second places in the Route du Rhum (1982 and 1986), a brace of seconds in the Route of Discovery and Round Europe (1988 and 1989), plus a third place in the Quebec–St Malo and fifth in the OSTAR/Transat (1988) prove that he attracted the sponsorship, had the boats and had the skill to be one of the best of his generation.

Besides being one of the inspirations behind the Trophée Jules Verne, Bruno demonstrated similar imagination with a no-rules/no-limits race, which he called simply The Race, that started on new year's eve 2000. His vision was a direct head-to-head competition for the giant multihulls – which normally voyaged alone, and picked their own start time according to the weather routing forecasts, in Jules Verne attempts.

Of the two, Bruno is the more taciturn. Loïck is the media darling, with an impish sense of humour and the most expressive of faces. Four decades on, both give interviews freely and are very accessible to the public, a key factor in France's success in transocean sailing.

Loïck brought his big multihull experience to two America's Cup teams, Switzerland's Alinghi (2010) and Sweden's Artemis Racing (2013 and 2017). A rare setback for Bruno and Loïck was their failure to secure funding for their own French America's Cup team for the 2013 series, at the very time the switch to high-performance catamarans seemed to have created an excellent opportunity for them. If history is any guide, it will not hold them back for long.

*'The common denominator is the wind and the sea, so hopefully I know what to do, but the main difference is that on multihulls it's a lot more stressful. That's why I have so much white hair. [laughs] I'm not so old, you know?'*

**Loïck Peyron** after Transat, 2008

between 1996 and 2002; the solo OSTAR/Transat three times (1992, 1996 and 2008); the two-handed Transat Jacques Vabre twice (1999 and 2005); contested seven solo Route du Rhums, retiring three times and winning once (2014); won the Trophée Clairfontaine eight times (between 1995–2011); and set the Jules Verne record once (2011).

No wonder he has been appointed skipper by some of the biggest backers of French sailing, such as Fujicolor, Banque Populaire and Benjamin de Rothschild.

## Ocean Greats
# James Spithill

*'That's the great thing about sport and in life, that, you know, if it's not over, if they haven't handed the trophy over, you still have a shot.'*

**James Spithill** | America's Cup, 2013

### Vital stats

**Name:** James (Jimmy) Spithill

**DoB:** 28/06/1979

**Nationality:** Australian

**Known for:** Being the youngest winning America's Cup skipper

B oats and the water were on the doorstep for the Spithill family. They lived at Elvina Bay, Pittwater, north of Sydney, Australia, and the only way to school or to the shops was by boat. So Jimmy Spithill learned early.

He was also exposed to the event that has defined his life, the America's Cup, at a young age. Still a teenager, Spithill was the youngest-ever skipper in the America's Cup aged 19, in 1999, and the youngest-ever winning skipper, aged 30, in 2010.

He has a barely formed childhood memory of Australia winning the 1983 America's Cup, the first ever challenger to do so. The celebrations around Pittwater were as enthusiastic as anywhere, and the joy of it all made an impact on the four-year-old Spithill. The Beashals, whose son Colin was mainsail trimmer on *Australia II*, were nearby neighbours.

As a youngster, Spithill's sailing career didn't follow the normal path. The family budget

couldn't stretch beyond windsurfers and a Hobie cat, so Spithill started crewing on bigger boats, side-stepping the usual progression through dinghy classes.

Australia had a strong youth keelboat programme, and by 1998 he'd collected a couple of match racing titles. At the Australian Yachtsman of the Year awards dinner, Spithill met offshore legend Syd Fischer and was recruited to steer his 16-m (50-ft) *Ragamuffin*.

This led directly to Fischer, whose competitive top-level career started in the 1960s, to re-use his 1995 America's Cup challenger in the 2000 Cup as *Young Australia*. The budget was so tight that the crew made their own sandwiches, but the opportunity Fischer gave his young guns was immense.

Spithill adopted the Fischer mantra about hard, successful sailing: 'Lead by example; from the front.' Spithill was skipper of the

▽ From 1:8 down and one race from losing, Spithill leads Oracle Team USA to a successful 9:8 defence of the America's Cup in 2013 against Emirates Team New Zealand.

▷ Spithill's team celebrating victory in the 2013 America's Cup, dubbed the biggest comeback in sports history. Spithill and crew had reason to be jubilant.

youth team and his prowess in match racing saw the youngest crew in the oldest boat take some notable scalps in the start sequence.

Fellow Aussie Peter Gilmour signed up Spithill for the 2003 America's Cup for the big US team, OneWorld, happy to step back and give Spithill the helm. When the Italians recruited him for the Luna Rossa team for the 2007 America's Cup, it meant that Spithill had spent ten years straight sailing big, heavy, slow keelboats.

Ironic, then, that in the 2010 America's Cup, by which time Russell Coutts had hired Spithill for Larry Ellison's BMW Oracle Racing/Oracle Team USA, he should end up in multihulls, completing the circle right back to his childhood sailing on Pittwater.

The 2010 multihulls were nothing like Hobie cats, and were arguably the most extreme boats ever seen in the competition. Spithill threw himself at the task of sailing a boat with a solid wing sail that was, at 72m (232ft), the biggest wing ever built, bigger even than a Boeing 747 or Airbus 380 wing.

With Spithill at the helm, *BOR90* beat *Alinghi V 2:0* in the battle of the giants off Valencia in 2010, with a demonstrably faster boat. But in 2013 in San Francisco it was a different story. Oracle Team USA started with a -2 deficit on the score line in the first-to-nine-wins series, because of a jury penalty relating to illegal modifications in the AC45 class used the preceding America's Cup World Series.

In the giant AC72s, Emirates Team New Zealand were faster and more polished, yet Spithill's crew mounted one of the greatest fightbacks in sport, reversing a 1:8 score line to win 9:8. CNN said Spithill's crew had done the 'unthinkable'. The *New York Times*, so long the chronicler of the America's Cup, said the team had 'completed a voyage into history.'

Heady stuff. Spithill, for all the jubilation, remembered in his moment of triumph the sage advice of Syd Fischer about not getting carried away by such moments. 'Syd used to say when something was going good, remember this: "Be careful, you can be the rooster one day, and a feather duster the next."'

## Ocean Greats
# Seve Jarvin

### Vital stats

**Name:** Seve Jarvin

**DoB:** 02/05/1986

**Nationality:**
Australian

**Known for:** Holding
the greatest number
of 5.5-m (18-ft) skiff
world titles

From an unpromising start – reduced to tears when taken afloat for the first time as a five-year-old – Seve Jarvin has matured into the best of the best amongst helmsmen in the 18ft skiff class.

By 2015, he'd already got seven world titles to his name and his work hadn't finished.

'I was forced into it by my dad because I come from a big sailing family,' remembers Jarvin of his baptism into sailing. 'I didn't really get into it until I was about eight. Dad's really big into sailing, he's been to the Olympics and sailed around the world. I guess he's really happy that I'm still doing it.'

Jarvin comes from a long line of Sydney-siders whose prowess in the three 18-ft skiff classes brought them recognition around the world. It's a funny coincidence that Jarvin has achieved his success in the *Gotta Love It 7*. Iain Murray won five titles as helmsman in *Color 7* in the consecutive years 1977–82, while the same Channel 7 TV company is Jarvin's backer. With Murray still on the books in what must be one of the longest personal sponsorship deals in the sport, he's acted as mentor and team manager to Jarvin and his crew.

To his seven J.J. Giltinan trophy titles (the 18-ft skiff class world championships), Jarvin added an eighth when he crewed Euan McNichol's *Club Marine* in 2005. The trophy was first put up by James J. Giltinan, who was secretary of the Australian 18-footers League and wanted to encourage what was to become the class's premiere prize.

By reputation, the annual J.J. Giltinan is a tough championship to win. Since its first running in 1938, there have been only 11 multiple winners

and only three have won more than two titles. Jarvin is one of an elite crop of sailors.

Jarvin's father Steve was an America's Cup sailor and Etchells world champion in his own right. His son worked his way up through the smaller dinghy classes, sailing Sabots, Flying 11s and 29ers.

He was then enlisted in the Youth Sailing Academy run by the Cruising Yacht Club of Australia out of Rushcutters Bay. In the 2002/3 season he was crowned 29er class national champion, as well as youth match racing champion, all at the age of 17.

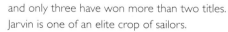

Instead of sticking with keelboat match racing, Jarvin jumped into the 18ft skiffs, a class that has stood at the forefront of high-performance, small-boat innovation in design, construction and technique for decades.

Given his father's own career, and the strong links between mentor Iain Murray and the Oatley family's interest in top-level racing, it came as no surprise that Seve Jarvin was signed up by Robert Oatley when in 2014 it looked as it he was going to launch his own America's Cup campaign.

Jarvin proved his versatility in a highly specialized class by winning not just in Sydney Harbour. The 2008 win was taken in San Francisco and in big wind conditions, with the characteristic hard chop that the ebb tide can kick up. 'Like riding a bicycle on a tightrope in a gale,' was how he described the testing conditions.

In 2015 he joined the Extreme Sailing Series, the stadium-style catamaran event staged in cities throughout Europe.

△ The most successful combination ever in 18-ft skiff racing – Seve Jarvin's crew and *Gotta Love It 7*.

# Ocean Greats
# Eric Tabarly

Eric Tabarly was short in stature but a giant of the sport; a softly spoken and shy man, with a vice-like handshake and a reputation as the toughest seaman of all — the epitome of a Breton from that granite corner of France he called home.

Born in Nantes in 1931, sailing was in Eric's blood. He was still a baby when his parents first took him afloat in *Annie*, a cutter. Then his father bought another cutter, called *Pen Duick* — a Breton name for a little black-headed seabird — a marque that was to become one of the best-known names in sailing.

The yacht, built in Ireland just before the turn of the century before last, and designed by William Fife of Scotland, was laid up in a mud berth during the Second World War in a vain bid to both hide and preserve her. The keel lead was removed and, although the boat survived hostilities, the wooden structure suffered badly.

In 1958, Tabarly completed the rebuild of the gaff cutter, making a new hull from glassfibre. Tragically, in 1998, he lost his life from the same beloved yacht. He'd celebrated *Pen Duick's* centenary at a regatta in Bénodet, south Brittany, in May, and in June was en route to a regatta for Fife boats in Scotland when he fell overboard in the Irish Sea.

Tabarly was an old-school sailor, eschewing safety harness and lifejacket and preferring instead to rely on his experience, his empathy with his boat and the sea, his fitness and his agility.

'I'd rather spend an hour in the water than be tied on with a harness,' he'd once said.

In a building breeze, an unsettled sea and at night, Tabarly progressively reduced *Pen Duick's* sail, working on the bowsprit with a dexterity that belied his 66 years but spoke legions about his skill. Typically, when the mainsail is lowered on a gaff-rigged yacht, there are awkward moments when the gaff spar can arc above the deck while the sail is gathered and before the gaff is made secure. In one particularly violent roll, the gaff swung outboard and then returned, striking Tabarly and knocking him into the sea. His body was found five weeks later.

France's greatest sailor was lost from the yacht that he held so dear throughout his life. He was an icon, the quiet man who had achieved great things, beating the Anglo Saxons at their own sport, becoming his country's first national sailing hero and winning the *Légion d'Honneur*.

▽ The schooner *Pen Duick III* was Tabarly's own creation. She won the 1967 Sydney–Hobart race.

This singular man declined dinner with president General de Gaulle to mark this honour, as it clashed with a particularly low tide, that would have allowed him to work on the hull of his boat.

In the late 1950s, Tabarly was serving in the French navy when he targeted the second solo transatlantic race in 1964. Francis Chichester had won the first race, which he'd co-created, in 1960 with a time of 40d 12h. Tabarly built the ketch *Pen Duick II* and won the 1964 event. He was nearly two weeks faster across the Atlantic from Plymouth to Newport in 27d 3h.

There followed a string of boats and though he did not have an engineering or design background, Tabarly was very inventive in commissioning their design. *Pen Duick III* was variously a sloop and a wishbone schooner. *Pen Duick IV* was a 19-m (60-ft) ketch-rigged aluminium trimaran. In 1968 she was considered impossibly big and powerful for one man to sail. Her successor was a pioneer in using water ballast. In 1973/4 he contested the first Whitbread fully crewed round-the-world race, and though the 23-m (73-ft) *Pen Duick V* was conventional, her denser-than-lead spent-uranium keel was definitely not.

Testament to Tabarly's cussedness and stamina was the fact that he raced the same boat solo in the 1976 OSTAR transatlantic race as he'd competed with in the Whitbread with more than ten crew. Early in the race from Plymouth to Newport, the self-steering failed. Tabarly considered turning back, but pressed

on, hand steering for nearly 2,000 miles. Out of contact, fears for him were growing in France. The French navy, for whom he remained an emblematic figure, were considering mounting a search when he suddenly sailed out of the fog at the Rhode Island finish.

His most radical yacht was the trimaran *Paul Ricard*. With foils on her outrigger floats, she set a new transatlantic record in 1980.

▽ The *Pen Duick IV* was constructed for Tabarly in 1968. Constructed from aluminium, she was the first oceangoing multihull racing sailboat, and quickly dominated the ocean races with her superior speed. Later renamed *Manureva*, the boat sadly disappeared during a violent storm along with her skipper Alain Colas during the first Route du Rhum in 1978.

# Ocean Greats
# Olivier de Kersauson

## Vital stats

**Name:** Olivier de Kersauson

**DoB:** 02/07/1944

**Nationality:** French

**Known for:** Being a two-time Jules Verne record holder

In terms of magnificence, Oliver de Kersauson de Pennendref has the name, the family and the title – vicomte – without compare.

With his long locks and distinguished face, you feel that de Kersauson would only need a ruffled shirt, cape, feathered wide-brimmed hat and sword to become one of Alexandre Dumas's musketeers. A musketeer who looks as if he'd ridden the length of France, eating and drinking with abandon and not caring to wash, that is.

By the time de Kersauson was an established sailing star, his idiosyncratic character and carefree grooming and wardrobe encouraged a second career on both radio and TV as a pundit. In talking-head panel debates, de Kersauson played the part of grumpy contrarian to perfection.

A sense of de Kersauson's character is encapsulated by something he once said: 'If I had not been a sailor, I would have been a sailor!' He is not a man to fit neatly into a pigeonhole.

For such a French Frenchman, the origin of the family name can be traced back to 1030. 'Sauzon' or 'Sauson' means an English Breton, indicating the family was one of the tribes who crossed the Channel and settled in Brittany.

De Kersauson's immediate family is no less interesting. The seventh of eight children, he was born in July 1944 in Sarthe, which then was on the brink of liberation after the D-Day landings. One of his brothers, Yves, was an admiral in the French navy responsible for intelligence. Another brother, Florent, co-created the Route du Rhum transatlantic race.

He sailed during his childhood from the sailing hotspots in Brittany such as Morlaix on the

Channel coast and La Trinité-sur-Mer on the Biscay coast. Finishing his national service in the marines in 1967, he was recruited by Eric Tabarly to the crew of *Pen Duick III*.

It was to prove the start of a strong relationship between the men; Tabarly appreciated de Kersauson's strength, commitment and humour, while the latter prospered in the hands of such a mentor, finding the sea a great leveller.

De Kersauson completed the inaugural 1973/4 Whitbread Round-the-World Race on *Pen Duick VI* as Tabarly's right-hand man, before becoming a skipper in his own right with *Kriter II* in the 1974/5 London–Sydney–London FT Clipper Race. He won the first leg and followed up by coming fourth in the first Route du Rhum race in 1978, in *Kriter IV*.

He was not an easy man to sail with, and some of his crews spoke of a regime of 'wild domination'. It is no surprise that he moved into multihulls and generally sailed with solo, two-handed or unusually small crews.

In 2005/6 he participated with *Geronimo* in the Qatari-backed Oryx Cup round-the-world event. He then achieved a series of passage-record voyages in the Pacific, chalking up fastest times around Australia, Sydney–Tahiti, Los Angeles–Honolulu, San Francisco–Yokohama, Yokohama–Hong Kong and Yokohama–San Francisco.

In October 1992, the idea of lapping the planet faster than the fictional Phileas Fogg had managed in Jules Verne's *Around the World in 80 Days* was formalized, with a body to set rules and validate attempts. De Kersauson was president of the Jules Verne Association, and he made no fewer than seven cracks at the Jules Verne record himself.

He proved successful in becoming the skipper to set the third and fifth records for the Trophée Jules Verne, setting a new record of 71d 22h 8m in the 27.4-m (90-ft) trimaran *Sport-Elect* in 1977. It was a brave voyage, leaving Europe and the Ushant start line in March, which was perilously close to the onset of the southern-hemisphere winter in the Southern Ocean. This put him and his six-man crew three days ahead of the previous record, set by *ENZA*, skippered by Sir Peter Blake and Sir Robin Knox-Johnston, a record that de Kersauson held for five years.

For the Frenchman it was a case of second time lucky, having been beaten by *ENZA* three years earlier by some two days. The first attempt made

in 1993 aboard *Charal* was halted by hull damage south of Cape Town, and others were aborted in the early stages when the requisite sling-shot start down the Atlantic to the equator failed to live up to the forecast winds. But de Kersauson was to be successful again in 2004, when *Geronimo* cut the record to 63d 13h 59m.

In later life de Kersauson settled in Polynesia, and he spends much of his time in Moorea. His biographical book about sailing, life and the sea, *Ocean's Song*, became a bestseller in France, selling 250,000 copies.

△ The multihull *Geronimo*, skippered by Kersauson, after the start of the February 2005 Oryx Quest Round The Globe yacht race in Doha, Qatar.

# Ocean Greats
# Michel Desjoyeaux

## Vital stats

**Name:** Michel Desjoyeaux

**DoB:** 16/07/1965

**Nationality:** French

**Known for:** Being a two-time Vendée Globe winner

If you are given 'Le Professeur' as a nickname, you have a lot to live up to. Michel Desjoyeaux has done exactly that. At 20, he was signed up by Eric Tabarly for his first around-the-world event – the Whitbread/Volvo Ocean Race – and it proved to be the first step of a glittering career.

Desjoyeaux was given his nickname by his peers, acknowledging both the meticulous detail he goes into when conceiving his boats and his studious approach to computer meteo files when using his routing software when competing on the oceans of the world.

The result is that he has won most of the great solo races and done so over a long period of time: true testament to his range of skills, talent and steely determination.

Desjoyeaux became the first sailor to win the Solitaire du Figaro three times – in 1992, 1998 and 2007 – and what is noteworthy is that, in the race that many sailors use to set out their stall at the start of their solo careers, Desjoyeaux went back 25 years after his first victory to revalidate himself against a younger generation.

He has also won the biggest round-the-world race, the Vendée Globe – not once, but twice in 2000/1 and 2008/9 – and the two premier transatlantic events, the Route du Rhum (2002) and the Transat/OSTAR (2004).

His record in two-handed events is no less impressive, winning the Transat AGR2 in 1992 and the Transat Jacques Vabre in 2007. This versatility has made him an in-demand sailor for both multihull and monohull crewed events. He's also won the 2011 Vulcain Trophy on Lake Geneva, and sailed in the Decision 35 catamaran class as well as parts of the European Tour in the MOD 70 one-design trimaran class.

Besides his first Whitbread/Volvo with Eric Tabarly on *Cote d'Or* in 1985/6, Desjoyeaux has sailed on certain legs in the 1989/90, 1993/4 and 2013/4 events on *Charles Jourdan*, *La Poste* and *Mapfre*.

The ubiquity of canting keels on grand-prix race boats can be traced back to Desjoyeaux trying one out in the 1991 Mini Transat race. He won the second leg.

Desjoyeaux was shaped at a young age by his outward-looking mother and father. 'My parents were people who lived on the fringes of normality,' he says. 'They were free thinkers before free thinking was cool. They taught me to do what I wanted without worrying what people thought about it. They taught me to do whatever I wanted – as long as I did it with full commitment.'

It was this ethos that led his father, Henri Desjoyeaux, to become one of the co-founders of the Glénans Sailing School in 1947. It grew into Europe's largest, instrumental in opening up the sport to hundreds of thousands of newcomers who might not otherwise have had the chance. He also helped the Port la Forêt marina get off the ground. The growth of marinas all over France in the 1960s onwards was another key step in the democratization of the sport.

'The Professor' has channelled all that he has learnt into a multi-discipline pro-sailing business called Mer Agitée. This embraces everything from working with designers and builders in making non-standard optimizations to full project management.

Scratch the surface of the some of the top-level French projects of the last 20 years and you'll find Desjoyeaux's service company behind them, either supporting himself or other top skippers.

The specialisms run deep in Desjoyeaux's company, including custom configurations and systems for autopilots, and canting keel systems. In Formula 1 terms, he would be the world-champion-calibre driver who also trebled-up as the design director and team boss.

A cornerstone of his technical interest in sailing was co-creating the CDK boatyard in La Foret Fouesnant with his brother Hubert, fellow skipper Jean Le Cam and naval architect Marc van Peteghem.

Given the vast amount of open-ocean racing Desjoyeaux has undertaken, is comes as no surprise that he is no stranger to setbacks. Amongst these have been pulling out of the 2008 Transat when *Foncia* hit a whale. Later, the same Open 60 was dismasted 600 miles from Cape Town in the South Atlantic, when he and Francis Gabert were favourites in the 2011 two-handed Barcelona World Race.

△ *Géant*, Michel Desjoyeaux's multihulled boat, during the 2004 Transat, which he later went on to win.

## Ocean Greats
# Florence Arthaud

## Vital stats

**Name:** Florence Arthaud

**Dates:** 28/10/1957–09/03/2015

**Nationality:** French

**Known for:** Winning the 1990 Route du Rhum

When yachtswoman Florence Arthaud was killed with other celebrities taking part in a TV reality show in Argentina in early 2015, France lost a trailblazer.

She had already dodged death twice. The first time was in a car accident when she was 17, which took two years to recover from. The second time was sailing alone between Corsica and Elba in 2011, when she fell overboard.

Arthaud had her phone in her pocket and was able to call her mother in Paris, who alerted the rescue services. She was located via her phone signal after two hours in the water, describing her recovery as a miracle.

During her earlier racing career she'd known several friends lost at sea. In the 1986 Route du Rhum transatlantic, Arthaud had been the nearest competitor to Loïc Caradec when he sent a Mayday message. First to reach his position, she'd been unable to locate Caradec.

This memory, and others, led Arthaud to say of her own overboard experience: 'I knew I wasn't certain to survive.' So it was especially tragic that it was not the sea that took her life, but a mid-air collision between two helicopters carrying the TV show contestants.

Her sailing career started when she left home after her car accident, compelled to go to sea, leaving a simple note for her family: 'I need to be free.' Her parents understood this wanderlust. Her father, as publisher of Editions Arthaud, had brought many books by adventurers, explorers and photographers to the French market, including those of Bernard Moitessier.

At 21, Arthaud finished 11th in one of France's biggest races, the Route du Rhum solo transatlantic. In the eyes of the French headline writers, she'd become 'la petite fiancée de l'Atlantique' ('the Atlantic's small fiancée').

Arthaud wasn't the first woman to take on a male-dominated sport – Naomi James, Claire Francis and others preceded her – but she brought a vitality and verve to it that made her undeniably cool.

She still bore the scars of the car crash, but slim, lithe and with flowing hair, Arthaud certainly had a certain je ne sais quoi. Sponsors knew it, too, as her boats such as Miss Dubonnet and Biotherm attested.

Above all, she was a superb and gritty sailor. Her landmark victory was the 1980 Route du Rhum in the 19-m (60-ft) trimaran Pierre 1er. Already a magnet for the media cameras with gold metallic hulls, highlighted in silver reflective accents, Arthaud's boat stormed across the finish line, with Arthaud herself standing high above the water on the windward hull as Pierre 1er sped on under autopilot. The photos taken that day summed up

everything Arthaud had brought to the sport, and the moment had something of the mould-breaking glamour of the 1930s aviatrixes about it.

'But sailing is not easy for a woman,' she later said. 'It's a hard, tough world. You're on boat here, there and everywhere. For years, I didn't have a home. I lived on a boat. I was 36 by the time I gave birth to my only daughter. I certainly didn't follow the traditional path. I lived like an adventuress.'

Arthaud blazed a trail since followed by other French yachtswomen such as Isabelle Autissier, Catherine Chabaud, Karine Fauconnier and Christine Guillou. Prior to her death, she had been working on creating a women-only race in the Mediterranean. Gone too soon, she is a great loss to the sailing world.

▷ Florence Arthaud waves at the start of the Transat race on 5 June 1988 in Plymouth, UK. Arthaud was solo sailing's first female superstar. She lost her life in 2015 in a helicopter crash while filming a reality TV show.

# François Gabart

## Vital stats

**Name:** François Gabart

**DoB:** 23/03/1983

**Nationality:** French

**Known for:** Being the youngest and fastest winner of the Vendée Globe

Picture a blond-haired five year old, shinning up the mast of his parents' cruising boat, sitting on a spreader and grinning happily at the photographer back down on the deck.

That kid is François Gabart, so at home on a boat that he now reckons his life at sea began 'in my mother's belly'. By the time the kid was 29, he had won the 2012/3 Vendée Globe solo round-the-world race – not just the youngest ever to do so, but in a time so fast (78d 2h 16m) that he crushed the previous winning time by over six days.

Gabart's parents, Dominique and Catherine, a dentist and a magistrate, took their three children cruising while they were young, expanding their horizons in every way. It was during a stop in the US that François tried out the Optimist singlehander class and began racing.

Not only was Gabart good, but he revealed a seriously competitive nature. At 13, he was France's Optimist national champion, following that up at 15 in the bigger Moth class. He moved on to the two-person Tornado catamaran, then an Olympic class, and became the world junior champion in 2004.

Gabart tried for Olympic selection for the 2008 Games, while combining it with his engineering-degree studies at INSA in Lyon. In all, he spent six years on the French sailing team, though ultimately missing out on Olympic selection. By then, he'd already had a taster of the life of a pro sailor when he crewed as part of Antoine Koch's young crew in the ORMA 60 trimaran Sopra, in the 2006 Round Europe Race.

It set him on a path that's he's remained on ever since. He joined the Figaro class which, like the Classe 6.50 Mini Transat boats, are incubators for emerging solo sailors. In 2007, with Laurent Pellecuer, Gabart finished second in the Cap Istanbul race. A year later he won the Challenge Espoir Région Bretagne, an academy-type school/event whose more illustrious alumni have included Franck Cammas, Yann Eliès, Sébastien Josse and Armel le Cléac'h.

While at the academy, Gabart stepped up to the IMOCA 60 monohull for the first time, racing *Groupe Bel* with Kito de Pavant to second place in the 2009 Transat Jacques Vabre. The same year saw insurance giant sponsor Macif sign Gabart up as their skipper for the intense and ultra-competitive Figaro circuit. Gabart repaid his backer's faith by being crowned the 2010 champion.

He was now ready for a fully funded campaign with a brand-new IMOCA 60. Macif gave Gabart the means to build a new boat, hiring Michel Desjoyeaux's expertise to optimize the design and build the latest-generation boat from designers VPLP and Guillaume Verdier.

As second-youngest skipper in the fleet, Gabart was reckoned to be a strong contender in the 2012/3 Vendée Globe, but not a favourite. The attritional nature of the race, where a third of the fleet is routinely knocked out by incidents,

injury and gear failure, meant that other skippers in comparable boats but with previous race experience were fancied ahead of him.

At the equator on the outbound leg, Gabart was part of a leading clutch of six boats. This was reduced to four by the time the longitude of the Cape of Good Hope was passed, before Gabart moved to the front, duelling all the way through the Southern Ocean with Armel le Cléac'h. Gabart managed to break clear after Cape Horn and lead home up the Atlantic to reach Les Sables d'Olonne finish line as the winner. A new French star had arrived.

Gabart says he has no particular sailing role model, but names Eric Tabarly, Paul Elvstrøm, Michel Desjoyeaux, Loïck Peyron, Franck Cammas and Ben Ainslie amongst those who have inspired him. Interestingly, they combine Olympic and trans-oceanic skills, intuitive talent and structured education, level-headedness and burning determination.

Gabart followed up his Vendée Globe with a new *Macif*, a 31-m (100-ft) trimaran whose race programme will culminate in a 2019 bid to set the fastest solo circumnavigation.

▽ Gabart on the way to winning the 2012/3 Vendée Globe in *Macif*, the youngest-ever skipper to do so.

## Ocean Greats
# Sir Ben Ainslie

### Vital stats

**Name:** Ben Ainslie

**DoB:** 05/02/1977

**Nationality:** British

**Known for:** Being the most successful sailor in Olympic history

Even as a teenager, Ben Ainslie was known inside the British Sailing Team as 'Big Ben' – not for his stature, but for his towering talent and tangible sense of greatness.

Now that his Olympic sailing career has ended, the record confirms Ainslie as the greatest sailor in Olympic history. His tally from five successive Olympic Games from 1996 to 2012 is one silver and four golds. Like rowers, sailors can only compete in one event at each Games, but his peers rank Ainslie alongside the multiple medal winners such as Mark Spitz and Michael Phelps.

The tense finale of the last race of the 2012 Olympics in London saw a place change between two key rivals on the penultimate leg that brought Ainslie his fourth Olympic title. Only Brazil's Torben Grael and Robert Scheidt can count a grand total of five Olympic medals; only Denmark's Paul Elvstrøm has four golds. Ainslie has both.

This win ended a year of suffocating pressure for Ainslie. He was the very first person to start the Olympic torch parade, and the media inked him in as a gold-medal winner-in-waiting months before his home Games commenced. He'd been asked to lead the British team as flag bearer at the opening ceremony, but the imminent start of his own competition in Weymouth precluded this.

As a 19 year old in 1996, Ainslie was pipped to the gold in the Laser singlehanded by Robert Scheidt. The supremely talented Brazilian was a little older and more street-smart than Ainslie, and finessed him into a premature start in the final race. Scheidt could afford to drop the race and still win gold. Ainslie could not.

Four years later in Sydney, Ainslie – whose

self-confessed maxim is, 'I never give up' – repaid Scheidt by racing him out of gold to win the medal himself. It showed a steel that has been manifest in Ainslie's career ever since. He will not accept being beaten until the last breath has expired from the last moment of the last race of any competition.

It was this winning aura and nous about how to manage the end-game of a major competition that Ainslie brought to *Oracle Team USA*'s crew, when he was moved onboard from the sub's bench to win the America's Cup in 2013.

Ainslie had been involved the America's Cup three times before, but always shoe-horning it around his Olympic sailing. He did the same with Oracle Team USA, but a week after winning at London 2012, he was back in San Francisco for the critical final 12 months of the 2013 America's Cup. For 2017, he is heading his own team, Land Rover Ben Ainslie Racing, hoping to become the first-ever British winner of the America's Cup.

Having won his silver and gold medals in the Laser, Ainslie moved up to the heavier Finn singlehanded class. It is a vastly more complex boat than the Laser, with a very sensitive, tuneable rig. Ainslie mastered it in short order. He also re-engineered his body, adding 15kg (33lb) of fighting-weight muscle. He completely dominated the Finn class from 2001–12, winning the world championship Gold Cup in 2002, 2003, 2004, 2005, 2008 and 2012. In all, he has 11 world titles and nine European titles to his name.

Ainslie comes from a sailing background. His father, Roddie, skippered the 22-m (71-ft) *Second Life* in the inaugural 1973/4 Whitbread Round the World Race. Ainslie and his sister, Fleur, sailed with

their parents on their cruising boat. The turning point in his life came when the family moved from Cheshire to Restronguet, Cornwall. Aged eight, Ainslie was given an Optimist children's singlehander. One day, his father pushed him off and said, 'We'll see you round the headland.'

By the age of ten Ainslie was racing, and by 12 he was competing in his first international competition. He became part of the Royal Yachting Association's British Sailing Team shortly afterwards, exposing him to international competition from a young age and culminating in him becoming Youth Sailing World Champion in 1995.

Rod Carr, the then RYA chief executive and former Olympic coach, described Ainslie as 'the best British sailor of a generation.' Time and results have proven that he is even better than that.

△ Ainslie, whose fifth medal and fourth gold, won at London 2012, made him the most successful sailor in Olympic history.

# Ocean Greats
# Paul Elvstrøm

*'One has not won, if, in the process of winning, one has lost the respect of one's competitors.'*

**Paul Elvstrøm**

**Vital stats**

**Name:** Paul Elvstrøm

**DoB:** 28/02/1928

**Nationality:** Danish

**Known for:** Winning four Olympic gold medals

Called 'The Great Dane' with good reason, Paul Elvstrøm was the first sailing superstar in the Olympic Games.

Sailing had been part of the modern Olympics ever since the second Games in 1900 staged in Paris, when racing took part on the River Seine and off Le Havre. This was yacht racing as a pursuit for the privileged, and so it largely remained until after the Second World War.

Elvstrøm helped change that with the London Games of 1948 and a sailing competition in Torbay, winning the gold medal as a precocious 20 year old in the Firefly class. He then took successive golds in the more powerful Finn class at the 1952, 1956 and 1960 Games.

The Dane built his own training bench at home, allowing him to condition his physique for extending hiking out of the dinghy, such was his focused pursuit of success on the race course.

For all his physical prowess and relentless training, Elvstrøm was not invincible. He admitted that the mental pressures of being expected to win leeched away his confidence in Naples in 1964, when going for a fifth straight gold medal. Failed involvements in putative America's Cup efforts from Switzerland and Denmark also dented his confidence.

Elvstrøm bounded back in 1968, coming within a hairsbreadth of a bronze medal in the Mexico Games regatta at Acapulco, having switched to the two-man Star class. He just missed the same medal again in a Tornado catamaran in 1984, in Pusan, Korea, when he sailed his teenage daughter Trine.

In all, Elvstrøm won world titles in five different classes, a marker of his talents. For generations

of aspiring racing sailors, he was their first hero, not only for his superlative record, his innovations (such as the low-drag, through-hull dinghy bailer) and his bestselling texts explaining the racing rules, but also for his integrity.

'One has not won, if, in the process of winning, one has lost the respect of one's competitors,' he once said.

A true measure of the man is that his impact continues many decades after he won his first gold medal.

△ Elvstrøm competing with his daughter, Trine, at the 1988 Olympics. He came within .75 of a point of winning a fifth Olympic medal.

◁ A young 'Great Dane', winner of four gold medals at successive Olympics from 1952 to 1960.

# Ocean Greats
# John Bertrand

*'Any boss who sacks someone for not turning up to work today is a bum.'*

**Bob Hawke** | Australia's prime minister in 1983 on John Bertrand sailing – and winning – the America's Cup

## Vital stats

**Name:** John Bertrand

**DoB:** 20/12/1946

**Nationality:** Australian

**Known for:** Skippering the first-ever challenger to win the America's Cup

For a one-sentence summary, Australian John Bertrand holds a unique claim: skippering the first-ever challenger to win the America's Cup.

How big an achievement was this? Well, it ended the longest winning streak in sports history, of 132 years, and sent his home country into delirium. The following day, Australian prime minister Bob Hawke appeared on breakfast TV, having watched events unfold overnight on the other side of the world, and declared, 'Any boss who sacks anyone not turning up to work today is a bum.'

Talk about television gold. This was 1983 and the gem is still there to be seen on YouTube. The gist of the comment was that *Australia II*'s victory was one of the great nation-uniting and nation-defining events in a sports-mad country. Coles, Australia's biggest food-store chain, pinpointed the win as a turnaround time from recession to increasing earnings. The number of citizenship applications rose, and champagne and green-and-gold ribbon both sold out. Australia felt good about itself. Even now, the Australian Confederation of Sport calls it 'the greatest team performance in 200 years'.

The man at the wheel of Alan Bond's *Australia II* was skipper and helmsman John Bertrand. This was the man with the tanned face, moustache and gold-gilet crew uniform. It was the time of Bondy, the self-made billionaire who was later to crash at the centre of Australia's biggest corporate fraud. And it was a time when Newport, Rhode Island, resonated to the Men at Work song 'Down Under', playing up and down the waterfront during that tumultuous America's Cup summer.

Overturning 132 years of American dominance wasn't likely to happen quietly, and so it proved in the 23rd match for the America's Cup. *Australia II* had a radical keel, not just 'upside down' for being wider at the bottom than the top, but one sprouting wings. The New York Yacht Club spent the summer of 1983 claiming that it was illegal under nationality rules, suggesting that designer Ben Lexcen had got more help than just testing facilities from the Dutch test tank and aerospace lab he had used.

In the climatic contest, *Australia II* was faster than Dennis Conner's *Liberty*, but went 1:3 down before coming back and passing *Liberty* on the penultimate leg of the seventh race to win 4:3.

By then, Bertrand was already a significant

△ A broken mainsail headboard was one of several failures that almost thwarted *Australia II*'s historic victory in the 1983 America's Cup.

△ A come-from-behind win in the deciding seventh race made Bertrand the first challenging skipper to win the America's Cup and defeat the USA.

sailor. He won an Olympic bronze medal in the 1976 Toronto Olympics at the regatta in Kingston, in the Finn singlehander class. He had also already earned the nickname 'Aero', having written a paper on the aerodynamics of America's Cup sails. After graduating from Monash, he went to the US to complete a masters in ocean engineering at the Massachusetts Institute of Technology.

This, and sailing, was already in his family. His great-grandfather Thomas Pearkes had been an engineer for two of Sir Thomas Lipton's challenges for the America's Cup. His brother Lex built boats with John, and raced against him when they were kids.

'Winning in 1983 changed the game. It showed other countries it could be done,' says Bertrand. 'It is the most prestigious sporting event in the world. It's different.'

By the time Bertrand won the America's Cup, he'd been to two Olympics and six world championships, and had been on the team for four previous Cups, as well as being one of 'young guns' that North Sails' founder Lowell North employed to drive its worldwide expansion.

On winning, Bertrand found 'contentment' at his 'Everest moment' and chose to move away from sailing. He went into business, targeting real estate and emerging media. However, by 1995 he was ready for a comeback, this time leading a team backed by blue-chip corporate sponsorship, oneAustralia. In San Diego, the only team better was Team New Zealand, the ultimate winner of the Cup that year, though Bertrand's challenge was set back by the spectacular sinking of *AUS 35*. From the first crack across the deck to the mast disappearing under the Pacific waves, only two minutes elapsed.

It was the first and only time since 1851 that an America's Cup yacht had sunk. For Bertrand, reacquiring the high of 1983 was a compelling but challenging goal. No one expected it to end this way.

Bertrand remains a significant figure in sport. Not just an ongoing presence at each America's Cup, in 2013 he took on the presidency of Swimming Australia, arguably his country's greatest Olympic sport. He also runs a leadership lecture series at Monash University that invites former prime ministers and current CEOs of global corporations to speak, chairs Australia's sporting Hall of Fame and is selector for the Australian Olympic sailing team. All in all, it's quite a CV.

# Ocean Greats
# Torben Grael

◁ Torben Grael, with fellow Olympic great
Robert Scheidt, during the 2009 Maxi Yacht Rolex
Cup in Porto Cervo, Sardinia.

In the pantheon of Olympic sailors there is Britain's Sir Ben Ainslie (four golds, one silver), Denmark's Paul Elvstrøm (four golds), Russia's Valentin Mankin and Germany's Jochen Schümann (three golds and one silver), plus the Brazilian pair of Robert Scheidt and Torben Grael.

These men have accrued more medals than any others since yachting become part of the modern Olympics in 1900. Mankin, a Ukrainian from Kiev, and Schümann, an East German from East Berlin, were both products of the former Eastern Bloc state-supported Olympic programmes, and recorded their successes before and after the break-up of the Soviet bloc.

Brazil's Grael and Scheidt, by contrast, have the traditional background of being kickstarted in sailing by their families.

Scheidt has won two golds, two silvers and one bronze from five successive Olympic Games in the Laser singlehanded class and two-man Star keelboat. Grael's record is only marginally behind

this, counting two bronzes to Scheidt's one, but is remarkable for its longevity, spanning the period from 1998 to 2004.

Even in his mid-50s Torben Grael wasn't sated, aiming for another shot at the Olympics, this time at his home Games in Rio de Janeiro in 2016. This ambition created an interesting problem for the Brazilians, as Grael, his brother Lars and Robert Scheidt were all targeting the Star class, with only one place per nation, per event available.

What really sets Torben Grael and Robert Scheidt apart is the sheer breadth of the former's success, while Scheidt has remained a two-class Olympic specialist.

Grael won his Olympic medals in the three-man Soling and two-man Star classes, but he also has world titles in the Snipe, One Ton and 12-metre classes. This means he's won in everything from a two- to an 11-person crew. He also has Brazilian national titles in five further classes.

After such a superlative record in inshore day racing, Grael took the plunge into round-the-world racing, skippering *Brasil 1* to third place in the 2005/6 Volvo Ocean Race and *Ericsson* to victory in the next race in 2008/9.

Add in three America's Cup campaigns with Italy's Prada/Luna Rossa team in 2000, 2003 and 2007, and Grael's claim to be one of the world's finest racing sailors is irrefutable.

Not for nothing did Torben Grael get the nickname 'Turbine' for making boats go fast, though for the past 20 years it is his uncanny wind-sensing ability that has made watching him compete so absorbing.

He is fully prepared to race the breeze rather than cover his opponents. Often derided as a high-stakes style of racing, particularly in two-boat-only America's Cup match racing, Grael nonetheless has consistently high percentages in reading the conditions better than his opponent.

The Graels are Brazil's first family of sailing. Younger brother Lars is himself a double Olympic medallist, with two bronzes in the Tornado catamaran class. Their grandfather, Preben, pioneered sailboat racing in Brazil and their two uncles, Axel and Erik, were among the first countrymen to succeed in international competition.

So strong is the family heritage that Torben owns the 6-m (19.7-ft) *Aileen* that his grandfather Preben purchased in 1929. Her rig has been updated from gaff to Bermudan, and she has modern sails and fittings as she is raced keenly.

Torben and Andrea Grael's children are proving to be formidable sailors, too. Martine Grael, with Kahena Kunze, won the 2014 ISAF Worlds in the 49er FX class, and her brother Marco is showing strongly in the men's 49er class. Quite a pedigree.

△ Five Olympic medals in the tight confines of inshore racing and outright victory with *Ericsson* in the 2008/9 round-the-world Volvo Ocean Race; Grael is one of sailing's true greats.

# The Boats

# Olympic

## International 470

**Crew:** 2 (single trapeze)
**LOA:** 4.7m (15.4ft)
**Beam:** 1.69m (5.5ft)
**Draft:** 0.5–1.06m (1.6–3.5ft)
**Weight:** 120kg (260lb)
**Main/jib:** 3.58m² (38.5 sq ft)
**Spinnaker:** 13m² (140 sq ft)
**Website:** www.470.org

The 470 is a double-handed monohull planing dinghy with a centreboard, Bermuda rig and centre sheeting. It is equipped with spinnaker and trapeze, making teamwork necessary to sail it well. It has a large sail-area-to-weight ratio, and is designed to plane easily.

The 470 is a popular class with both individuals and sailing schools, offering a good introduction to high-performance boats without being excessively difficult to handle. It is not a boat designed for beginners, but its earlier-designed smaller sister, the 420, is a stepping stone to the 470. The 470 is an International Sailing Federation International Class and has been an Olympic class since the 1976 games.

## Laser

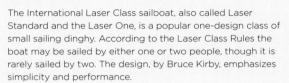

**Crew:** 1
**LOA:** 4.2m (13.8ft)
**Beam:** 1.39m (4.6ft)
**Draft:** 0.787m (2.6ft)
**Weight:** 58.97kg (130lb)
**Main/jib:** 7.06m² (76 sq ft)
**Spinnaker:** N/A
**Website:** www.laserinternational.org

The International Laser Class sailboat, also called Laser Standard and the Laser One, is a popular one-design class of small sailing dinghy. According to the Laser Class Rules the boat may be sailed by either one or two people, though it is rarely sailed by two. The design, by Bruce Kirby, emphasizes simplicity and performance.

The Laser is one of the most popular single-handed dinghies in the world. In addition to its durability, a commonly cited reason for its popularity is that it is robust and simple to rig and sail. The Laser also provides very competitive racing, due to the very tight class-association controls that eliminate differences in hull, sails and equipment.

## Laser Radial

**Crew:** 1
**LOA:** 4.2m (13.8ft)
**Beam:** 1.39m (4.6ft)
**Draft:** 0.787m (2.6ft)
**Weight:** 58.97kg (130lb)
**Main/jib:** 5.76m² (62 sq ft)
**Spinnaker:** N/A
**Website:** www.laserinternational.org

The Laser Radial is a popular one-design class of small, singlehanded sailing dinghy. It is a variant of the Laser, with a shorter mast and reduced sail area, allowing light sailors to sail in heavy winds. The International Class is recognized by the International Sailing Federation.

The Laser Radial is generally sailed and raced by lighter-weight sailors and is usually the choice of women Laser sailors. Men typically sail the Laser, which has a larger sail. Most larger regattas for the Laser class generally have separate races for the Laser, Laser Radial and Laser 4.7.

## Finn

**Crew:** 1
**LOA:** 4.5m (14.4ft)
**Beam:** 1.47m (4.3ft)
**Draft:** 0.17m (4.10ft)
**Weight:** 107kg (236lb)
**Mainsail area:** 10.6m² (114 sq ft)
**Mast height:** 6.66m (21.10 ft)
**Website:** www.finnclass.org

Designed in 1949 by Swedish boat designer Rickard Sarby, the single-handed Finn was initially only meant to compete in the 1952 Helsinki Summer Olympics. It has since become so successful that multi-medallist Ben Ainslie sailed it to Olympic gold in the 2012 games in Great Britain (*picture left*).

This Finn dinghy design has competed in every summer Olympics since 1952, making it one of the most prolific Olympic sailboats and the longest-serving dinghy in the Olympic Regatta. It currently fills the slot for the Heavyweight Dinghy at the Olympic Games. It has been contended that the Finn is the most physical and tactical singlehander sailboat in the world.

## RS:X

**Crew:** 1
**LOA:** 2.86m (9.4ft)
**Beam:** 0.93m (3.1ft)
**Draft:** N/A
**Weight:** 15.5kg (34lb)
**Main/jib:** Men 9.5m² (102 sq ft);
women/youth 8.5m² (91 sq ft)
**Spinnaker:** N/A
**Website:** www.rsxclass.com

The RS:X came about as a result of a successful bid by Neil Pryde Windsurfing to supply one-design windsurfing equipment for the 2008 Olympic Games in China. The RS:X was designed by Jean Bouldoires and Robert Stroj in 2004 and went into production in 2005.

The RS:X design features a high technology rig, with carbon mast and boom, and a 'wide-style' board that merges modern windsurf board design with a centreboard, thus enabling competition to be held in virtually any conditions from 3 to 30 knots. This means that the RS:X is always a dynamic, versatile class to observe, and racing is always close, exciting and visually appealing.

## Nacra 17

**Crew:** 1
**LOA:** 4.2m (13.8ft)
**Beam:** 1.39m (4.6ft)
**Draft:** 0.787m (2.6ft)
**Weight:** 58.97kg (130lb)
**Main/jib:** 5.76m² (62 sq ft)
**Spinnaker:** 19.5m² (210 sq ft)
**Website:** www.nacra17class.com

The Nacra 17 is a performance catamaran used for racing. It was first designed in 2011 and went into production in 2012. Specially designed to fulfil ISAF specifications, the Nacra 17 is 250mm (10in) longer and 100mm (4in) wider than an F16-class catamaran. It also has a taller mast, more sail area and curved dagger boards. The curve boards give an added dimension to the sailing, and the boat is able to carry a wider range of crew weight than the F16 while being considerably lighter than the F18.

In May 2012, the International Sailing Federation chose the Nacra 17 as the equipment for the mixed multihull at the 2016 Olympic Sailing Regatta and 2020 Summer Olympics in Tokyo.

## International 49er

**Crew:** 1–2
**LOA:** 4.995m (16.4ft)
**Beam:** 2.9m (9.5ft)
**Draft:** 1.447m (4.7ft)
**Weight:** 74kg (163.5lb)
**Main/jib:** 19.97m² (215 sq ft)
**Spinnaker:** 38m² (409 sq ft)
**Website:** www.49er.org

The 49er (*picture right*) is a two-handed, skiff-type high-performance sailing dinghy. The two crew work on different roles, with the helm making many tactical decisions, as well as steering, and the crew doing most of the sail control. Both of the crew are equipped with their own trapeze and sailing is handled while 'flying'.

The 49er was designed by Julian Bethwaite, the son of Frank Bethwaite, designer of the Tasar and the popular Laser 2 classes. The boat was selected by the ISAF after a series of trials and has been in every Olympics since its debut in the Sydney Olympics of 2000.

## International 49erFX

**Crew:** 1–2
**LOA:** 4.995m (16.4ft)
**Beam:** 2.9m (9.5ft)
**Draft:** 1.447m (4.7ft)
**Weight:** 94kg (208lb)
**Main/jib:** 17.5m² (188 sq ft)
**Spinnaker:** 35m² (377 sq ft)
**Website:** www.49er.org

The 49erFX is an identical platform to the Olympic International 49er, with a smaller mast and suit of sails. The smaller version was created for and adopted by the Olympics for all female competition and will be raced in the Rio 2016 Games for the first time.

The planing hull has fixed wings to provide greater leverage for the crew, resulting in a very fast but demanding and acrobatic boat. The boat is frequently sailed by non-Olympic crews looking for a boat as fast as the International 49er that is much more manageable.

# Centreboards

## 29er

**Crew:** 2
**LOA:** 4.4m (14.4ft)
**Beam:** 1.7m (5.6ft)
**Draft:** 0.7m (2.3ft)
**Weight:** 90kg (198lb)
**Main/jib:** 13.19m² (142 sq ft)
**Spinnaker:** 16.83m² (181.15 sq ft)
**Website:** www.29er.org

The 29er is a true high-performance skiff – a two-man, single trapeze, asymmetric spinnaker boat. 29ers are built to exceedingly strict one-design standards, and under the strict control of the International Sailing Federation (ISAF). The boats are rugged, well equipped and fully competitive. Failures are rare, sails are durable and the expense of running the boat is modest.

The 29er was designed by Australian skiff legend Julian Bethwaite, with a team of internationally recognized dinghy sailors. Constructed from hi-tech composite-foam sandwich, the hull is ultra-lightweight with a self-draining cockpit. Although the design was originally targeted to youth sailors as a feeder class to the Olympic 49er, the 29er is a super class on its own merits.

## International 420

**Crew:** 2
**LOA:** 4.2m (13.8ft)
**Beam:** 1.63m (5.3ft)
**Draft:** 0.965m (3.2ft)
**Weight:** 80kg (180lb)
**Main/jib:** 10.25m² (110.3 sq ft)
**Spinnaker:** 8.83m² (95 sq ft)
**Website:** www.420sailing.org

The International 420 Class Dinghy (*picture left*) is a double-handed monohull planing dinghy with centreboard, bermuda rig and centre sheeting. The name describes the overall length of the boat in centimetres (the boat is exactly 4.2 metres long). The hull is fibreglass with internal buoyancy tanks. The 420 is equipped with spinnaker and optional trapeze, making teamwork necessary to sail it well. It has a large sail-area-to-weight ratio, and is designed to plane easily. It can be rigged to be sailed singlehanded.

The 420 was designed specifically to be easier to handle than its larger, higher-performance cousin, the 470. Both were designed by French engineer Christian Maury, the 420 as a stepping stone for club and youth sailing to the 470.

## International 505

**Crew:** 2
**LOA:** 5.05m (16.6ft)
**Beam:** 1.88m (6.2ft)
**Draft:** 1.05m (3.4ft)
**Weight:** 127.4kg (282lb)
**Main/jib:** 16.3m² (175 sq ft)
**Spinnaker:** 27m² (291 sq ft)
**Website:** www.int505.org

Designed in 1953 by John Westell as a smaller version of his 5.48-m (18-ft) Coronet Olympic design, the 505 was given International status in 1955. The first World Championship was held in 1956 in La Baule and since then World Championships have been held annually, hosted by 20 different countries.

The sail plan and hull shape are tightly controlled by the measurement rules, but considerable freedom in the rigging, internal layout and size and shape of the foils allow the boat to be set up in many ways, to suit sailors over a wide weight range. Apart from spars, there are no restrictions on the materials that can be used, enabling the class to evolve over the years. The modern materials now used mean that today's boats are significantly stronger and have long competitive lives.

## B14

**Crew:** 2
**LOA:** 4.25m (13.9ft)
**Beam:** 3.05m (10ft)
**Draft:** N/A
**Weight:** 64kg (141lb)
**Main/jib:** 17.2m² (185 sq ft)
**Spinnaker:** 29.2m² (314 sq ft)
**Website:** www.b14.org

The B14 is a two-man monohull dinghy, designed by Julian Bethwaite in 1984. It is recognized as an International Class by the International Sailing Federation.

The B14 is designed with a low centre of gravity for added stability and an open transom, to help the boat drain itself quickly without the need for a self-bailer. The mast is set far back in the boat to make room for the large, asymmetric spinnaker. The boat has a fast handicap, designed with racing in mind. For this reason, it is highly suitable for more experienced sailors. The boat does not have a trapeze, but instead makes use of wide wings.

## Byte

**Crew:** 1
**LOA:** 3.6m (11.8ft)
**Beam:** 1.3m (4.3ft)
**Draft:** N/A
**Weight:** 45.5kg (101lb)
**Main/jib:** 5.65–6.8m² (60.8–73 sq ft)
**Spinnaker:** 13.94m² (150 sq ft)
**Website:** www.bytecii.com

The Byte CII is a fast and fun, singlehanded one-design dinghy. The CII's carbon two-piece mast and fully battened mylar sail are self depowering, allowing sailors with a wider weight range to sail in a vast range of conditions. The smaller Byte CI utilizes the same hull with a smaller, more manageable rig. Using the same top section as the Byte CII with a smaller sail and shorter lower mast section, the CI caters for the lighter end of the weight range. The two-piece mast makes the jump from CI to CII easy, and a Byte is the perfect transition from smaller boats such as the Optimist, providing the skills to move on to larger boats such as the Laser.

## Cadet

**Crew:** 2
**LOA:** 3.2m (10.5ft)
**Beam:** 1.38m (4.5ft)
**Draft:** 0.16m (0.5ft) without centreboard
**Weight:** 54kg (119lb)
**Main/jib:** 17.2m² (185 sq ft)
**Spinnaker:** 29.2m² (314 sq ft)
**Website:** www.cadetclass.org.uk

In 1947, *Yachting World* organized a design competition for a beginners' sailing dinghy that the current Cadet design won. The boat sails with a bermuda-rigged mainsail, jib and spinnaker.

The Cadet is a class of sailing dinghy designed to be sailed by two children up to the age of 17. It is a one-design class, originally designed by Jack Holt. Cadets are sailed worldwide in at least 18 countries.

## Contender

**Crew:** 1 (trapeze)
**LOA:** 4.9m (16ft)
**Beam:** 1.5m (4.9ft)
**Draft:** 1.4m (4.6ft)
**Weight:** 83kg (183lb)
**Main/jib:** 10.8m² (116 sq ft)
**Spinnaker:** N/A
**Website:** www.sailcontender.org.uk

The International Contender is a single-handed, high-performance sailing dinghy, designed by Australian Bob Miller, latterly known as Ben Lexcen, in 1967 as a possible successor to the Finn dinghy for Olympic competition. The Contender is recognized as an International Class by the International Sailing Federation.

The boat has a trapeze that allows the sailor to use his or her weight more effectively. Sailors wishing to master the Contender must learn how to trapeze and steer the boat at the same time, and how to move about the boat while keeping it level. Unlike older and heavier dinghy designs, the Contender requires the centreboard to be lowered at least somewhat to avoid quick capsizes when reaching and running in a breeze.

## Enterprise

**Crew:** 2
**LOA:** 4m (13.1ft)
**Beam:** 1.6m (5.2ft)
**Draft:** 0.2–1.2m (8in–3.9ft)
**Weight:** 94kg (208lb)
**Main/jib:** 18 m² (194 sq ft)
**Spinnaker:** Not normally used
**Website:** www.sailenterprise.co.uk

The Enterprise is a two-man, sloop-rigged hiking sailing dinghy with distinctive blue sails. Despite being one of the older classes of dinghy, it remains popular and is used for both cruising and racing. It has a combination of size, weight and power that appeals to all ages. The Enterprise is accredited as an International Class by the ISAF.

The Enterprise is most often sailed with no spinnaker. However the international class rules allow the decision of whether to allow spinnakers to be made by the national authority. They are relatively unstable in comparison with other dinghies of similar performance, but they have handling characteristics that would generally be associated with much faster designs.

## Europe

**Crew:** 1
**LOA:** 3.35m (11ft)
**Beam:** 1.38m (4.5ft)
**Draft:** 0.15m (0.5ft)
**Weight:** 45kg (99lb)
**Main/jib:** 7m² (75 sq ft)
**Spinnaker:** N/A
**Website:** www.europeclass.org.uk

The Europe is a one-person dinghy designed in Belgium in 1960 by Alois Roland as a class-legal Moth dinghy. The design later changed into its own one-design class. Ideal for sailors weighing 50–75kg (111–166lb), the hull is made of fibreglass. The mast is made of carbon fibre and specially designed to the sailor. A soft mast is best for light sailors, while heavier sailors use stiffer masts. Sails are also specially designed according to mast stiffness and crew weight.

The Europe was introduced as an Olympic class in the 1992 summer Olympics as the women's single-handed dinghy. It was replaced by the Laser Radial in the 2008 Games.

## Fireball

**Crew:** 2 (single trapeze)
**LOA:** 5m (16.4ft)
**Beam:** 1.4m (4.6ft)
**Draft:** 1.22m (4ft)
**Weight:** 79kg (175lb)
**Main/jib:** 13.3m² (143 sq ft)
**Spinnaker:** 13m² (140 sq ft)
**Website:** www.fireball-international.com

Originally designed by Peter Milne in 1962, the Fireball is a one-design, high-performance sailing dinghy. The Fireball is sailed by a crew of two, and sports a single trapeze, symmetric spinnaker and chined hull. The class is strictly controlled, but has adapted to advances in building techniques. The performance of the boat is very dependent on tuning, as the Fireball's rig can be adjusted in numerous ways.

The Fireball is a highly competitive dinghy, with large fleets worldwide and state, national, continental and world championships held annually.

## Flying Dutchman

**Crew:** 2
**LOA:** 6.06m (19.9ft)
**Beam:** 1.78m (5.8ft)
**Draft:** 0.15–1.07m (0.5–3.5ft)
**Weight:** 130kg (290lb)
**Main/jib:** 18.6m² (200 sq ft)
**Spinnaker:** 21m² (230 sq ft)
**Website:** None

The Flying Dutchman (FD) is a one-design, high-performance, two-person monohull racing dinghy. Developed in the early 1950s, its large sail area per unit weight allows it to plane easily when sailing upwind. It made its Olympic debut at the 1960 Games.

The FD is still one of the fastest racing dinghies in the world. It carries a mainsail, a very large foresail genoa and a large spinnaker for running and reaching. The FD has been the basis for many important innovations in sailing over the past half century, largely because it was left as an 'open' one-design class, where innovation and development in the boat is allowed and encouraged.

## Flying Junior

**Crew:** 2
**LOA:** 4m (13.1ft)
**Beam:** 1.5m (4.9ft)
**Draft:** 0.76m (2.5ft)
**Weight:** 95kg (210lb)
**Main/jib:** 9.3m² (100 sq ft)
**Spinnaker:** 7.4m² (80 sq ft)
**Website:** None

The International Flying Junior (FJ) is a sailing dinghy that was originally designed in 1955 in the Netherlands, by renowned boat designer Van Essen and Olympic sailor Conrad Gülcher. The FJ was built to serve as a training boat for the then Olympic-class Flying Dutchman.

In 1960 the Flying Junior formed its own class organization, and by the early 1970s it was accorded the status of an International Class. In the US, many high-school sailing and Intercollegiate Sailing Association programmes own fleets of FJs. It is ideal for teaching young sailors the skills of boat handling and racing.

## GP14

**Crew:** 2
**LOA:** 4.27m (14ft)
**Beam:** 1.54m (5.1ft)
**Draft:** 1.2m (3.9ft)
**Weight:** 133kg (294lb)
**Main/jib:** 12.85m² (138 sq ft)
**Spinnaker:** 8.4m² (90 sq ft)
**Website:** www.gp14.org

The GP14 is a popular sailing dinghy, used for both racing and cruising. The boat is relatively heavy but stable, and the weight and the freeboard, together with its lines, combine to make this an excellent sea boat. It is also an ideal boat to learn to sail in.

The class is raced competitively and offers excellent close racing. The boat is a very forgiving and easy boat to sail, but a very challenging, demanding and immensely rewarding boat to sail really well. At the highest level of competition the standard is world class, and it is not unusual to find reigning or past Olympic champions entering the major GP14 championships and being defeated.

## International 14

**Crew:** 2
**LOA:** 4.27m (14ft)
**Beam:** 1.54m (5.1ft)
**Draft:** 1.2m (3.9ft)
**Weight:** 132.9kg (294lb)
**Main/jib:** 12.85m² (138 sq ft)
**Spinnaker:** 8.4m² (90 sq ft)
**Website:** www.international14.org

The International 14 is a double-handed racing dinghy, one of the very first true international racing-dinghy classes recognized by the International Sailing Federation.

It is a development class being controlled by a set of rules that allow for innovation and changes in hull and rig design, as long as they fall within a set of specific limitations such as length, weight, beam and sail area. The class has permitted its rules to be revised at various times in order to keep the class at the forefront of dinghy-racing development, and can now best be described as an ultralight, dual-trapeze sailing dinghy with a large sail area.

## Laser 4.7

**Crew:** 1–2
**LOA:** 4.2m (13.8ft)
**Beam:** 1.39m (4.6ft)
**Draft:** 0.787m (2.6ft)
**Weight:** 58.97kg (130lb)
**Main/jib:** 4.7m² (51 sq ft)
**Spinnaker:** N/A
**Website:** www.laser.org.uk

The Laser 4.7 is a one-design dinghy class in the Laser series, all of which are built to the same specifications. Lasers are cat-rigged, meaning they have only one sail. The Laser 4.7 uses the same hull and top mast section as the Laser, but has a different bottom mast section and a smaller sail.

The Laser 4.7 has been increasing in popularity around the world since the late 1990s. In some areas it is less favoured than the Byte dinghy, a very similar class also designed as a youth single-handed racing trainer, but the interchangeability of the rigs of the Laser series has always made them popular.

## Laser II

**Crew:** 2 (single trapeze)
**LOA:** 4.4m (14.4ft)
**Beam:** 1.4m (4.6ft)
**Draft:** approx. 1m (3.3ft) (daggerboard)
**Weight:** 76kg (168lb)
**Main/jib:** 11.52m² (124 sq ft)
**Spinnaker:** 10.2m² (110 sq ft)
**Website:** www.laser2.de

The Laser 2 is a light and fast two-person dinghy with trapeze and spinnaker. The strict one-design boat was designed in 1980 by the Australian Frank Bethwaite and it is a recognized ISAF class. The Laser 2 is solidly built (like the original Laser), thus older boats can compete on the same level as new boats without any disadvantage. The ideal crew weight is between 120 and 170kg (265 and 376lb), which also makes it an ideal boat for mixed crews and youth sailors. With its light hull and portable mast, the Laser 2 is easy to rig and easy to handle, both on land and at sea.

## Lightning

**Crew:** 3
**LOA:** 5.8m (19ft)
**Beam:** 1.98m (6.5ft)
**Draft:** 1.5m (4.9ft)
**Weight:** 320kg (700lb)
**Main/jib:** 16.4m² (177 sq ft)
**Spinnaker:** 28m² (300 sq ft)
**Website:** www.lightning368.org

The Lightning is a sloop-rigged sailing dinghy originally designed by Olin Stephens of Sparkman & Stephens in 1938. More than 15,000 Lightnings have been built since then, and there are over 500 fleets of Lightnings worldwide, many of which participate in dinghy racing.

Awarded ISAF International Class status, the Lightning is sailed in more than 13 countries and in the Pan-American Games, and the class provides a professionally managed association that is among the largest in all of one-design sailing. A World Championship is held every two years. North American, South American and European Championships are held each year, as are innumerable regional and district championships.

## Mirror

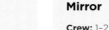

**Crew:** 1–2
**LOA:** 3.3m (10.8ft)
**Beam:** 1.4m (4.6ft)
**Draft:** 0.76m (2.5ft)
**Weight:** 45.5kg (100lb)
**Main/jib:** 6.5m² (70 sq ft)
**Spinnaker:** 4.4m² (47.3 sq ft)
**Website:** www.mirrorsailing.org

The Mirror is a small, light, easy-to-sail, easy-to-transport, pram dinghy. It is the classic dinghy for training, cruising and racing. A stable family boat suitable for all ages and abilities, it is raced widely and actively in many countries. Its ease of handling makes it a great singlehander sailed with main and jib, and with a crew of two it's an ideal International Class racing boat – many top sailors started in a Mirror.

## Moth

**Crew:** 1
**LOA:** 3.4m (11.2ft)
**Beam:** N/A
**Draft:** N/A
**Weight:** Unrestricted
**Main/jib:** N/A
**Spinnaker:** N/A
**Website:** www.mothboat.com

Classic Moth boats are a class of small, fast, singlehanded racing sailboats that originated in the US in 1929. Designed by Joel Van Sant, the Classic Moth is a monohull development class using a modified version of the International Moth rule in effect pre-1969. With a 3.4m (11.2ft) overall length, a maximum beam of 1.5m (4.9ft), a minimum hull weight of 33.8kg (75lb), a sail area of 6.5m² (72 sq ft) and very few other restrictions, a Classic Moth can be a skiff, pram, scow, skinny tube, dinghy or any combination thereof. The Moth is an ideal class for amateur designers, builders and tinkerers, and can easily be built from inexpensive materials.

## Musto Performance Skiff

**Crew:** 1
**LOA:** 4.55m (14.9ft)
**Beam:** 2.3m (7.5ft)
**Draft:** 1.074m (3.5ft)
**Weight:** 55kg (121.6lb)
**Main/jib:** 11.5m² (124 sq ft)
**Spinnaker:** 15.5m² (167 sq ft)
**Website:** www.mustoskiff.com

The Musto Performance Skiff was designed and developed with the following brief in mind – to produce an elegant yet simple dinghy with blistering performance that is highly enjoyable to sail.

As with any true skiff, the deck layout is extremely simple, leaving the sailor free to focus on sailing the boat. The spinnaker hoist and recovery system allows the sailor to hoist and drop the kite in seconds due to the low friction blocks and wide chute mouth. Another bonus is that the system is not prone to jamming or ropes twisting up, which can lead to problems in extreme situations.

## O'pen BIC

**Crew:** 1
**LOA:** 2.75m (9ft)
**Beam:** 1.3m (4.3ft)
**Draft:** 0.85m (2.8ft)
**Weight:** 45kg (99lb) (hull only)
**Main/jib:** 4.5m² (48 sq ft)
**Spinnaker:** N/A
**Website:** www.openbic.com

The O'pen Bic, often simply referred to as the Open Bic, is a singlehanded sailboat designed for younger sailors. Developed by Vitali Design, the boat was launched in 2006. It is an International Class, as recognized by the International Sailing Federation. The ideal weight for a user of this boat is 30–65kg (66–144lb), but it can accommodate up to 90kg (199lb), making it suitable for children and young teens, the same people who would sail Optimist dinghies and are looking for a more exciting boat.

## OK Dinghy

**Crew:** 1
**LOA:** 4m (13.1ft)
**Beam:** 1.42m (4.7ft)
**Draft:** 0.787m (2.6ft)
**Weight:** 72kg (159lb)
**Main/jib:** 8.95m² (96 sq ft)
**Spinnaker:** N/A
**Website:** www.okdinghy.co.uk

In 1957, Axel Dangaard Olsen of Seattle, USA, asked the Danish yacht designer Knud Olsen to prepare drawings for a light and fast singlehanded sailing dinghy based on conventional plywood construction. The resulting design was named the OK, using Knud Olsen's initials in reverse.

The OK was intended as a preparation class for the Olympic Finn, and it has followed its technical evolution ever since. The choice of mast, sail and fitting must fit within the class rules but can suit the sailor's own requirements. Consequently, every OK develops to suit the owner's style of sailing, while the shape of the hull is defined by a comprehensive set of strict one-design rules, ensuring a long competitive life span.

## Optimist

**Crew:** 1
**LOA:** 2.36m (7.7ft)
**Beam:** 1.12m (3.7ft)
**Draft:** 130mm (5in)
**Weight:** 35kg (77lb)
**Main/jib:** 3.3m² (35 sq ft)
**Spinnaker:** N/A
**Website:** www.optimistsailing.org.uk

The Optimist is a small, singlehanded sailing dinghy intended for use by children up to the age of 15. It is one of the most popular sailing dinghies in the world, with over 150,000 boats officially registered with the class and many more built but never registered.

A monograph-style 'IO' insignia (after IODA – the International Optimist Dinghy Association) on the sail is a registered trademark and may only be used under licence from the International Optimist Association. Optimists also have a national sail number using the Olympic abbreviation of their country and a sequential numbers, e.g. GBR for Great Britain.

## RS Feva

**Crew:** 2
**LOA:** 3.64m (11.9ft)
**Beam:** 1.42m (4.7ft)
**Draft:** N/A
**Weight:** 63kg (139lb)
**Main/jib:** 8.6m² (92.5 sq ft)
**Gennaker:** 7m² (75 sq ft)
**Website:** www.rssailing.org

Designed by Paul Handley in 2003, the RS Feva has been the bestselling two-person sailboat ever since. Primarily known as an internationally successful junior racing class, the Feva is also popular within clubs and training centres due to its user-friendly characteristics, sparkling performance and robust roto-moulded polyethylene construction.

The RS Feva is raced by two sailors, with a main, jib and gennaker, giving exciting sailing and a great introduction to double-handed techniques on the pathway from entry-level boats to double-handed skiffs or other dinghies.

## RS Aero

**Crew:** 1
**LOA:** 4m (13.1ft)
**Beam:** 1.4m (4.6ft)
**Draft:** N/A
**Weight:** 30kg (66.3lb)
**Mainsail options:** 5, 7 or 9m² (54, 75 or 97 sq ft)
**Spinnaker:** N/A
**Website:** www.rssailing.org

Designed by Jo Richards and RS Sailing in 2014, at just 30kg (66.3lb) the RS Aero weighs less than an Optimist and completely re-sets the standard for pure exhilaration in a simple singlehander. Three rig sizes allow the boat to be enjoyed by youths, women and men.

With an epoxy glass/carbon-fibre composite hull and carbon-fibre spars, the RS Aero makes use of the latest material and production technology to reduce weight within a realistic cost. Ultra-light weight makes the boat user-friendly onshore and afloat, and it can be rigged in moments.

## Snipe

**Crew:** 2
**LOA:** 4.8m (15.7ft)
**Beam:** 1.5m (4.9ft)
**Draft:** 1.96m (6.4ft)
**Weight:** 171kg (381lb)
**Main/jib:** 11.5m² (128 sq ft)
**Spinnaker:** Not permitted
**Website:** www.snipe.org

A radical departure from tradition for the yacht-racing world was set in motion in Florida in July 1931, when *Rudder* editor Bill Crosby designed and published plans for a racing sailboat that could be trailered to regattas in his magazine. The name 'Snipe' was chosen in accord with *Rudder*'s custom of naming all its designs for sea birds.

By early September, reports of boats being completed from the plans were coming in, the first one from 14-year-old Jimmy Brown of Mississippi, who had built the boat with the help of his father. By July 1936, it was the world's largest racing class, with fleets worldwide. In 1958, the Snipe received IYRU's recognition as an International Class.

## Splash

**Crew:** 1
**LOA:** 3.5m (11.5ft)
**Beam:** 1.3m (4.3ft)
**Draft:** N/A
**Weight:** 55kg (121lb)
**Main/jib:** 6.3m² (68 sq ft)
**Spinnaker:** N/A
**Website:** www.splashdinghy.org.uk

The Splash is capable of speeds of over 10 knots on a broad reach, and has performance very similar to a Laser 4.7. As with all one-design classes, all Splash dinghies are identical, meaning that it is the sailor's ability rather than the equipment that is emphasized in fleet racing. The boats employ an unstayed mono rig, which makes the class easy to handle by lighter-weight sailors. This, combined with the low hull weight, allow the class to serve as a stepping stone between the Optimist dinghy and boats such as the Laser Radial, suiting sailors from around 13 to 21 years.

## Sunfish

**Crew:** 1–2
**LOA:** 4.19m (13.7ft)
**Beam:** 1.24m (4.1ft)
**Draft:** 0.89m (2.9ft)
**Weight:** 54kg (120lb)
**Main/jib:** 7m² (75 sq ft)
**Spinnaker:** N/A
**Website:** www.sunfishclass.org

The Sunfish is a beach-launched sailing dinghy with a pontoon-type hull. It carries a lateen sail mounted to an unstayed mast. It was developed by Alcort, Inc. and first appeared around 1952 as the 'next generation' improvement on their original boat, the Sailfish. In contrast, the Sunfish has a wider beam for more stability, increased freeboard and the addition of a footwell for a more comfortable sailing position. Having a lateen sail, with its simple, two-line rigging, makes a Sunfish simple to set up and learn to sail on. Upgrades can be added to enhance sail control for competitive sailing, making the boat attractive to both novice and experienced sailors alike.

## Tasar

**Crew:** 2
**LOA:** 4.5m (14.8ft)
**Beam:** 1.75m (5.7ft)
**Draft:** N/A
**Weight:** 68kg (149lb)
**Main/jib:** 11.9m² (128 sq ft)
**Spinnaker:** N/A
**Website:** www.tasar.org.uk

The Tasar is a high-performance sailing dinghy, designed to be sailed and raced by a man and a woman. A lightweight, low-drag, planing hull, a rotating mast and a jib and fully battened mainsail with efficient sail controls provide exhilarating sailing without the need for spinnaker or trapeze.

Designed by Frank Bethwaite of Sydney in 1975, the Tasar is technologically advanced. Aimed at a husband and wife/parent and child crew, it is designed for a combined crew weight of 140kg (309lb). The wide beam and a cockpit designed for comfortable hiking make the Tasar easy, fun and very exciting to sail in winds up to 25 knots.

## Topper

**Crew:** 1
**LOA:** 3.4m (11.2ft)
**Beam:** 1.2m (3.9ft)
**Draft:** 1.5m (4.9ft)
**Weight:** 43kg (95lb)
**Main/jib:** 5.3m² (57sq ft)
**Spinnaker:** N/A
**Website:** www.toppersailboats.com

The Topper (*see photograph*) is sailed all around the world and is a true one-design boat thanks to its unique production techniques. It was designed in the 1970s by Ian Proctor, a prolific boat designer who won two Design Council awards, one of which was for the Topper.

The boat is injection moulded out of polypropylene, meaning that all hulls are identical in weight and specification. This unique construction makes it almost indestructible. Clever design features include a swivelling mast gate that enables you to erect the mast singlehanded and the rudder system, which allows the blade to be set and locked in any position at the flick of a wrist.

## Vaurien

**Crew:** 2
**LOA:** 4.08m (13.4ft)
**Beam:** 1.47m (4.8ft)
**Draft:** 0.98m (3.2ft)
**Weight:** 70kg (155lb)
**Main/jib:** 10.5m² (113 sq ft)
**Spinnaker:** 9.4m² (101 sq ft)
**Website:** www.vaurien.org

The Vaurien is an international two-person racing dinghy. It was designed by the French sailor and boat designer Jean-Jaques Herbulot in 1951. Since 1961 the Vaurien has been recognized as an international one-design class by ISAF.

The hard-chined construction gives the Vaurien very stable sailing characteristics, meaning that it can easily be controlled, even by beginners. An all-up weight of only 95kg (210lb) makes handling the Vaurien a simple task, both while sailing and ashore. It is therefore great for learning to sail. Managing a Vaurien at optimum speed, however, requires great skill at the helm and good teamwork.

## Zoom8

**Crew:** 1
**LOA:** 2.65m (8.7ft)
**Beam:** 1.45m (4.8ft)
**Draft:** 0.75m (2.5ft)
**Weight:** 37kg (82lb)
**Main/jib:** 4.8m² (52 sq ft)
**Spinnaker:** N/A
**Website:** www.zoom8.org

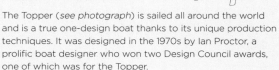

Designed in Finland by Henrik Segercrantz, based on the ideas gathered from young dinghy sailors, the Zoom8 is fast, safe and easy to handle. It was accepted as an International Class by ISAF in March 2005.

The Zoom8 is considered an excellent transition dinghy between the Optimist and the more physically demanding dinghies such as the Laser, Europe and 29er. Many attempts have been made by other classes to fill this gap, and the Zoom8 dinghy is one of the few to have succeeded.

# Keelboats

## 2.4 Metre

**Crew:** 1
**LOA:** 4.16m (13.6ft) (Mark III)
**Beam:** 0.805m (2.6ft)
**Draft:** 1m (3.3ft) (Mark III)
**Weight:** 260kg (570lb)
**Main/jib:** 7.5m² (81 sq ft) (Mark III)
**Spinnaker:** N/A
**Website:** www.inter24metre.org/

The International 2.4mR is a one-person keelboat. While there is a small but active group of amateur designer/builders around the world, around 90 per cent of boats are the commercially produced Norlin Mark III, designed by yacht designer Peter Norlin of Sweden.

The boat is primarily used for racing, and in some countries it features mainly as a class for sailors with a disability. The 2.4mR is ideal for handicap-integrated sailing, since the sailor does not move in the boat, and everything is adjustable from right in front of the sailor. Both hand-steering and foot-steering are possible. In 2002 and 2005 there were handicapped World Champions. In the 2012 British Summer Paralympics, Dutch Thierry Schmitter (*picture left*) won bronze in the International 2.4mR.

## 5.5 Metre

**Crew:** 3
**LOA:** About: 9.5m (31.2ft)
**Beam:** Min. 1.92m (6.3ft)
**Draft:** Max. 1.35m (4.4ft)
**Weight:** Min. 1,700–2,000kg
         (3,700–4,400lb)
**Main/jib:** 26.5–29m² (285–312 sq ft)
**Spinnaker:** 50m² (538 sq ft)
**Website:** www.5.5class.org

The International 5.5 Metre Class was created to yield a racing keelboat giving a sailing experience similar to that of the International 6 Metre Class, but at a lower cost.

The main class regulation is a restriction on a single quantity output from a formula involving the boat's rating length, weight and sail area; the regulation states that the output of this formula must not exceed 5.5 metres. There is considerable scope for variation in design while still meeting this restriction, and as a result each 5.5m boat is unique.

## 6 Metre

**Crew:** Maximum 6
**LOA:** 11.2m (36.8ft)
**Beam:** 2.03m (6.7ft)
**Draft:** 1.65m (5.4ft)
**Weight:** 4,060kgs (8,959lb)
**Main/jib:** 45m² (484 sq ft)
**Spinnaker:** 65m² (699 sq ft)
**Website:** www.6mr.org.uk

The International Rule, with which these yachts must comply, was formed in the early 1900s and resulted in three-quarter decked, inshore racing yachts, without accommodation. During the 1920s and 1930s these were the smallest of the rated class yachts, and were often at the forefront of sail-, rig-, and hull-design development. The Rule allows a designer a degree of freedom in the set-offs of hull shape and weight against sail area. The description 'six metre' does not, somewhat confusingly, refer to the length of the yacht, but rather to the product of the formula. The yachts are, on average, 10–11m (33–36ft) long.

## 12 Metre

**Crew:** 11
**LOA:** 19.21m (63ft)
**Beam:** 3.64m (11.9ft)
**Draft:** 2.72m (8.9ft)
**Weight:** 22,150kg (48,952lb)
**Main/jib:** 175m² (1,883 sq ft)
**Spinnaker:** variable within formula
**Website:** www.12mrclass.com

The metre formula is the result of several international meetings that took place in 1906. In summary, for a 'Twelve' the formula is length in metres added to the square root of the sail area and divided by 2.37. The result must be 12 metres (39.3ft). Thus, different designers are left free to explore different design concepts, varying hull shape, length, depth, width, weight and sail area. The class is restricted, so that, as well as meeting the required 12 metres, under the formula there are other requirements on accommodation and so forth.

Twelves were used in the America's Cup competition from 1958 to 1987.

## Hansa 2.3

**Crew:** 1–2
**LOA:** 2.3m (7.5ft)
**Beam:** 1.25m (4.1ft)
**Draft:** 0.9m (3ft)
**Weight:** 70kg (155lb)
**Main/jib:** 5.8m² (62.4 sq ft)
**Spinnaker:** N/A
**Website:** www.hansasailing.com

The original accessible sailboat and most popular of the Hansa range has proven that sailing really is for everyone. Now sailed in over 30 countries and with numbers growing steadily around the world, the Hansa 2.3 has been designated an International Class by the ISAF.

The Hansa 2.3 is available in single-seat and wide-seat (two-person) models, both with the same innovative design features. Easy to sail, safe and stable, the Hansa 2.3 is the ideal boat for anyone learning to sail.

## Hansa 303

**Crew:** 1–2
**LOA:** 3.03m (9.9ft)
**Beam:** 1.35m (4.4ft)
**Draft:** 1.1m (3.6ft)
**Weight:** 90kg (199lb)
**Main/jib:** 5.8m² (62 sq ft)
**Spinnaker:** N/A
**Website:** www.hansasailing,com

The Hansa 303 features two sails and is available in single-seat and wide-seat models. Like the 2.3, the wide-seat boat can be sailed by one or two persons, but the 303 has a greater carrying capacity, along with more ballast and sail area. Over 1,000 of this ISAF-accredited class are sailing worldwide.

The 303 offers better performance while retaining the simplicity and safety features of the 2.3. It is an ideal boat for recreation and introductory racing on waterways that are less protected.

## Hansa Liberty

**Crew:** 1
**LOA:** 3.6m (11.8ft)
**Beam:** 1.35m (4.4ft)
**Draft:** 1.1m (3.6ft)
**Weight:** 75kg (166lb)
**Main/jib:** 8.75m² (94 sq ft)
**Spinnaker:** N/A
**Website:** www.hansasailing.com

The Hansa Liberty, with its high freeboard design, high-stability ballasted centreboard and unique reefing system, provides safe and stable performance sailing that can be enjoyed by elite-level competitors and sailors with limited mobility. An ISAF-accredited class, Hansa Liberty World Championship competitors include sailors with quadriplegia and paraplegia.

The Hansa Liberty opens up high-performance sailing to everyone. The boat can be sailed at extreme angles of heel, yet the skipper remains dry and in control. This is a unique craft that enables safe yet exciting racing or recreational sailing in open waters.

## Dragon

**Crew:** 2–4
**LOA:** 8.9m (29.2ft)
**Beam:** 1.95m (6.4ft)
**Draft:** 1.2m (3.9ft)
**Weight:** 1,700kg (3,700lb)
**Main/jib:** 27.7m² (298 sq ft)
**Spinnaker:** 23.6m² (254 sq ft)
**Website:** www.intdragon.net

The Dragon is a one-design keelboat designed by Norwegian Johan Anker in 1929. In 1948 the Dragon became an Olympic Class, a status it retained until the Munich Olympics in 1972. The Dragon's long keel and elegant metre-boat lines remain unchanged, but today Dragons are constructed using the latest technology to make the boat durable and easy to maintain.

The World Championships are held in every odd year and the European Championships are held annually. The Gold Cup, which can only be held in certain specified European countries, is unique in that all six races count without discard. It is held annually and often attracts over 100 entries, usually starting in one fleet.

## Etchells

**Crew:** 3–4
**LOA:** 9.3m (30.5ft)
**Beam:** 2.11m (6.9ft)
**Draft:** 1.5m (4.9ft)
**Weight:** 1,508kg (3,325lb)
**Main/jib:** 27.1m² (292 sq ft)
**Spinnaker:** 37m² (400 sq ft)
**Website:** www.etchells.org

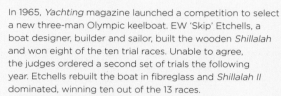

In 1965, *Yachting* magazine launched a competition to select a new three-man Olympic keelboat. EW 'Skip' Etchells, a boat designer, builder and sailor, built the wooden *Shillalah* and won eight of the ten trial races. Unable to agree, the judges ordered a second set of trials the following year. Etchells rebuilt the boat in fibreglass and *Shillalah II* dominated, winning ten out of the 13 races.

At the completion of the trials the judges chose the Soling over *Shillalah II*, in spite of her success. However, the boat's performance had won converts and the boat entered production. The class became known as the E22, and 32 boats had been built by Etchells' company by the end of 1969.

## Flying Fifteen

**Crew:** 2
**LOA:** 6.1m (20ft)
**Beam:** 1.5m (4.9ft)
**Draft:** 0.76m (2.5ft)
**Weight:** 307kg (677lb)
**Main/jib:** 14m² (150 sq ft)
**Spinnaker:** 14m² (150 sq ft)
**Website:** f15international.org

The Flying Fifteen is a two-person keelboat designed by Uffa Fox in 1947. It quickly became a popular one-design racing boat. The most famous Flying Fifteen in the class is *Coweslip*, presented to the Duke of Edinburgh and Princess Elizabeth as a wedding present. Uffa Fox and Prince Philip frequently sailed together at Cowes.

The Flying Fifteen has been modernized over the years, with Uffa Fox agreeing to changes towards the end of his life to improve the design specification and sail plan. The first World Championships were held in Perth, Australia, in 1979 and subsequently have alternated between the northern and southern hemispheres biennially.

## H-Boat

**Crew:** 3–4
**LOA:** 8.28m (27.2ft)
**Beam:** 2.18m (7.2ft)
**Draft:** 1.3m (4.3ft)
**Weight:** 1,450kg (3,200lb)
**Main/jib:** 25m² (269 sq ft)
**Spinnaker:** 36m² (388 sq ft)
**Website:** www.h-boat.org

The H-Boat is a one-design keelboat designed by Fin Hans Groop in 1967, with some minor modifications by Paul Elvstrøm in 1971. The boat gained international status in 1977. Since 1967 over 5,000 hulls have been made, making it one of the most popular yacht classes in the world.

The boat is mostly sailed and raced in Nordic countries and central Europe, although there are a few boats in the UK and the US. It is still a popular cruising/racing yacht, with 69 boats participating in 2007 H-boat World Championships. Used H-boats are fairly inexpensive, so it is popular for people looking for their first yacht.

## J/22

**Crew:** 3–5
**LOA:** 6.86m (22.5ft)
**Beam:** 2.44m (8ft)
**Draft:** 1.19m (3.9ft)
**Weight:** 812kg (1,790lb)
**Main/jib:** 20.7m² (222.7 sq ft)
**Spinnaker:** 34m² (370 sq ft)
**Website:** www.jboats.com

The International J/22 is a popular fixed-keel, one-design, racing sailboat normally raced with a crew of three or four people (total crew weight is restricted to 275kg/605lb). It races with the 'class jib', a non-overlapping jib, a mainsail and a large spinnaker. The boat is capable of planing on reaches and runs.

There are over 1,600 J/22s now sailing in 65 active fleets in 18 countries on three continents. Recognized by the ISAF, the International J/22 Class Association promotes activities and regattas worldwide. There is a very active class website and association newsletters. For class racing, sails are restricted to only a main, small jib and spinnaker.

## J/24

**Crew:** 3–5
**LOA:** 7.32m (24ft)
**Beam:** 2.71m (8.9ft)
**Draft:** 1.22m (4ft)
**Weight:** 1,406kg (3,100lb)
**Main/jib:** 24.26m² (261 sq ft)
**Spinnaker:** 41.7m² (449 sq ft)
**Website:** www.jboats.com

The J/24 is an international one-design keelboat designed in 1975 by Rodney Johnstone, who designed all J-class boats. The J/24 was created to fulfil the diverse needs of recreational sailors, such as cruising, one-design racing, day sailing and handicap racing.

In the summer of 1975, Rodney Johnstone designed and built hull number one in his garage in Stonington, Connecticut. *Ragtime* would serve as the master mould for the subsequent hulls, and allowed him to start the very successful J/Boat company with his brother, Bob. By 1978 the class was popular enough to hold a one-design regatta in Key West with 20 boats on the line, and it became one of the most popular racing boats in its class.

## J/70

**Crew:** 3–5
**LOA:** 6.93m (22.7ft)
**Beam:** 2.25m (7.4ft)
**Draft:** 1.45m (4.8ft)
**Weight:** 794kg (1755lbs)
**Main/jib:** 26m² (280 sq ft)
**Spinnaker:** 45m² (484 sq ft)
**Website:** www.jboats.com

The J/70 is a sailboat class designed by Alan Johnstone. It is J/Boats' first ramp-launchable keelboat – designed to fulfil the growing need for an easy-to-own, high-performance one-design that is exciting to sail, a stable enough sailboat for the family and built to last.

J/70's high aspect, all-carbon rig provides spirited performance and stability that feels like a much larger boat upwind. The asymmetrical spinnaker helps in downwind, moderate breezes. This new hull design has in its short life become very popular globally; it is the fastest keelboat class to receive ISAF International Class status in history, with over 20 fleets worldwide.

## J/80

**Crew:** 3–5
**LOA:** 8m (26.2ft)
**Beam:** 2.51m (8.2ft)
**Draft:** 1.49m (4.9ft)
**Weight:** 1,315kg (2,906lb)
**Main/jib:** 31.4m² (338 sq ft)
**Spinnaker:** 65m² (699 sq ft)
**Website:** www.j80.org

Designed in 1993 by Rod Johnstone of J/Boats, the J/80 has set the gold standard for international sportboat competition and training, thanks to its unique combination of stability, speed, durability and low maintenance. One of the first keelboats to feature a retractable carbon-fibre sprit and asymmetric spinnaker, the J/80 ushered in a more 'age-friendly' deck layout including a 3.7-m (12-ft) cockpit and high boom. Most major J/80 regattas see competitors aged from 10 to 70 sailing, and there are now more than 1,500 J/80s sailing in 20-plus countries across four continents.

## Melges 20

**Crew:** 3–5
**LOA:** 6.1m (20ft)
**Beam:** 2.1m (6.9ft)
**Draft:** 1.4m (4.6ft)
**Weight:** 520kg (1,146lb)
**Main/jib:** 24.2m² (260 sq ft)
**Spinnaker:** 40m² (430 sq ft)
**Website:** www.melgeseurope.com

In September 2007 Melges confirmed rumours that they would release a 6-m (20-ft) boat named Melges 20. The release is a group effort, as the boat has been designed by Reichel Pugh Yacht Design and built by McConaghy Boats.

A one-design class sailboat with a keel, the Melges 20 is anticipated to be used most commonly in racing. It fulfils the need for a more compact yet spacious, fast, well-built sportboat, and ushers in the next generation of sailboats. Simple to sail, made with high-quality materials and easy to rig, it will appeal to many ages and skill levels.

## Melges 24

**Crew:** 3–5
**LOA:** 7.8m (25.6ft)
**Beam:** 2.5m (8.2ft)
**Draft:** 1.5m (4.9ft)
**Weight:** 809kg (1,783lb)
**Main/jib:** 33m² (355 sq ft)
**Spinnaker:** 56m² (670 sq ft)
**Website:** www.melgeseurope.com

The Melges 24 is a one-design class of sailboat commonly used for racing. The monohull sportsboat is notable for its ability to plane over the water downwind in modest winds, and for its combination of a simple design that is highly tunable.

The Melges 24 is the most popular design produced by Melges Performance Sailboats, a US company founded by Harry Melges, father of former Olympic sailor Buddy Melges. The boat was designed in 1992 by the Reichel Pugh design team, and went into production in 1993.

## Melges 32

**Crew:** 5+
**LOA:** 9.7m (31.8ft)
**Beam:** 3m (9.8ft)
**Draft:** 2.13m (7ft)
**Weight:** 1,712kg (3,775lb)
**Main/jib:** 65m² (699 sq ft)
**Spinnaker:** 100m² (1,113 sq ft)
**Website:** www.melgeseurope.com

The Melges 32 was designed by the Reichel Pugh design team and went into production in 2005. The boat's hull is made from lightweight fibreglass, and the mast, rudder, bowsprit and keel fin are made from carbon fibre for light weight. The hull is generally flat on the bottom, making it plane easily, while the keel fin and keel bulb can retract up to the hull bottom to make it easier to put on a trailer.

The boat is generally raced with a crew of five or more. Because the boat sails faster with a heavier crew, class rules for racing limit crew weight to 629kg (1,390lb) total.

## Micro

**Crew:** 3
**LOA:** About 9.5m (31.2ft)
**Beam:** Min. 1.92m (6.3ft)
**Draft:** Max.1.35m (4.4ft)
**Weight:** 1,700–2,000kg (3,757–4,420lb)
**Main/jib:** 26.5–29m² (285–312 sq ft)
**Spinnaker:** 50m² (538 sq ft)
**Website:** www.micro-class.org

The Micro class was created in 1977, on the initiative of the French magazine *Bateaux*. They provided the foundations of a measurement intended to sail in elapsed time on small, easily transportable yachts. This formula was intended only for one yearly event, the 'Micro Cup', and was based on the dimensions of existing boats, like the Corsaire. This led to the development of a large fleet of boats from Bénéteau (First 18) and Jeanneau (Microsail), and several smaller manufacturers produced their own Micro (Challenger, Neptune and Kelt). Individuals built some very innovative prototypes such as Nuits Blanches and Les Copines. The French market was soon saturated with small, second-hand boats, most of which are still sailing more than 25 years later.

## Platu 25

**Crew:** 4+
**LOA:** 7.49m (24.6ft)
**Beam:** 2.56m (8.4ft)
**Draft:** 1.58m (5.2ft)
**Weight:** 1,240kg (2,740lb)
**Main/jib:** 17.6m² (189.4 sq ft)
**Spinnaker:** 44.5m² (479 sq ft)
**Website:** www.platu25.com

The Platu 25 was designed by Farr Yacht Design, led by Bruce Farr. The first boat was built by McDell Marine in New Zealand in the early 1990s, and the International Platu 25 Class Association was soon formed to support the class and promote racing amongst owners. This led to the class being recognized by the ISAF in November 2006, entitling it to hold World Championships.

The current two boat builders for the Platu 25 are Bénéteau in France and Extreme Sailing Products in Singapore.

## RC44

**Crew:** 8
**LOA:** 13.35m (43.8ft)
**Beam:** 2.75m (9ft)
**Draft:** 2.9m (9.5ft)
**Weight:** 3,560kg (7,868lb)
**Main/jib:** 130m² (1,399 sq ft)
**Gennaker:** 170m² (1,829 sq ft)
**Website:** www.rc44.com

The RC44 is a light-displacement, high-performance, one-design racing yacht. Co-designed by five-time America's Cup winner Russell Coutts with naval architect Andrej Justin, the boats are strictly identical in terms of construction, shape of hull, appendages and weight/height distribution, as well as a 50–50 split between amateurs and professionals in each eight-person crew.

Each year, the five events of the RC44 Championship Tour are hosted by some of the most beautiful and diverse sailing venues around the world. Every event is made up of two elements – one day of match racing where the pro skippers or owner-drivers get their chance to shine at the helm, followed by four days of owner-helmed fleet racing.

## SB20

**Crew:** 3
**LOA:** 6.15m (20.2ft)
**Beam:** 2.15m (7.1ft)
**Draft:** 1.5m (4.9ft)
**Weight:** 685kg (1,514lb)
**Main/jib:** 27.3m² (293.7 sq ft)
**Spinnaker:** 46m² (495 sq ft)
**Website:** www.sb20class.com

Designed by Tony Castro and launched in 2002, the SB20 is a one-design, open keelboat designed for racing with a crew of three, whose maximum weight must not exceed 270kg (597lb). Very stable and also quite fast due to the substantial sail area, the SB20 is unique in that it does not allow hiking. There is a small, stainless-steel bar that prevents this, allowing competitive crews of all shapes, sizes and ages to compete.

There are over 600 boats worldwide, sailed in over 20 countries. Growth in fleets internationally enabled the class to successfully apply to the ISAF for the right to host a world championship, the first of which was hosted in Dublin in 2008.

## Shark

**Crew:** 2–3
**LOA:** 7.3m (24ft)
**Beam:** 2.08m (6.8ft)
**Draft:** 0.97m (3.2ft)
**Weight:** 1,256kg (2,776lb)
**Main/jib:** 17.7m² (190.5 sq ft)
**Spinnaker:** 22.35m² (240.6 sq ft)
**Website:** www.sb20class.com

The Shark 24 is a Canadian-designed 7.3-m (24-ft) sailing yacht that has earned itself a reputation of extraordinary reliability and longevity among sailors in both North America and central Europe. Having been designed by George Hinterhoeller back in 1959 to cope well even with the harshest conditions found in the Great Lakes region, the vessel has proven to be well suited for extended leisure trips as well as for tough racing.

There have been a number of cosmetic changes to the design but, by and large, one-design standards have been maintained. The Shark 24 was awarded international status by the ISAF in 2000.

## Soling

**Crew:** 2–3
**LOA:** 8.2m (26.9ft)
**Beam:** 1.9m (6.2ft)
**Draft:** 1.3m (4.3ft)
**Weight:** 1,035kg (2,287lb)
**Main/jib:** 23.7m² (255 sq ft)
**Spinnaker:** 30m² (323 sq ft)
**Website:** www.soling.com

The Soling was designed as a day racer/sailer (without any compromising cruising accommodations) by Jan Linge. In 1968, after a series of trials, the ISAF selected the Soling (over a number of designs created for the occasion) to be the Olympic three-man keelboat. Despite the subsequent appearance of vast numbers and varieties of similarly sized keelboats, it was selected for every Olympics from 1972 until the Sydney Olympics in 2000.

The Soling provides ease of handling combined with unusually sensitive responsiveness to sail and hull trim, meaning that it is the boat most commonly used in commercial sail-training schools all over the world.

## Sonar

**Crew:** 3-5
**LOA:** 7m (23ft)
**Beam:** 2.4m (7.9ft)
**Draft:** 1.2m (3.9ft)
**Weight:** 950kg (2,100lb) of which 408kg (902lb) is ballast
**Main/jib:** 23.2m² (250 sq ft)
**Spinnaker:** 22.8m² (245 sq ft)
**Website:** www.sonar.org

The Sonar, a one-design keelboat, was designed in 1979 by Bruce Kirby, designer of the popular Laser dinghy. Since then, over 800 boats have been built. Most of the fleet is in the USA, with smaller fleets in Britain and Canada. Since its adoption as a Paralympic class, the Sonar has spread to many other countries as well.

The Sonar showcased disabled sailing at the 1996 Paralympics in a demonstration event, and sailing (using Sonars for the three-person keelboat) has featured in every subsequent Paralympics. The Sonar is well suited for disabled sailing because of its large, open cockpit, making adaptations easy.

## Star

**Crew:** 2
**LOA:** 6.9m (22.6ft)
**Beam:** 1.7m (5.6ft)
**Draft:** 1m (3.3ft)
**Weight:** 671kg (1,483lb)
**Main/jib:** 26.5m² (285 sq ft)
**Spinnaker:** N/A
**Website:** www.starclass.org

The Star is one of the most prolific keelboats in the world for a reason: it is an incredible boat to sail. Designed in 1911 by Francis Sweisguth, it has proven to be a classic in every sense. An Olympic class from 1932 to 2012, the Star is supported by a worldwide association – one of the best organized in sailing – with over 8,500 yachts built over its 104-year history, and 2,000-plus actively racing today.

The design, sails and equipment of the Star are governed by stringent class rules, created to improve competition on the basis of skill and control cost. This has also served to help the longevity of the design, keeping older boats competitive through careful evolution.

## Tempest

**Crew:** 2
**LOA:** 6.66m (21.8ft)
**Beam:** 1.92m (6.3ft)
**Draft:** 1.1m (3.6ft)
**Weight:** 480kg (1,0601lb)
**Main/jib:** 23.11m² (248.7 sq ft)
**Spinnaker:** 25.9m² (278.7 sq ft)
**Website:** www.tempestclass.com

The Tempest is a one-design, high-performance keelboat with a trapeze. It was designed by Ian Proctor for the 1965 trials for the new Olympic keelboat, which it won convincingly. In the last few years the rules have allowed a bigger spinnaker, longer spinnaker pole and the use of epoxy resin in the construction of the hull.

The Tempest has an unusual aspect in that it is a keelboat but also has a trapeze, a rigging element usually only found on certain dinghies. As a result the Tempest is just as exciting to sail as fast dinghies, but is much more forgiving and is unable to be capsized.

## Yngling

**Crew:** 2-3
**LOA:** 6.37m (20.9 ft)
**Beam:** 1.7m (5.6ft)
**Draft:** 1.05m (3.4ft)
**Weight:** 645kg (1,425lb)
**Main/jib:** 15.84m² (170.4 sq ft)
**Spinnaker:** Max. 20m² (215 sq ft)
**Website:** www.yngling.org

The Yngling is a sleek and seaworthy small racing keelboat, an agreeable cross between a planing dinghy and a keelboat. Its design is classic, and its construction is durable. It can be regarded as a smaller version of the Soling, although there are differences in sailing characteristics, proportion and tuning requirements between the two classes.

It was designed in 1967 by Jan Herman Linge, who wanted to build a keelboat for his young son. He named it Yngling, the Norwegian word for 'youngster'. The Yngling received ISAF International Class status in 1979 and was chosen as the Olympic Women's Keelboat for 2004 and 2008.

# Multihulls

## A-Class Catamaran

**Crew:** 1
**Min. overall boat weight:** 75kg (166lb)
**Max. overall boat length:** 5.49m (18ft)
**Max. overall boat width:** 2.3m (7.5ft)
**Max. sail area (including mast):** 13.94m²
(150 sq ft)
**Website:** www.a-cat.org

A-Class catamarans are the fastest single-handed racing boats in the world.

It is a development class, and a combination of modern materials and innovative sail-craft design means that the A-Class catamaran has been able to really push the boundaries. Speeds exceeding 24 knots have been recorded and it has superb handling, due to sailors taking advantage of the very few design limitations placed on the class. Design aspects such as hull and sail shape, as well as mast length and shape, are unrestricted. Only the basic measurements of maximum hull length, maximum beam, maximum sail area and minimum weight must adhere to certain limits.

## Formula 16

**Crew:** 1–2
**Max. overall length:** 5m (16.4ft)
**Max. overall width:** 2.5m (8.2ft)
**Min. overall weight:** 1-up: 104kg
(230lb); 2-up: 107kg (236lb)
**Max. mast height:** 8.5m (27.9ft)
**Max. mainsail (including mast):** 15m²
(161 sq ft)
**Max. jib:** 3.7m² (40 sq ft)
**Max. spinnaker:** 17.5m² (188 sq ft)
**Website:** www.formula16.net

Formula 16 is a multi-manufacturer class for beach catamarans, and any boat that adheres to a certain limited set of general design specifications may participate in all the official class races.

Designed to sail equally well with one person or two, the F16 can be sailed and even launched and righted singlehandedly thanks to its lightweight construction. This, as well as an asymmetric spinnaker and generous sail area, means that it is speedy, too. There are few restrictions on materials, yet it is comparable in cost to other race catamarans. Practical and fast, it is a lot of fun to sail.

## Dart 18

**Crew:** 2
**LOA:** 5.5m (18ft)
**Beam:** 2.3m (7.5ft)
**Draft:** minimal
**Weight:** 130kg (287lb)
**Main/jib:** 16m² (172 sq ft)
**Spinnaker:** 15.5m² (167 sq ft) (not legal for racing)
**Website:** www.dart18.com

The Dart 18 (*picture left*) is a one-design, glass-fibre sailing catamaran. It is designed to be sailed by two people and can achieve speeds of up to 20 knots.

The boat was designed in 1975 as a one-design class by Rodney March, who was also responsible for the design of the Olympic Tornado-class catamaran. The very first Dart 18, designed and built in Falmouth, UK, is now owned by the National Maritime Museum in Cornwall. Up to the present, a number of improvements have been made, but the original concept was preserved though strict class rules.

## Hobie 14

**Crew:** 1-3
**LOA:** 4.3m (14ft)
**Beam:** 2.3m (7.5ft)
**Draft:** 0.2m (0.7ft)
**Weight:** 108kg (239lb)
**Main/jib:** 48.93m² (526 sq ft)
**Spinnaker:** N/A
**Website:** www.hobieclass.com

The Hobie 14, designed by Hobie Alter, is the original catamaran. The general shape and design of the boat is very similar to the later Hobie 16, the two sharing many of the same parts. The 14 was originally designed to be sailed as a unirig with just a main sail. Quick and light, Hobie 14s are great for younger sailors who want a solo-able multihull that can be held down without much weight. The boat does not carry passengers well, but used boats can be found quite cheaply.

It is possible to convert a standard 14 into a Hobie 14 'Turbo' by adding a jib, trapeze and dolphin striker.

## Formula 18

**Crew:** 1-2
**LOA:** Max. 5.52m (18.1ft)
**Beam:** Max. 2.6m (8.5ft)
**Draft:** minimal
**Weight:** Min. 180kg (398lb)
**Main/jib:** 17m² (183 sq ft)
**Spinnaker:** N/A
**Website:** www.f18-international.org

The Formula 18 (F18) class is a formula-design, sport-catamaran class. It was started in the early 1990s and quickly grew to a full-sized class recognized by the ISAF. Before the turn of the century, the F18 class was attracting up to 150 boats and crews to their world championships. Since then, a limit has been placed on attendance (maximum 150), and therefore qualifier rounds for the world championships are held worldwide.

Because the F18 class is a formula class, any boat that adheres to the limited set of general design specifications may participate in all F18 races. This has led to a score of homebuilders and professional builders designing and racing their own F18 boats.

## Hobie Dragoon

**Crew:** 3
**LOA:** 3.91m (12.8ft)
**Beam:** 2.2m (7.2ft)
**Draft:** minimal
**Weight:** 98kg (217lb)
**Main/jib:** 11.7m² (126 sq ft)
**Spinnaker:** 8.1m² (87.2 sq ft)
**Website:** www.hobieclass.com

The Dragoon is the result of a collaboration between sailing schools and Hobie Cat. It has been specially designed to train sailors from initiation through to performance racing. This catamaran is equipped to start sailing in regattas, then evolve into highly competitive competition. With twin trapeze and spinnaker options, the boat is ideal for introducing young sailors to high-performance multihulls, and the target age is 12 to 14 years. The class has ISAF Class status.

## Hobie 16

**Crew:** 1–4
Length: 5.04m (16.5ft)
**Beam:** 2.41m (7.9ft)
**Draft:** 0.25m (0.8ft)
**Weight:** 145kg (320lb)
**Main/jib:** 20m² (215 sq ft)
**Spinnaker:** 17.65m² (190 sq ft)
**Website:** www.hobieclass.com

The 16 is the most popular Hobie cat, both for recreational and racing purposes and as a one-design racer. As with the 14, it is intended to be sailed from the beach through the surf, and to be surfed back in on the waves to the beach. Instead of daggerboards or centreboards, the 16 has asymmetrical hulls that act like foils and keep the boat from crabbing, or slipping sideways from the force of the wind.

One notable difficulty in sailing this boat is the tendency of the boat to 'pitchpole' when running downwind; sailors compensate for this by putting their weight as far aft as they can while running downwind.

## Hobie Wild Cat

**Crew:** 2–3
**LOA:** 5.46m (17.9ft)
**Beam:** 2.59m (8.5ft)
**Draft:** 0.18m (0.6ft)
**Weight:** 180kg (399lb)
**Main/jib:** 42m² (452 sq ft)
**Spinnaker:** N/A
**Website:** www.hobieclass.com

The Hobie Wild Cat is a Formula 18 developed by Hobie Cat Europe as a one-design within the Formula 18 rules. Introduced in Jaunary 2009, the class was recognized by the ISAF in November 2010. It was designed to replace the Hobie Tiger as a more up-to-date and competitive design within the Formula 18 fleet.

Elegant, functional touches include wave-piercing bows, an integrated wing-mast section, high-aspect ratio daggerboards and rudders, dual trapezes, a spinnaker launching-and-retrieval system and seriously fast fibreglass hulls. The Wild Cat is Hobie's next-generation, extreme-racing machine, and its current Formula 18 design.

## Hobie Tiger

**Crew:** 2–3
**LOA:** 5.51m (18ft)
**Beam:** 2.6m (8.5ft)
**Draft:** 1.74m (5.7ft)
**Weight:** 180kg (398lb)
**Main/jib:** 20.5–21.2m² (221–228 sq ft)
**Spinnaker:** 19–21m² (204–226 sq ft)
**Website:** www.hobieclass.com

The Hobie Tiger is a Formula 18 developed by Hobie Cat Europe as a one-design within the Formula 18 rules. Created in 1995, it rapidly became an ISAF International Class.

The Hobie Tiger is an excellent boat for mixed teams. The small jib and spinnaker option allows performance for smaller crews without compromising the performance for larger crews. Most top cat sailors will have once sailed a Hobie Tiger. Tiger fleets are particularly large in Europe, the United States and Australia.

## SL16

**Crew:** 2
**LOA:** 4.8m (15.7ft)
**Beam:** 2.32m (7.6ft)
**Draft:** minimal
**Weight:** 145kg (320lb)
**Main/jib:** 17.5m² (188 sq ft)
**Spinnaker:** 17m² (183 sq ft)
**Website:** www.sl16.co

Designed in 2003, the SL16 is the culmination of 40 years of research and development carried out by the architect Yves Loday, Olympic gold medallist in Tornado in 1992. Using the same platform as the KL15.5 but with a larger rig, it is a sporty and powerful catamaran, fast and exciting but still easy to handle.

The official multihull for the ISAF Youth Sailing World Championship and the FFVoile Youth Sailing French Championship, the SL16 is the perfect catamaran for young crews, providing a springboard to the F18 and Nacra 17.

## Nacra F18 Infusion

**Crew:** 1–3
**LOA:** 5.5m (18ft)
**Beam:** 2.6m (8.5ft)
**Draft:** 0.18m (0.6ft)
**Weight:** 180kg (399lb)
**Main/jib:** 42m² (452 sq ft)
**Spinnaker:** N/A
**Website:** www.nacrasailing.com

The Nacra F18 Infusion represents the very latest F18 design and is one of the fastest-growing catamaran classes in the world. The boat is named after the method used in construction, and is the only production catamaran made with this modern infusion system. It allows better material weight distribution within the hulls, yielding greater stiffness where it is needed, and stiffness equals speed.

Hull volume, larger than other F18s, means that the Infusion drives hard with handling that is rapid and precise. Wave-piercing technology reduces drag and improves speed in all conditions, meaning that the Infusion wins in big seas and big winds just as well as gliding on a lake in flat water.

## Tornado

**Crew:** 2
**LOA:** 6.09m (20ft)
**Beam:** 3.08m (10.1ft)
**Draft:** 0.15m (0.5ft)
**Weight:** 155kg (343lb)
**Main/jib:** 21.9m² (236 sq ft)
**Spinnaker:** 25m² (269 sq ft)
**Website:** www.tornado-class.org

The Tornado is a double-handed multihull class recognized as an International Class by the ISAF. It was used for the Olympic catamaran discipline for over 30 years.

The boat was designed in 1967 by Rodney March, from the Isle of Sheppey, England. At the IYRU Olympic Catamaran Trials for international status, it easily defeated the other challengers. To increase its performance even further, the Tornado was modified in 2000, with a new sail plan that included a spinnaker and spinnaker boom, as well as increasing the sail area of the existing sails. An additional trapeze was also added, and the jib was made self-tacking.

## Topcat K1

**Crew:** 2–4
**LOA:** 5.5m (18ft)
**Beam:** 2.5m (8.2ft)
**Draft:** minimal
**Weight:** 175kg (387lb)
**Main/jib:** 18.9m² (203 sq ft)
**Spinnaker:** N/A
**Website:** www.topcatsailing.com

In the mid-1970s, two German A-Cat sailors, Bernd Breymann and Klaus Enzmann, were unhappy with the complicated transport and assembly of their boats. Klaus Enzmann built a first prototype without daggerboards or rudders, similar to the Spanish 'Patin-Vela', but with many of the successful details of the later boats. The first Topcat catamaran was born.

The flagship of the Topcat fleet, the Topcat K1 is one of the fastest catamarans without daggerboards in the world and always responds reliably, even at top speed.

## Viper

**Crew:** 1–2
**LOA:** 5m (16.4ft)
**Beam:** 2.5m (8.2ft)
**Draft:** 0.5m (1.6ft)
**Weight:** 129kg (285lb)
**Main/jib:** 18.7m² (201 sq ft)
**Gennaker:** 18.8m² (202.3 sq ft)
**Website:** www.viperclass.org

The Viper is a performance catamaran used for racing. A one-design boat within the Formula 16 class, it is recognized by the ISAF. The Viper class has been created as a strict one-design catamaran, and the true test when racing is between crews and not boats and equipment. The fundamental objective of these class rules is to ensure that this concept is maintained.

# Yachts

## Class 40

**Crew:** 1–2
**LOA:** 12.19m (40ft)
**Beam:** 4.5m (14.8ft)
**Draft:** 3m (9.8ft)
**Weight:** 4,500kg (9,945lb)
**Main/jib:** 96.19m² (1,035 sq ft)
**Spinnaker:** N/A
**Website:** www.class40.com

The Class 40 Association, based in Paris, France, has a simple, stringent, 'box' rule, within which parameters anyone may design a monohull yacht, with a maximum length of 12.19m (40ft), intended for competition in offshore or transoceanic events. The aim is that a fleet of simple, seaworthy, economic, performance-orientated yachts will be produced, which then compete, offshore, with a single – or a small number – of crew, but otherwise without any handicap. High-performance racing boats, the Class 40 can be built by anyone provided the defined rules are followed.

## Farr 30

**Crew:** 7
**LOA:** 9.43m (30.9ft)
**Beam:** 3.08m (10.1ft)
**Draft:** 2.1m (6.9ft)
**Weight:** 2,069kg (4,572lb)
**Main/jib:** 46.81m² (504 sq ft)
**Spinnaker:** 100m² (1,076 sq ft)
**Website:** www.farr30.org

Designed by Farr Yacht Design in 1995, the first of these yachts was called the 'Mumm 30', as it was sponsored by Champagne Mumm. This sponsorship ended in 2007, and thereafter the class was known as the International Farr 30 One Design. The design concept was for a state-of-the-art, offshore design that would be fast and exciting yet uncomplicated and economical. The International Farr 30 One-Design Association is an ISAF-recognized class.

## Farr 40

**Crew:** 10
**LOA:** 12.41m (40.7ft)
**Beam:** 4.03m (13.2ft)
**Draft:** 2.6m (8.5ft)
**Weight:** 4,945kg (10,928lb)
**Main/jib:** 87.36m² (940 sq ft)
**Spinnaker:** 170m² (1,829 sq ft)
**Website:** www.farr40.org

A design developed by Farr Yacht Design from some of their previously designed yachts, the Farr 40 (*picture left*) was intended as a modern Grand Prix-type yacht, for both one-design and IRC competition.

From a first launch in 1997, there are now some 152 yachts in 19 countries worldwide. Strict class rules ensure good one-design racing, particularly with the 'owner-steering' requirement.

## Maxi

**Crew:** 27
**LOA:** 30.48m (100ft)
**Beam:** 6.8m (22.3ft)
**Draft:** 5.5m (18ft)
**Weight:** 24,500kg (54,145lb)
**Main/jib:** variable
**Spinnaker:** variable
**Website:**
internationalmaxiassociation.com

The original Maxi yachts were built in the 1970s and 1980s, when the racing of seagoing yachts was conducted under the International Offshore Rule (IOR). This meant that there was an upper rating limit, and yachts built to that limit – which was generally around 25m (82ft) in length – were known as 'maxis'.

The IOR rule later gave way to the International Measurement System (IMS), which then gave way to IRC (a system of handicapping boats for the purpose of racing). Under IRC, the 'modern maxi' (sometimes referred to as a 'super maxi') has evolved, having an overall length of 30.48m (100ft). Examples of super maxis are ICAP Leopard 3, Comanche and Wild Oats XI.

## J/111

**Crew:** 8
**LOA:** 11.1m (36.4ft)
**Beam:** 3.29m (10.8ft)
**Draft:** 2.19m (7.2ft)
**Weight:** 4,218kg (9,322lb)
**Main/jib:** 61.6m² (663 sq ft)
**Spinnaker:** 130m² (1,399 sq ft)
**Website:** www.j111class.org

In 1975 American Rod Johnstone launched *Ragtime*, a 7.4-m (24-ft) yacht that was the beginning of the J/24 class. The number of J/24s now exceeds 5,000 and there are other 'J' boats ranging in size from the International J/22 up to the J/65.

The J/111 is one of the range, a sleek, speedy, one-design boat. The large cockpit and easy-to-tune rig mean that the crew can sail fast and in control, going to windward at 7+ knots and hitting double-digit speeds downwind. There are J/111 one-design fleets in the USA and Europe, with J/111s also sailing in Australia, Hong Kong, Columbia and South Africa.

## IMOCA 60

**Crew:** 1–2
**LOA:** 18.6m (60ft)
**Beam:** 6.5m (21.3ft)
**Draft:** 4.5m (14.8ft)
**Weight:** 10,500kg (23,205lb)
**Main/jib:** variable
**Spinnaker:** variable
**Website:** www.imoca.org

IMOCA 60 are a type of monohull sailing yachts administrated by the International Monohull Open Class Association (IMOCA). An 'open' class, based in Paris, France, and recognized by the ISAF, IMOCA 60 yachts must meet a 'box' rule limiting the length to 18.6m (60ft) and subjecting them to other restrictions or requirements (particularly a minimum stability).

The monohulls are high-performance racing boats, designed principally for single-handed competition. Typically, yachts to this rule are sponsored and push the envelope of accepted parameters for ocean-racing yachts, being more akin to a multihull than a conventional monohull.

## Soto 40 OD

**Crew:** 10
**LOA:** 12.3m (40.3ft)
**Beam:** 3.75m (12.3ft)
**Draft:** 2.6m (8.5ft)
**Weight:** 4,290kg (9,481lb)
**Main/jib:** 86.19m² (927 sq ft)
**Spinnaker:** 182m² (1,959 sq ft)
**Website:** www.soto40.org

The Soto 40 OD is a high-performance, one-design racing yacht designed by Javier Soto Acebal and built by M Boats, in Argentina. The yacht is rigged as a fractional sloop, but carries mast-head spinnakers set from a bow prodder. The hull is wedge shaped, with high-aspect ratio foils (keel, fin with bulb and spade-type rudder).

There are stringent class rules aimed at keeping the boats as near to identical as possible, so that the only variable will be the crew.

## Swan 45

**Crew:** 12
**LOA:** 13.83m (45.4ft)
**Beam:** 3.91m (12.8ft)
**Draft:** 2.8m (9.2ft)
**Weight:** 8,850kg (19,559lb)
**Main/jib:** 112.82m² (1,214 sq ft)
**Spinnaker:** 153m² (1,647 sq ft)
**Website:** www.swan45class.org

Designed by Germàn Frers as a 'cruiser-racer' and built by Nautor's Swan, the first Swan 45 was launched in 2001. The class was recognized by the ISAF in 2005, and continues to race around the world.

Swan 45s are relatively high performance, but with a luxury fit-out. The hull shape is modern, with fin and bulb keel and spade rudder; the rig is fractional sloop. They race in class, as a level boat, or compete in IRC and PHD fleets.

## Swan 60

**Crew:** 2–14
**LOA:** 18.86m (61.9ft)
**Beam:** 5.09m (16.7ft)
**Draft:** 3.6m (11.8ft)
**Weight:** 18,700kg (41,327lb)
**Main/jib:** 221m² (2,378 sq ft)
**Spinnaker:** 320m² (3,444 sq ft)
**Website:** www.nautorswan.com

The combination of designer Germàn Frers and builder Nautor's Swan has produced four generations of 18.6-m (60-ft) Swans, all aimed at the dual-purpose market of comfortable cruiser but competitive racer.

The latest iteration, the Mark II RS, was built from 2015. Designer Germàn Frers says, 'The new Swan 60 combines a voluminous interior, a large, protected cockpit and racing performance ... The yacht can be sailed easily by two persons with the aid of powered winches and a layout that allows the helmsman to get involved in the manoeuvre if needed.'

## Transpac 52

**Crew:** 16
**LOA:** Max. 15.85m (52ft)
**Beam:** 3.96–4.42m (13–14.5ft)
**Draft:** Max. 3.2m (10.4ft)
**Weight:** 7,600–7,800kg
(16,796–17,238lb)
**Main/jib:** variable
**Spinnaker:** variable
**Website:** www.transpac52.org

The Transpac 52 (TP52) is a class of yacht used for competitive yacht racing. The class has grown from a non-registered club of like-minded yachtsmen to a fully member-controlled, registered and ISAF-recognized class.

These yachts are the ultimate fully crewed, grand-prix racer, constructed with carbon hulls, carbon-fibre spars and minimal interior fit-out. The TP52 was originally conceived as a 'box' rule, within which sporting 16-m (52-ft) yachts could be built and then compete on a boat-for-boat basis both across oceans and around the buoys. The rule has been tweaked several times, with the boats now tending to be used more for buoy regattas than ocean races.

## X-35

**Crew:** 3+
**LOA:** 10.61m (34.8ft)
**Beam:** 3.27m (10.7ft)
**Draft:** 2.15m (7.1ft)
**Weight:** 4,300kg (9,503lb)
**Main/jib:** 74m² (796 sq ft)
**Spinnaker:** 105.7m² (1,137 sq ft)
**Website:** www.x-35.com

Having not built a one-design class since 1985, Niels Jeppesen, the designer, set himself a challenge. In 2006, X-Yachts launched the X-35 with over 100 models already sold off the plans. They became an official ISAF-recognized class that same year, holding a world championships every year since. The model has an open, ergonomic cockpit and refined control systems, providing a rapid cruising option with a highly functional, partly removable interior. When not racing in a one-design fleet, the X-35 is highly successful racing under handicap.

## X-41

**Crew:** 6+
**LOA:** 12.35m (40.5ft)
**Beam:** 3.64m (11.9ft)
**Draft:** 2.5m (8.2ft)
**Weight:** 6,800kg (15,028lb)
**Main/jib:** 98.3m² (1,058 sq ft)
**Spinnaker:** 147.6m² (1,588 sq ft)
**Website:** www.x-41.com

On the back of the fantastic success of the X-35, a bigger and more widely appealing sister was born. The X-41 became an officially ISAF-recognized class in 2008. Its optional removable anchor locker and optional below-deck headsail furler appealed to the racer and cruiser, as did her nicely crafted teak-veneered interior and white bulkheads. An elegant carbon mast, boom and wheel along with sleek hull lines and heavy, bulbed T-keel ensured it sailed as well as it looked, and the X-41 proceeded to win the title of 'Best Crossover' by the Boat of the Year judges on its launch.

## Volvo Open 65

**Crew:** 15
**LOA:** 22.14 m (72.6 ft)
**Beam:** 5.60 m (18.4 ft)
**Draft:** 4.70 m (15.4 ft)
**Weight (empty):** 12,500 kg (27,557lb)
**Mainsail area:** 151m² (1,625 sq ft)
**Website:** www.volvooceanrace.com

The Volvo Ocean 65 is the successor to the
Volvo Open 70 yacht that was used from
2005 to 2012. This new Farr Yacht design first saw action in
the 2014–15 race, but will continue for at least another edition
in 2017–18, marking the first time in its history that the Volvo
Ocean Race will become a one-design event.

Doubts were voiced over the overall safety of the ageing and
expensive Volvo Open 70 series after a lot of breakages and
accidents during the 2011–12 Volvo Ocean Race, due to many
of the boat designers opting for speed while failing to meet
safety requirements.

In becoming a one-design event, the new fleet has become
more cost effective and adopts a similar strategy to that of
the Clipper Round The World Race. The SCA team (right) is
the first all-female team competing in the Volco Ocean Race.

# Index

# Thank you

The author would like to extend special thanks to Sir Ben Ainslie for taking time out of his busy schedule to write the foreword for this book.

The creative team at The Urban Ant would like to extend their heartfelt thanks to a few key people who, in the true spirit of ocean sailors, heeded our Mayday call when we needed help to launch this project.

First and foremost we'd like to thank Vanessa Dudley, who helped us structure and shape this book and opened a great deal of doors to us that would otherwise have remained closed. Thanks also to Robert Green, who helped us with his expert knowledge and advice, and who managed to connect us with contributors far outside our reach. And finally, thanks to the following individuals who generously donated their photos – it would not have been possible to put this together without you: Amy Martindale at Clipper Ventures Ltd, Mike Golding, Tasha Hacker, Graham Snook, KM Yachtbuilders, Perfect Prints, Jean-Marie Liot, Sally White at Whitespace Design, Ian MacWilliams, Helena Darvelid and Paul Larson, Giles Pearman, Kurt Arrigo and Rolex.

# Acknowledgements

The publisher would like to thank the following for permission to reproduce their material. Every effort has been made to trace copyright holders. However, if there have been any unintentional omissions or failure to trace copyright holders, we apologize and will, if informed, endeavour to make corrections in any future edition.

1 © Aurora Photos/Alamy Stock Photo; 2-3 © Clipper Race/www.clipperroundtheworld.com; 4-5 © Clipper Race/www.clipperroundtheworld.com; 6 © Bluegreen Pictures/Alamy Stock Photo; 8-9 © Bluegreen Pictures/Alamy Stock Photo; 10-11 © Kos Picture Source Ltd/Alamy Stock Photo; 12-13 © Andrew Lloyd/Alamy Stock Photo; 14-15 © Library of Congress, Prints & Photographs Division, Detroit Publishing Company; 16 © David Gordon/Alamy Stock Photo; 18 © Library of Congress, Prints & Photographs Division, Detroit Publishing Company; 20 © Stockmaritime, Trademark of GentCom GmbH/Alamy Stock Photo; 21 © ZUMA Press, Inc./Alamy Stock Photo; 22-23 © AJAXNETPHOTO/COLLECTIONS/Alamy Stock Photo; 24-25 Pedro Armestre/AFP/Getty Images; 26 © Stephen Bardens/Alamy Stock Photo; 29 © Chad Ehlers/Alamy Stock Photo; 30-31 © Stephen Bardens/Alamy Stock Photo; 32 © Photos 12/Alamy Stock Photo; 33 © Sergey Komarov-Kohl/Alamy Stock Photo; 34 © Bob Fisher/PPL; 35 © Aurora Photos/Alamy Stock Photo; 36-37 © Aurora Photos/Alamy Stock Photo; 38-39 © Chris Cheadle /Alamy Stock Photo; 40-41 © All Canada Photos/Alamy Stock Photo; 41 top © Royal Vancouver Yacht Club/vicmaui.org, 41 bottom © Sally White – Whitespace Design/vicmaui.org; 42-43 © Getty Images; 45 © Keystone-France/Getty Images; 46-47 © Sea&See/Kos Picture Source/Getty Images; 48 © Nature Picture Library/Alamy Stock Photo; 49 © Getty Images; 50-51 © Bluegreen Pictures/Alamy Stock Photo; 52-53 © Jean-Marie Liot/www.jmliot.com; 55 © Jean-Marie Liot/www.jmliot.com; 56 © Andrea Francolini; 57 © Clipper Race/www.clipperroundtheworld.com; 58 © Australian National Maritime Museum; 59 © PPL; 60 © Andrea Francolini; 61 © Andrea Francolini; 63 © PPL; 64 © Eniz Umuler/Alamy Stock Photo; 66 © Aurora Photos/Alamy Stock Photo; 69 © Bluegreen Pictures/Alamy Stock Photo; 70-71 Gillian Moore/Alamy Stock Photo; 71 © sthelenaonline.org; 73 © Gallo Images/Alamy Stock Photo; 74 © Rolex/Kurt Arrigo; 75T © Rolex/Kurt Arrigo 75B © Alvov/Shutterstock.com; 76 © JONATHAN EASTLAND/Alamy Stock Photo ; 77 © JONATHAN EASTLAND/Alamy Stock Photo; 78 JONATHAN EASTLAND/Alamy Stock Photo; 80 L © JONATHAN EASTLAND/Alamy Stock Photo, R © AFP; 81 © Bluegreen Pictures/Alamy Stock Photo; 82 © Hemis/Alamy Stock Photo; 84 © Gamma-Rapho/Getty Images; 85 © Action Plus Sports Images/Alamy Stock Photo; 87 © Marcel Mochet/AFP/Getty Images; 88 © Aurora Photos/Alamy Stock Photo; 89 © Nature Picture Library/Alamy Stock Photo; 90-91 © Jean-Marie Liot/www.jmliot.com; 92-93 © AFP/Stringer/Getty Images; 93 T © JOHN MOTTERN/Stringer/Getty Images; 95 © Niday Picture Library / Alamy Stock Photo; 98 © JONATHAN EASTLAND/Alamy Stock Photo; 98-99 © Bluegreen Pictures/Alamy Stock Photo; 101 © Ian MacWilliams; 103 © Allsports/Getty Images; 104 © Graham Snook; 105 © epa european pressphoto agency b.v./Alamy Stock Photo; 106-107 © Clipper Race/www.clipperracearoundtheworld.com; 108 © Simon Littlejohn/Alamy Stock Photo; 111 T © JONATHAN EASTLAND/Alamy Stock Photo, B © JONATHAN EASTLAND/Alamy Stock Photo; 112-113 © Amory Ross/Team Alvimedica/Volvo Ocean Race/Getty Images; 114 © Onne Van Der Wal /PPL; 115 © JONATHAN EASTLAND/Alamy Stock Photo; 116 © Bluegreen Pictures/Alamy Stock Photo; 117 © François Chevalier; 118-119 © Nature Picture Library/Alamy Stock Photo; 119 © 2006 Kos Picture Source/Getty Images; 120-121 © Bluegreen Pictures/Alamy Stock Photo; 122 © AFP/Getty Images; 123T © Jean-Marie Liot/www.jmliot.com; 124 © PPL; 125 © AFP/Getty Images; 126 © Bluegreen Pictures/Alamy Stock Photo; 127T © Royal Australian Navy, C © Royal Australian Navy/PPL, B © Royal Australian Navy/PPL; 128-129 © Tasha Hacker/www.turftosurf.com; 131 © Simon Littlejohn/Alamy Stock Photo; 132 © Clipper Ventures Plc; 133 © Clipper Ventures Plc; 134-135 Nature Picture Library/Alamy Stock Photo; 136 © Thierry Martinez/Kos Picture Source/Getty Images; 137 © PPL; 138 © Jean-Marie Liot; 140 © Mike Golding Yacht Racing; 141 © Thierry Martinez/Kos Picture Source/Getty Images); 142 © epa european pressphoto agency b.v./Alamy Stock Photo; 145 © Bluegreen Pictures/Alamy Stock Photo; 146 - 147 © Nature Picture Library/Alamy Stock Photo; 148-149 © ZUMA Press, Inc./Alamy Stock Photo; 151 © one-image photography/Alamy Stock Photo; 152 © Fritz Stoltenberg; 153 T © mediacolor's/Alamy Stock Photo; 153 B © RThiele; 154 © Andrea Francolini; 155 © Jack Atley/Bloomberg News/Getty Images; 157 © JONATHAN EASTLAND/Alamy Stock Photo; 159 © JONATHAN EASTLAND/Alamy Stock Photo; © Bluegreen Pictures/Alamy Stock Photo; 161 © Bluegreen Pictures/Alamy Stock Photo; 162-163 © Dave Willis/Alamy Stock Photo; 163 TL © Hilary Morgan/Alamy Stock Photo; 163 TR © robertharding/Alamy Stock Photo; 164-165 © Christopher Ison/Alamy Stock Photo; 166-167 © Gilles Martin-Raget; 168 © Gilles Martin-Raget; 169 © Gilles Martin-Raget; 170 © Guy Nowell; 171 © Guy Nowell; 172-173 © Chris Schmid/Eyemage Media/Alamy Stock Photo; 174-175 © Chris Schmid Photography/Alamy Stock Photo; 176-177 © RooM the Agency/Alamy Stock Photo; 178 © Andrea Francolini; 180 © Guy Nowell; 182 © zixia/Alamy Stock Photo; 185 © Loris von Siebenthal; 186-187 © Horizons WWP/TRVL/Alamy Stock Photo; 188 © Paolo Gallo/Alamy Stock Photo; 190 © Kos Picture Source Ltd/Alamy Stock Photo; 192-193 © Bluegreen Pictures/Alamy Stock Photo; 194-195 ©Rick Tomlinson/Kos Picture Source; 196-197 © Mark Lloyd/lloydimages.com; 198 © www.stadtdesign.com; 199 © Pool/Getty Images; 200-201 © JONATHAN EASTLAND/Alamy Stock Photo; 201 © sirpeterblaketrust.org; 202-203 © William Stevens/Gamma-Rapho/Getty Images; 204 © Helena Darvelid/Sailrocket; 205 © Helena Darvelid/Sailrocket; 206L © Keystone Pictures USA/Alamy Stock Photo, R © Keystone Pictures USA/Alamy Stock Photo; 208 © Clipper Race/www.clipperroundtheworld.com, 209 © Action Plus Sports Images/Alamy Stock Photo; 210 © JONATHAN EASTLAND/Alamy Stock Photo; 211 © Keystone Pictures USA/Alamy Stock Photo; 212 © JONATHAN EASTLAND/Alamy Stock Photo; 213 © Ajax News & Feature Service/Alamy Stock Photo; 214 © Chris Schmid Photography/Alamy Stock Photo; 215 © ZUMA Press, Inc./Alamy Stock Photo; 216-217 © Gilles Martin-Raget; 218 © SPUTNIK/Alamy Stock Photo; 219 © Fedor Konyukhov/PPL; 221T © Ian Dear Archive/PPL; 221B © Bernard Moitessier; 222 © Stéphanie Billarant/Energy team; 222-223 © Corbis; 224-225 © Jean-Marie Liot; 226 T © Christopher Ison/Alamy Stock Photo, 226-227 © Corbis; 228-229 © epa european pressphoto agency b.v./Alamy Stock Photo, 230 © Newzulu/Alamy Stock Photo, 230-231 © Christophe Favreau; 232T © JONATHAN EASTLAND/Alamy Stock Photo; 234L © Corbis, 235 © Pascal Le Segretain/Getty Images; 236 © Aurora Photos/Alamy Stock Photo; 237 © Ajax News & Feature Service/Alamy Stock Photo; 238-239 Andre Durand/AFP/Getty Images; 240 T © Aurora Photos/Alamy Stock Photo; 240-241 © Aurora Photos/Alamy Stock Photo; 242 © Christopher Ison/Alamy Stock Photo; 243 © Action Plus Sports Images/Alamy Stock Photo; 244-245 © Daniel Forster/The LIFE Images Collection/Getty Images; 245 © Keystone/Getty Images; 246T Bettmann/Getty Images; 248 © ZUMA Press, Inc./Alamy Stock Photo; 249 © Oskar Kihlborg/Ericsson Racing Team/Getty Images; 250 © Photomakers/Perfect Prints; 252 © Dorset Media Service/Alamy Stock Photo; 255 © Aurora Photos/Alamy Stock Photo; 256 © one-image photography/Alamy Stock Photo; 265 © Michael Austen/Alamy Stock Photo; 266 © Dorset Media Service/Alamy Stock Photo; 274 © Holden Travel/Alamy Stock Photo; 278 © Kos Picture Source Ltd/Alamy Stock Photo; 282-283 © Alvov/Shutterstock.com.